D0181868

DISCARD

My cameraman Glenn Evans and I with a sleepy polar bear cub and its mother, both of whom have been sedated. Their blood-stained fur is the result of a successful morning hunt: an unlucky seal.

**Right:** The bald eagle is a conservation success story.

**Below:** Orangutans are losing their rainforest homes at an alarming rate, and poachers are adding insult to injury.

**Above:** An elusive Bengal tiger on the prowl in Ranthambore National Park, near Jaipur, India.

**Below:** There are only about 700 mountain gorillas left in the world. Their survival is caught in a complicated net of social problems, poaching, and habitat destruction.

**Above:** The critically endangered bamboo lemur is one of the rarest mammals in the world.

**Below:** The po'ouli, a native Hawaiian bird, is now extinct.

At left and below: The majestic California condor; above: The discovery of a wild condor chick gives conservationists hope.

**Above:** The rare 'alala, Hawaii's only native crow.

**Below:** A young Tasmanian devil at the Trowunna Wildlife Park in Tasmania. Its massive jaw is stronger than that of a pit bull.

**Above:** A sea otter lounging off the coast of Monterey, California. Sea otters are one of an estimated 1,930 species of threatened marine mammals.

**Below:** The resilient black-footed ferret, once thought to be extinct, is making a comeback.

An orphaned chimp named Ikuru at Ngamba Island Chimpanzee Sanctuary, in a somber mood after losing her mother at the hands of poachers.

A rare Sumatran rhinoceros, the most endangered rhino species on Earth.

**Above:** An Asiatic one-horned rhino in what we thought was 4 or 5 feet of water... until it stood up.

**Right:** In Africa, many young elephants lose their mothers to poaching for ivory. Tactile creatures, elephants are dependent on a mother's touch and are highly emotional animals.

**Above:** A cheetah on the hunt in the tall grass.

**Below:** At a cheetah conservation ranch in Namibia, helping to rehabilitate a young cheetah that suffered a run-in with a rancher.

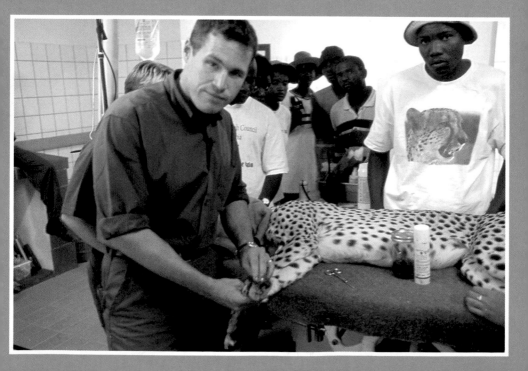

**Above:** Time is running out for Panama's national bird and the largest and most powerful raptor in the Americas, the harpy eagle.

**Below:** A portrait of poaching—dwarf crocodiles, which are threatened with extinction, for sale in commercial markets. Crocodiles are kept bound and alive until butchered.

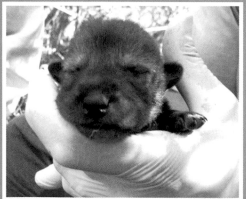

**Above and left:** My gloved hands shook as I held these 3-week-old red wolf pups, born in the wild.

**Right:** There are only about 100 red wolves living in the wild. This male is about to be released to join them.

The gray wolf, an apex predator, plays a vital role in the ecosystem it inhabits.

# 100 HEARTBEATS

# 100 HEARTBEATS

## THE RACE TO SAVE EARTH'S
## MOST ENDANGERED SPECIES

# JEFF CORWIN

RODALE

© 2009 by Jeff Corwin

Rodale books may be purchased for business or promotional use or for special sales. For information, please write to:

Special Markets Department, Rodale Inc., 733 Third Avenue, New York, NY 10017

Printed in the United States of America

Rodale Inc. makes every effort to use acid-free ∞, recycled paper ♻.

Photo credits: polar bears in Arctic © Glenn Evans; bald eagle © Tom Uhlman Photography; Jeff and orangutan © Jeff Corwin; wild tiger © Jeff Corwin; gorilla, courtesy of Great Ape Trust of Iowa; bamboo lemur © Peter Schlichting; po'ouli, courtesy of the San Diego Zoo Institute for Conservation Research; California condor (all photos) © Joe Burnett—Ventana Wildlife Society; 'alala, courtesy of the San Diego Zoo Institute for Conservation Research; sea otter © Jeff Corwin; black-footed ferret © Randy Matchett; young chimp © Jeff Corwin; Sumatran rhino © Terri L. Roth; Asiatic rhino © Jeff Corwin; elephant and Jeff © Shoshana Guy; cheetah (both photos) © Jeff Corwin; harpy eagle © Jeff Corwin; dwarf crocodiles © RG Ruggiero; red wolf cubs © Matthew Engel; Jeff with adult red wolf © Ryan Nordsven; Jeff with gray wolf © Jud Cremata

Book design by Chris Rhoads

**Library of Congress Cataloging-in-Publication Data**

Corwin, Jeff.
    100 heartbeats : the race to save earth's most endangered species / Jeff Corwin.
        p.    cm.
    Includes bibliographical references and index.
    ISBN-13 978–1–60529–847–4   hardcover
    ISBN-10 1–60529–847–6   hardcover
    1. One hundred heartbeats   2. Endangered species.   3. Wildlife conservation.
4. Wildlife conservationists.   I. Title.
QH75.C7185      2009
333.95'416—dc22                                                    2009023449

Distributed to the trade by Macmillan

2   4   6   8   10   9   7   5   3   1   hardcover

LIVE YOUR WHOLE LIFE™

We inspire and enable people to improve their lives and the world around them

For more of our products visit **rodalestore.com** or call 800-848-4735

Nothing is more priceless and more worthy of preservation than the rich array of animal life with which our country has been blessed. It is a many-faceted treasure, of value to scholars, scientists, and nature lovers alike, and it forms a vital part of the heritage we all share as Americans.

—PRESIDENT RICHARD NIXON, STATEMENT
UPON SIGNING THE ENDANGERED SPECIES
ACT OF 1973

To my daughters, Maya and Marina—you are both so very precious to your mother and me; your optimism and trust, reflected through a lovely lens of innocence, inspires us. And so I pray that you will inherit a natural world that is bountiful and pristine to cherish, recreate, and wisely harvest from. While at present the creatures who share Earth with us are in jeopardy, I have faith that my generation will make things right so you and your children will have the opportunity to thrive upon a rich, healthy, and diverse planet.

We will not fail you.

# CONTENTS

# ACKNOWLEDGMENTS

A very special thank-you to my beautiful wife, Natasha, and our precious daughters, Maya and Marina. No matter where I am in the world, my heart is always with you. To my parents, Marcy and Valerie, who nurtured my love for nature, thank you.

To all of the scientists and conservationists working to preserve animal species around the world, thank you. You are all heroes. *100 Heartbeats* would not have been possible without the generous contribution of time and expertise from my friends and colleagues in the conservation community. Thank you to Dr. Laurie Marker of Cheetah Conservation Fund, her lifetime work to save the cheetah has been a great inspiration; Dr. Ian Singleton, director, the Orangutan Conservation Program; Femka Den Haas, director, Jakarta Animal Aid Network; Dr. E. O. Wilson, an iconic scientist and conservationist; my good friends at Defenders of Wildlife; Steven C. Amstrup, PhD, senior polar bear scientist, USGS Alaska Science Center; Eric Regehr, PhD, research scientist, USGS Alaska Science Center; Adrienne E. Crosier, PhD, reproductive physiologist, Center for Species Survival, Smithsonian's Conservation & Research Center; Fateh Singh Rathore, PhD, first field director, Ranthambore National Park, India; Mahendra Shrestha, PhD, director of Save The Tiger Fund, National Fish and Wildlife Foundation; Carel van Schaik, PhD, primatologist, Duke University; John Seidensticker, PhD, biologist, Smithsonian Institution's National Zoological Park; Russell Mittermeier, PhD, chairman of the IUCN Species Survival Commission's Primate Specialist Group and president of Conservation International; Pat Chapple Wright, PhD, professor of anthropology, State University of New York, Stony Brook; Russell Ciochon, PhD, professor of anthropology, University of Iowa; Biruté M. F. Galdikas, PhD, director, Orangutan Foundation International; Jo Gayle Howard, DVM, animal-reproduction specialist, the Smithsonian Institution; Zhang Zhihe, PhD, director, Chengdu Research Base of Giant Panda Breeding; James Dietz, PhD, researcher, Golden Lion Tamarin Conservation Program; Benjamin Beck, PhD, director of conservation, Great Ape Trust of Iowa; Alan Lieberman, PhD, biologist, Keauhou Bird Conservation Center, San Diego Zoo's Conservation and Research for Endangered Species department; Carl Jones, founder and scientific director of the Mauritian Wildlife Foundation, fellow with the Durrell Wildlife Conservation Trust; Stanley A. Temple, PhD, Cornell University postdoctoral researcher associated with the Peregrine Fund; Peter Koopman, PhD, University of Queensland's Institute for Molecular Bioscience; Richard T. Watson, PhD, vice president and director, International Programs, The Peregrine Fund; Joe Burnett, PhD, wildlife biologist, Ventana Wildlife Society; Brian Gratwick, PhD, director of amphibian conservation, National Zoo, Washington, DC; Edgardo Griffith, PhD, director, Panama's El Valle Amphibian Conservation Center (EVACC); Bill Konstant, PhD, director of conservation and science, Houston Zoo; Ross Alford, PhD, professor of biology, James Cook University, Australia; Lee Berger, PhD, James Cook University, Australia; Reid Harris, PhD, professor of biology, James Madison University, Harrisonburg, Virginia; Karen Lips, PhD, associate professor, Southern Illinois University; M. Tim Tinker, PhD, biologist, USGS WERC Santa Cruz Field Station Long Marine Laboratory, UCSC; Dean Biggins, PhD, wildlife biologist, US Geological Survey; Dan

Roddy, PhD, biologist, Wind Cave National Park; Pete Gober, PhD, black-footed ferret recovery coordinator, USFWS; Richard G. Ruggiero, PhD, chief, Branch of the Near East, South Asia, and Africa of the USFWS Division of International Conservation; Lawrence Witmer, PhD, professor of anatomy, Ohio University; Eric Dinerstein, PhD, chief scientist, WWF; Terri Roth, PhD, director, Carl H. Lindner Jr. Family Center for Conservation and Research of Endangered Wildlife, Cincinnati Zoo; Debby Cox, AMMSc. Env, director, Chimpanzee Welfare Africa Programmes; Heather Eves, PhD, director, Bushmeat Crisis Task Force (BCTF); Natalie Bailey, MS, assistant director, BCTF; Vincent Opyene, Uganda Wildlife Authority lawyer, member of the Bushmeat-Free Eastern Africa Network; Ravi Chellam, PhD, faculty member, Wildlife Institute of India, Dehra Dun; Marta Curti, PhD, wildlife biologist, The Peregrine Fund; Doug Smith, PhD, Yellowstone Wolf Project Leader, Yellowstone National Park; Art Beyer, PhD, biologist, USFWS; Chris Lucash, PhD, biologist, USFWS; and Ryan Nordsven, PhD, biologist, USFWS.

I would also like to express my gratitude to my literary agent, Stephanie Tade; to Rodale Inc. and my editor, Julie Will; and to Toni Robino and Doug Wagner, whose editorial and research talents were instrumental in the creation of this book.

# INTRODUCTION

To waste, to destroy our natural resources, to skin and exhaust
the land instead of using it so as to increase its usefulness, will result
in undermining in the days of our children the very prosperity which
we ought by right to hand down to them amplified and developed.

—PRESIDENT THEODORE ROOSEVELT, 1907

THE ANIMAL KINGDOM is in critical condition. The affliction isn't a disease, but rather a crisis of endangerment that threatens to wipe out many of the world's animal species forever.

Ironically, the only species capable of saving these animals is the same one that's responsible for putting them in danger. The plight of the 16,928 species threatened with extinction is largely due to devastating man-made ecological changes such as habitat loss, pollution, climate change, and unsustainable exploitation.

The International Union for the Conservation of Nature (IUCN), whose classification system is widely considered to be authoritative, classifies a species as endangered when it has experienced a population loss of at least 50 percent in three generations or 10 years, whichever period is longer. In the United States, a species is officially considered endangered under the Endangered Species Act (ESA) if it's at risk for extinction throughout all or a significant portion of its range. The US Fish and Wildlife Service and the National Marine Fisheries Service share responsibility for implementing the ESA with the goal of conserving species as well as their ecosystems.

An "endangered" designation makes it illegal to hunt, harm, or otherwise kill or capture a species. Under the ESA, species are considered threatened if they're deemed likely to become endangered without intervention. Usually, threatened species receive the same protection as endangered species. "Critically endangered" is the highest-risk category assigned by the IUCN. Generally speaking, this designation is assigned to species that have experienced or are expected to experience population declines of at least 80 percent in three generations or 10 years, whichever is longer.

The animals featured in this book face varying degrees of endangerment; tragically, some of them have already lost their battle. But the stories I've chosen to share are those of the animals whose situations are representative of larger problems in our ecosystem—problems we can solve—and those whose loss has provided us with valuable wisdom.

The plight of the Asiatic cheetah (*Acinonyx jubatus venaticus*), an especially rare member of the Hundred Heartbeat Club, is symbolic of the critical condition of animals across the globe. With only 60 members remaining in the wild in Iran and an unknown but surely minuscule number in Pakistan, these powerful, graceful hunters that are a subspecies of the world's fastest terrestrial species (*Acinonyx jubatus*) unfortunately can't outrun the proverbial speeding bullet. A combination of poaching, habitat degradation, and poor genetics has conspired to critically endanger their existence.

The problems facing the cheetah date back to the last ice age, when populations were reduced so severely that today their genetic diversity is very limited. So I was elated to meet some of these beautiful, slinky creatures at a game reserve outside Lake Naivasha in Kenya 12 years ago. They were brothers who had been orphaned at 2 months old when a rancher shot their mother, and

I accompanied them on their first true test of survival. I'd spent the preceding days helping to train these brothers for the chase—the pursuit of prey they'd need to master in order to make it in the wild. The manager of the reserve had them chase lures, flashlight beams, and, to really build up their speed, a rope tied to the back of a speeding jeep. When they were ready, we drove them away from the reserve and nudged them out of our jeep. They were confused at first, probably wondering why we hadn't brought any "toys" for them to chase. But when they caught their first glimpse of a Thomson's gazelle (*Eudorcas thomsoni*), instinct took over. One brother charged after it at about 40 miles per hour, but his efforts weren't enough, and the gazelle outpaced him. Just as the gazelle began "pronking"—bouncing more than running—in celebration of its apparent victory, the other cheetah appeared from out of nowhere to finish the job.

Their teamwork had been flawless, but they still had one more thing to learn. Looking down at the gazelle, and then at one another, the brothers didn't seem sure of the next step. Just then the cheetah that had made the kill seemed to notice that he liked the taste in his mouth and bent down for another bite. Before we knew it, the brothers were feasting like seasoned gourmands. While they still had some training to undergo and their future was far from certain, this milestone was cause for hope.

———

I grew up as a city kid in Quincy, Massachusetts. When I was 6 years old and on a summer visit to my aunt downstate in Holbrook, I came face-to-face with a creature that I'd never seen before: a garter snake. When this scaly animal uncoiled itself like an unraveling turban and moved its long body deeper into my aunt's woodpile without the aid of legs, I may as well have been discovering a new life form. And when it slipped back into the stack of firewood as quickly as it had appeared, I panicked.

I picked up the heavy logs and heaved them behind me until the layer of mud and detritus beneath was within reach. And there, amid the spiderwebs and abandoned cocoons, was my new friend. With no preconceived notions to guide me, I reached out and gently grabbed hold of its coiled lower body. And it did the same, gliding over my wrist and "grabbing" onto my forearm with its upper body. Scared and exhilarated at the same time, I proudly took it inside, where, naturally, my aunt was less enthusiastic about my discovery.

"Get rid of it!" she screamed.

"No!" I shouted.

"Why?!"

There I was, a trembling, 3-foot-tall city boy utterly ignorant about the wild animal that was wrapped around my arm and inspiring such fear in my aunt. But I answered without hesitation.

"Because I love it!"

Somehow, amid the mayhem, she pried the snake off my arm and we put it back in the yard.

That was the day I became a naturalist. That was the defining moment when the light came on and I knew what I wanted to do with my life. For the next 2 years, I kept tabs on that snake as she lived her life. I learned about love and passion and birth and predation from her. Eventually, I wouldn't need to capture her to get an up-close look—I respected her space and she stopped fleeing at the sight of me. Snakes are creatures of habit, and at some point, she apparently accepted this little boy's presence as routine.

One day, as I watched her bask in the sun 4 feet from where I lay on my belly with my chin resting in my hands, I saw a sharp flash of metal and heard a sickening thud. The next thing I knew, she had been ripped in two, each half of her body flying in opposite directions as she helplessly bit at the air. As the pieces of her hit the ground, they writhed like the severed locks of a Medusa, her agony not quite over. When I looked up from the carnage, I saw the man who lived next door, shovel in hand and a stern, satisfied look on his face.

That was the day I became a conservationist.

Today, I'm a conservationist because I believe that my species doesn't have the right or option to determine the fate of *other* species, even ones that inspire fear in us. With 3,246 of the world's animal species classified as critically endangered, these animals need all the friends they can get. And whether we realize it or not, we need them. The biodiversity that results when millions of species share a planet benefits our species in ways that are easy to take for granted. We're inextricably bound with nature. When we put the survival of the natural world in jeopardy, we simultaneously put *our* survival in jeopardy.

As I write this introduction, with my daughter Maya's melodious laughter drifting down the hallway to my office and her baby sister, Marina, snuggled warmly in her crib, I lament the potential loss of 3,246 species of animals they may never see. I'm painfully aware that the world they will inherit may be in a state of ecological catastrophe. It is my hope that this book will serve as a catalyst, educating people about the state of our natural world and compelling them to help protect it for future generations. We have the chance to do it, and we *can* succeed. Every heartbeat matters.

# PART I

# GLOBAL WARMING AND HABITAT LOSS

# CHAPTER I

# THE RACE AGAINST EXTINCTION

FROM THE HELICOPTER, I can see an end-less stretch of Arctic ice. The downward curve of the horizon in the distance lets me know that I'm as close to the top of the world as I've ever been.

The landscape is otherworldly—starkly desolate and yet shock-ingly beautiful. I'm with Steve Amstrup, senior polar bear scientist with the US Geological Survey's Alaska Science Center, flying above the ice-locked village of Kaktovik, 300 miles north of the Arctic Circle.

We're searching for the mighty polar bear (*Ursus maritimus*), the apex predator that presides over the Arctic food chain. Spotting bear tracks as the snow blows across the ice is very difficult, so the pilot takes the chopper lower in an attempt to give us a better chance. I can see cracks and larger openings called *leads* in the ever-shifting labyrinth of ice. All day every day, millions of tons of ice are churned, crushed, and reconfigured. Cliffs form and leads open like gaping jaws. Wind scours the snow from the tundra, revealing silvery ice mirrors that intermittently blind us with the sun's reflection. We'd never survive on this ice, but polar bears can't survive *without* it.

Eric Regehr, another research scientist on Steve's polar bear team; my cameraman, Glenn Evans; and my sound guy, Jonah Torreano, are also on board. We're all excited when Steve points to the east and says, "There!" The pilot follows the tracks for nearly 30 miles before we finally catch our first glimpse of an enormous female running across the ice with her two young cubs, all 500 pounds of her massive body undulating beneath a layer of snowy white fur. The family is nearly invisible against the white backdrop of bluish white ice, and their camouflage is further enhanced by the sunlight bouncing off the ground. Even with my sunglasses on, I can feel a powerful headache coming on from the glare.

As the chopper closes the distance between us and the bears, they begin galloping at close to 20 miles per hour to escape what the mother perceives to be a giant flying predator. The female, who could run much faster if she wasn't being held back by her tiny offspring, doesn't know, of course, that the helicopter carries scientists who have devoted their lives to protecting her species. But despite her instinct to escape, she doesn't abandon her cubs. Even as the whirling cloud of snow created by the helicopter threatens to engulf her, she stops and allows them to catch up with her.

Steve loads a tranquilizer dart into his rifle, slides open the clear plastic window, and takes aim. *Pop!* The rifle fires as ice particles are sucked through the open window and prick our faces. It's a perfect shot, and within minutes the mother bear begins to slow and then sway drunkenly as she succumbs to the sedative. Steve takes a deep breath and sighs with relief, knowing that the data he gathers today can be added to the body of knowledge being used to conserve her species.

The familiar thrill of adventure rushes through my veins as I carefully step out onto the flat patch of snow-covered ice. I'm wearing $1,000 worth of high-tech, subzero weatherproof clothing, but with the –20°F temperature made even more frigid by the biting wind, I feel naked and helpless. The membranes of my eyes sting, and my breath instantly forms icicles on my face mask. Within minutes, the muscles in my face and lips begin to freeze, and when I speak I sound as if I, too, have been hit by a tranquilizer dart. But my inner adventurer loves every second of this experience, even the discomfort. I think back to the story I learned in fifth grade about the brave commander Robert E. Peary reaching the North Pole for the first time in 1909.

I've always been inspired by the accomplishments of other explorers and scientists. As a conservationist, I cherish the opportunity to be on the front lines in the race to save Earth's creatures. And as a biologist, I'm humbled by the fellowship of scientists joining together to make a critical difference in our uncertain future. Steve Amstrup is arguably one of the world's leading experts on polar bears. That he welcomed me to come on this research expedition is a great honor and privilege.

The pilot hands us our gear, and Steve rushes forward to the sow as Eric and I run after the cubs. We need to capture them and inject them with a mild sedative so that we'll be able to take measurements and then mark and tag them. But more importantly, we need to make sure they aren't separated from their mother. Polar bear cubs are dependent on their mothers until they're 2½ years old.

The young cubs don't make this an easy task, though, bolting away from us in single file. We sprint after them across the perilous ice, crossing the enormous tracks their mother left in the snow. Polar bear paws can measure 12 inches across and are wide enough to wrap around a man's head—and strong enough to crush it as easily as if it were an egg. Full-grown females weigh between 450 and 750 pounds; adult males are usually twice as heavy.

When I finally grab the first cub, scooping it up in my arms, I feel a little like I'm dreaming—I can't believe I'm holding a polar bear cub in its own habitat. Eric catches the other cub, and we gently inject them with sedatives, then tread—slowly and carefully this time—back across the treacherous landscape to reunite with Steve. We place the cubs next to their mother, and I sit on the ground to help Steve loop the radio collar around her neck. Steve has made sure she is lying in a safe position, snout pointed up and away from the ice; if she were lying facedown, she could suffocate in the snow and ice around her face.

Soon after we measure and mark the cubs, they begin to wake up and stretch. This time, they don't run from us. With the chopper still and silent, we simply appear to them to be some bipedal species that's significantly smaller than their mother. Having never encountered humans before, they have no reason to fear us, so they nuzzle us as they seek security and comfort. This is one of those moments when I understand how easy it is for people to anthropomorphize, projecting human feelings and qualities onto the instinctive behaviors of animals. Like other "poster animals" for endangered species—such as pandas, sea otters, and tiger cubs—the fluffy, white polar bear cubs, with their dark, round eyes and black button noses, evoke in us a strong emotional reaction to protect them as if they were our own children. Although I'm well aware that these are wild animals with sharp claws and teeth even at a young age, seeing them in this vulnerable state, without their mother's protection, instinctively tugs at my heart. I want them to live long and healthy lives in their natural habitat. In this moment, I don't allow my mind to dwell on the difficult future these cubs are destined to endure as their home melts away beneath their paws. There will be time enough to ponder these sobering thoughts when we return to the research lab, after our work here is finished.

For these precious 40 minutes, I honor the power and presence of these great white bears by being of service to one of their champions. With the considerable weight of the sow's massive head pressing into my lap, I pull off the magnetic switch on the radio collar so it begins transmitting the signal that will allow Steve to track her movements. All the while, I'm reveling in this once-in-a-lifetime experience, indelibly etching each moment into my memory.

This is the second trip I've made to Kaktovik to work with Steve. The first was while filming *Planet in Peril* in April 2007. Now, it's April 2008 and I'm filming a special for Animal Planet. Steve has been working with polar bears for 28 years. He understands these marine mammals better than anyone I've encountered, and he's gravely concerned about their future.

During the summer of 2008, Arctic sea ice receded to record levels—levels that 50 percent of climate modelers predicted wouldn't happen until 2050. Although the 2008 world population of polar bears is estimated to be more than 20,000, if Earth continues to warm at its current rate, forecasts developed by Steve's team at the US Geological Survey suggest that two-thirds of the polar bear's habitat will disappear by 2050. The bears would vanish from Alaska, Europe, and Asia. Their numbers and distribution also would decline in the Arctic Archipelago of Canada (the channels between the country's high Arctic islands) and areas off the northern coast of Greenland. By 2080, they would completely disappear from all of their current range except the Arctic

Archipelago and the adjacent continental shelves north of these islands. Even there, populations would probably be reduced.

"It's clear from all of the available research that the main threat to polar bears is the loss of their habitat as the result of global warming and that the global warming is being caused by increases in greenhouse gases. In fact, you can even take it one step beyond that," Steve says. "We know that the laws of physics dictate that more greenhouse gases in the atmosphere will lead to a warmer world. There are still going to be fluctuations in the climate— changes in oceanic circulation and atmospheric circulation can change the local temperatures or even the global mean temperatures, perhaps even for relatively extended periods of time—but whatever those temperatures are, they will be higher than they would have been had it not been for higher concentrations of greenhouse gases. So, to say 'Well, we're going to try to manage polar bears without managing greenhouse gases' is ignoring the larger, fundamental threat."

The polar bear has the unfortunate distinction of being the first animal to be listed as threatened due to climate change and the resulting loss of sea ice. Whereas most animals that are threatened or endangered have lost and continue to lose portions of their natural habitat, the polar bears' case is unique in that the ice itself is their home.

Polar bears have spent their entire evolutionary history adapting to the sea-ice environment. Less than 300,000 years ago, they diverged from brown bears (*Ursus arctos*) and began adapting to their frigid climate by developing fur on their feet to give them better purchase on the slippery ice. Their huge feet also act like snowshoes when the snow is soft underfoot. And their fur functions as a superefficient insulating and heating system. What look like white outer hairs are actually hollow, transparent tubes that tend to conserve heat. Polar bears are graced with a keen sense of smell—they can trace the scent of a seal that's under 6 feet of snow from a few miles away. They've adapted so well to their icy environment, in fact, that now they can't survive without it.

"They require the surface of sea ice to catch their food," Steve says. "They can come on land to den, and they can come on land to hang out or to cross peninsulas between bodies of water, but all of our data indicate they're only effective at catching prey from the surface of the ice." And as the sea ice diminishes, so, too, does our capacity to secure the survival of this remarkable species. Polar bears hunt mainly where water meets ice, and as that "shoreline" contracts, so do feeding opportunities. When they can't hunt for seals from late summer to late fall because there's no ice, they fast, losing more than 2 pounds a day. And studies in Canada's western Hudson Bay have revealed that these fasts now last about 3 weeks longer than they did 30 years ago.[1] This means that they have much less time for the hunting—and eating—that will build up the stores of fat required to sustain them until fall. Once the ice begins to form again, they can resume hunting. And there's one more ramification of the loss of sea ice: Despite the fact that polar bears are excellent swimmers buoyed by thick layers of blubber, scientists expect more bears to drown as the sea ice further recedes. Polar bears have been seen up to 200 miles from land, but the increased need to cross greater and greater expanses of open water raises the odds against them, no matter how well they can swim. It's one of the very cold truths of a warming world.

The plight of the polar bears is a grim reminder that if we don't bring global warming to a halt, even species with large populations face the risk of extinction within decades.

# GLOBAL WARMING —
# THE COLD, HARD FACTS

Polar bears aren't the only species suffering the effects of climate change. One study estimates that global warming will threaten 15 to 37 percent of terrestrial species with extinction by 2050. In India, scientists estimate that between 3 and 32 percent of the 12 most vulnerable Sundarban islands—home to both the world's largest mangrove forest and one of the world's largest Bengal tiger populations—will disappear by 2020 as a result of the rising sea level.[2]

Arctic sea ice has declined to its lowest levels since we began consistent satellite monitoring in 1979,[3] and in September 2007 the Northwest Passage—a direct shipping route from Europe to Asia through the Arctic Ocean—was ice free for the first time since records have been kept. It may have been a dream come true for mariners, but it was also a sure sign that disaster is closing in. The average global temperature rose 1.3°F from 1906 to 2005, according to the United Nations Intergovernmental Panel on Climate Change (IPCC), which predicts there will be an increase of 3.2° to 7.2°F in this century, depending on how effectively greenhouse gases are curbed.[4]

Despite conflicting reports you may have heard about whether global warming is actually occurring and whether, if it is, it's our fault, 97 percent of climate scientists surveyed about climate change in 2007 agreed that average global temperatures have increased during the past century.[5] Eighty-four percent of those scientists considered the warming to be caused by humans. Only a handful of those surveyed—5 percent—did not believe that human activity contributes to greenhouse warming. Interestingly, 5 percent of those surveyed also said government agencies or public officials have pressured them to "deny, minimize, or discount evidence of human-induced global warming."

According to the National Wildlife Federation, global warming is the most significant threat to wildlife today.[6] Scientists say warming must be reduced by 80 percent by 2050 to head off its worst possible effects, including erosion of coastlines, contamination of freshwater supplies, and the development of adverse growing conditions. Global-warming specialists are watching the Arctic especially closely because it's warming much more rapidly than other parts of the globe. Arctic warming has profound ramifications for the rest of the world as well, because the Arctic and the Antarctic help to moderate global temperatures. If these global refrigerators are turned off, temperatures around the world will rise even more rapidly. The area of permanent ice in the Arctic polar ice cap is contracting at a rate of 9 percent a decade. If this trend continues, the Arctic could melt completely in less than 100 years. And most scientists view the changes taking place in the Arctic as a sign of what's to come elsewhere.[7]

For example, the melting of glaciers and ice sheets exacerbates the rise in sea levels. Islands that support entire ecosystems and unique species of flora and fauna, coastal habitats, and even major cities such as Shanghai (which is just 6 feet above sea level) are at risk. The threat hits close to home for Americans, too. Scientists estimate that the sea level surrounding the United States could rise as much as 3 feet by 2100—an increase that would submerge 22,400 square miles of land along the Atlantic and Gulf coasts.[8] A warmer Arctic will have a negative impact on agriculture and limit the world's food production because it will affect weather patterns around the globe.

The IPCC reports that a temperature increase of more than 2°C (less than 4°F) during the next 50 to 100 years will produce major environmental disruptions. More than half of the climate scientists surveyed by the Statistical Assessment Service at George Mason University in Fairfax, Virginia, said they believe that, based on current trends, this tragedy will occur. But it doesn't have to. If we preserve the biodiversity that exists in areas like tropical rainforests, where there's an incredible convergence of different types of life forms, we'll go a long way toward protecting the planet as a whole. Becoming more responsible about oil and gas development—and the spills that inevitably come with it—could also make a profound difference. In an Arctic spill, polar bears, a variety of seabirds, and marine mammals, including seals and sea lions, would all be put at risk of extinction. When animals lick and ingest the oil from their fur or feathers, the effect is toxic and can induce kidney failure. These creatures also rely on their fur and feathers to stay warm; when those means of protection are coated with oil, an animal can freeze to death. Unless they're rescued—a monumental feat in remote regions—animals affected by oil spills typically die of hypothermia.

Oil exploration and development may also threaten polar bears' survival by creating stress, which can prompt mothers to leave maternity dens and abandon their cubs.[9] Maternal denning is the most sensitive time in the bears' life cycle because newborn cubs, who are extremely vulnerable to their harsh environment, need to remain in the den for nearly 4 months. Amstrup and other scientists have begun screening some areas of the Arctic with infrared devices to detect the presence of polar bear dens. Their goal is to win protection against oil operations in those areas.

Incidentally, Steve says that it was while he and a team of surveyors were investigating a denning area that he came face-to-face with an adult polar bear that was *not* sedated and could have killed him. Steve and his team had discovered a den and were waiting for the mother to leave so that they could measure it. "We were watching it and watching it, and we kept seeing signs that she was still there, so we didn't bother her," Steve says. The waiting went on for 3 days without the appearance of a single telltale paw print.

Then, to make matters murkier, a windstorm hit and filled in the entrance to the den, leaving only a dimple in the snow to signal its location. Three more days went by, and the tiny opening never got any bigger, even though most of the other bears in the area had already come out of *their* dens. It looked like the sow and her cubs had left and Steve's team had somehow missed their departure.

"So we went down there and we were going to dig into the den—remove the snow that had blown into the entrance—and then we were going to crawl in and measure it," Steve says. "I had a little shovel and I was digging in the entrance, and suddenly my right leg just went—*poof*—right through the roof of the den.

"The mother bear had moved over in the snow a couple of feet, and the den was actually under my feet, not where I was digging. And so I went through and just—*whoosh*—I was up to my waist in snow. I could hardly move and I was trying to pull myself out; and I looked, and there was the mother bear's head right next to my thigh. She just kind of looked up at me and, man, I rolled out of there so fast."

She burst from the den and gave chase for a few yards, but then she turned and ran in the opposite direction—toward a field assistant—before veering off in yet another direction, this time toward the sea ice. Now Steve's team was on the offensive, and with cool heads they got the job done. They caught the bear and returned her to the den, where they tagged her and her waiting cubs.

# Closing Enrollment in the Hundred Heartbeat Club

The title of this book, *100 Heartbeats*, refers to critically endangered species and subspecies that have 100 or fewer individuals alive in the wild today. I first read the term *Hundred Heartbeat Club* in "Vanishing Before Our Eyes," an article written by Pulitzer Prize–winning author Edward O. Wilson.[10] Those chilling words—*Hundred Heartbeat Club*—haunted me. The ill-fated membership list includes the Javan rhino, the Vancouver Island marmot, the Hawaiian crow, the Seychelles sheath-tailed bat, and the most endangered feline in the world, the Iberian lynx. These species literally have fewer than 100 hearts beating on our planet.

Most of the species in this book are not yet members of this club but are on a slippery slope toward the clubhouse door. In 2008, the IUCN listed as critically endangered 3,246 of the 44,838 species assessed. Seventeen of the mammalian species have fewer than 300 individuals, and another 15 of these species have been reduced to populations of between 350 and 1,000.

As scientists, we know that a species can number in the thousands yet vanish in the blink of an eye. And the threats to their existence, which often work in tandem, go far beyond global warming. Also conspiring against the animal kingdom are disease, pollution, toxic chemicals, the introduction of nonnative "invasive" species, and the loss, degradation, and fragmentation of habitat. Add to that the many lives that are stolen through illegal poaching and exploitation—activities that are, sadly, often made easier after the size of a species' natural habitat has been reduced—and the future looks bleak.

———

The Mediterranean monk seal (*Monachus monachus*), the world's most endangered pinniped, may be the most poignant example of what can happen when an animal faces multiple threats. The monk seal once lived in large numbers throughout the Mediterranean and

Black Sea regions and along the northwestern African coast, but the worldwide population is now estimated to be fewer than 400 and continues to decline. The main suspects: human encroachment on their habitat, collisions with commercial vessels, deadly encounters with fishermen, disease, pollution, and predation by sharks and killer whales.

Today, Mediterranean monk seals live only in remote areas in the Mediterranean and along the northwestern coast of Africa, where they can haul their 700-pound bodies out of the water and breed in coastal caves inaccessible by land. But unfortunately, the caves can be deadly to newborn pups when high surf and storm surges flood them. And when a Mediterranean monk seal occasionally forsakes the safety of a cave and hauls herself onto a beach to give birth, she risks interference from well-meaning people who think she's beached and can't make it back to water on her own. If they harass her until she goes back into the water, forcing her to go into labor and give birth at sea, she and her pup may die. Females bear only one pup at a time, and usually not every year. Because the rate of reproduction among the seals is much lower than it used to be—possibly due to inbreeding—every seal pup death is a major loss.

Until the mid-1990s, the Mauritania colony of Mediterranean monk seals at Cabo Blanco was the largest population and the only one still maintaining its social structure. But in 1997, a mysterious disease ravaged the colony. Scientists couldn't readily examine or treat the seals because local authorities didn't grant the needed permits in time. The population fell from about 310 to somewhere between 70 and 130. When the bodies of the dead seals were analyzed, scientists found that an algal bloom was the most likely culprit. These blooms can produce biotoxins, and they're often stimulated by pollution.

Another significant challenge posed to these resourceful creatures is the presence of fishermen in the eastern Mediterranean, many of whom blame the monk seals for lower-than-average catches. Competition for available food resources has become increasingly fierce as fish stocks in the Mediterranean steadily diminish, though overfishing is the most significant factor in this decline. Preying mainly on fish, octopus, squid, and mollusks in mostly shallow water, monk seals will on occasion chew through fishermen's nets. In an attempt to sustain their livelihoods, some fishermen respond by killing the seals despite their endangered status and legal protection. When MOm—the Hellenic Society for the Study and Protection of the Monk Seal—conducted an analysis of 130 monk seal deaths that occurred in the '90s, the leading cause proved to be deliberate killing. But thanks to the active involvement of organizations like MOm, the general public and fishing operations are becoming more educated about the seals and their critically endangered status. In Turkey, the World Wildlife Fund and the Underwater Research Society are working with fishermen to protect monk seals' breeding caves and increase fish stocks by creating no-fishing zones. But monk seals still need more habitat that's free of fishing boats, nets, and people. As of 2008, Greece was the only country that had dedicated a large area—the National Marine Park of Alonissos Northern Sporades in the Aegean Sea—to the preservation of the seals and their habitat.

Another monk seal species, the Caribbean monk seal (*Monachus tropicalis*), hasn't been sighted since 1952, and in June 2008 the National Oceanic and Atmospheric Administration's Fisheries Service reported that it's officially extinct. The third monk seal species, the Hawaiian monk seal (*Monachus schauinslandi*), has a population of about 1,200. Though that represents an all-time recorded low, the seals are being vigilantly protected in a reserve at French Frigate Shoals, off the coast of Hawaii, and are considered the greatest hope for the genus's survival.

As the monk seal makes all too clear, wildlife faces a daunting list of threats in the 21st century. But scientists, conservationists, and concerned individuals across the world have positively impacted the future of many species, such as the American bald eagle, whose population has been revived. And the California condor, whose population teetered precariously at an estimated 22 birds in 1987, is now nesting in the wild after intensive captive-breeding efforts helped bring the population to 321. The black-footed ferret was thought to be extinct but was rediscovered when a ferret found stealing food from a German shepherd turned out to represent a "lost colony" of 130. The Mauritius kestrel, a raptor native to the island of Mauritius, joined the Hundred Heartbeat Club in the 1960s. The presence of invasive species and the unregulated use of the pesticide DDT had chipped away at this bird population until there were just *10* birds in the wild by 1974; now, more than 500 Mauritius kestrels exist. This species is alive today because of the passionate work of conservationists. Throughout the pages of this book, you'll meet these creatures and others, as well as the many heroes who are working to save them.

It's important to understand that this is not a race to spare a handful of particular species because we feel an affinity for them and *want* to save them. That's a phenomenon referred to as *charismatic-species syndrome*, whereby we attach human-inspired values or characteristics to other species. We may rush to save the giant panda, but a venomous rattlesnake? We don't move as quickly—if at all. The reality is, each species, no matter how big or small, has an important relationship with other species in its ecosystem—and we're in a race to preserve as much of the animal kingdom as possible. Gray wolves have been vilified for generations, but their ecological role couldn't have been made clearer after they were hunted to the point of extinction in the northern Rocky Mountains. When the elk population became too large for the vegetation to sustain, many starved and others were shot to reduce their numbers. Coyotes became the region's top predators, and their population increased as they outcompeted smaller predators for the same prey. When Yellowstone National Park won the battle to reintroduce wolves in 1995, the predator-prey balance was restored, with the wolves once again keeping the coyote and elk populations in check. Clearly, all species in an ecosystem are dependent upon one another, and all are important to the health and survival of the ecosystem.

———

Enacted in 1973, the Endangered Species Act is the primary legislation in the United States that exists to conserve plants and animals at risk of extinction. The act's main directive is to recover threatened and endangered species to a state of health and stability in which they no longer require protected status. Before leaving office, President George W. Bush eliminated regulations that required proposed federal projects to be reviewed by independent scientists in order to assess their potential impact on protected animals and plants. This gave federal agencies the authority to build roads and power plants and lease sites for oil and gas drilling on public lands without an independent scientific analysis of the environmental impact. While in a perfect world this wouldn't present a problem, the pressures experienced by government scientists to approve various projects are significant. For a government that relies on checks and balances, this is a grave oversight that creates a troubling conflict of interest.

With habitat destruction prevailing as the biggest threat to wildlife—and with no end in sight to the human population growth that's driving the destruction—this is no time to make it easier to destroy that habitat.

# FEWER AND FEWER
# PLACES TO CALL HOME

As humans' need for food, water, housing materials, and space increases, the animal kingdom is likely to suffer the greatest losses in recorded history. According to the US Census Bureau, the current world population is 6.75 billion, and the UN projects that we'll pass the 9 billion mark by 2050. To produce enough food for all of those people, the global agricultural output will need to increase by at least 50 percent over the next 30 years. We have the technology and the workforce to meet that need, but we don't have the land. Eighty-three percent of the earth's total land surface and 98 percent of the land that can support rice, wheat, or corn crops has been affected to some degree by humans—that's how big our footprint is.[11] That's not to say that none of that land is available for new agricultural uses, but it gives you some idea of how close we are to running out of natural habitat. It's inevitable that a food crisis will accelerate habitat destruction as commercial farmers ramp up the productivity of their land by using more fertilizers and pesticides. When these measures are no longer enough, wilderness areas will be targeted for conversion to agriculture. Our population's growing demand for natural resources will be in direct competition with efforts to preserve the planet's fish and wildlife and their remaining natural habitat.

Habitat destruction—the deterioration of an environment to the point where it can no longer support an indigenous species—is the most significant cause of species extinction worldwide.[12] When habitat is destroyed, many of the animals and plants that had thrived there die or are displaced. While agriculture is the main source of this destruction, logging, mining, commercial fishing, homesteading, and urban sprawl also contribute to the problem. Conversion of land for agricultural use has also led to habitat fragmentation, which is the division of a species' habitat into smaller, unconnected parts. Habitat fragmentation occurs when native vegetation is cleared for uses such as farming, road construction, and urbanization. More than 75 percent of native vegetation has been destroyed in much of the East and the Midwest of America.[13]

Habitat destruction is disastrous for all species, including humans. Not only does it increase an area's chances for devastating natural disasters such as floods and droughts, it also heightens the potential for water contamination, crop failure, and the spread of disease. Habitat destruction has altered Earth's system of carbon exchange as well as levels of sulfur, nitrogen, and phosphorus. The result: more severe and frequent acid rain, sudden and sharp declines in fish populations referred to as "die-offs," and the increased presence of algal blooms. Habitat destruction also contributes to global climate change. Deforestation in the tropical rainforests alone has made it significantly more difficult for Earth to produce oxygen and process carbon dioxide—a main contributor to global warming. The Amazon rainforest accounts for 10 percent of the carbon stored among the world's ecosystems, and when trees are clear-cut, not only is all that greenhouse gas released, we also lose that source of storage forever.

If you're getting the impression that habitat degradation comes in a distressing multitude of forms, I regret to inform you that we've only just begun. Still more dangers are posed by pollutants, diseases, parasites, exploitation, and the introduction of nonnative species to ecosystems. And compounding it all is the dearth of protected lands. Only 7.3 million square miles of natural habitat are protected worldwide—approximately 13 percent of Earth's total land mass.[14] That's not a whole lot to work with. It's the terrestrial equivalent of trying to quarantine all the world's marine life in a body of water smaller than the Indian Ocean. Meanwhile, the world's forests are vanishing at a rate of 44,400 square miles a year,[15] and more than half of America's wetlands have disappeared in the past 2 centuries.[16] Ours is very much a shrinking world, and we simply can't afford to lose any more of it.

# SOMETIMES, WE DON'T KNOW WHEN TO STOP

Besides the loss of habitat that affects many animals, some endangered species are also threatened with extinction as a result of poaching—illegal hunting and fishing practices—and unsustainable hunting. (In Chapter 6, I'll share my experiences of witnessing these horrific practices firsthand.) Sustainable hunting—regulated, monitored, and managed by government fish and wildlife departments—keeps animal populations and their ecosystems healthy. Unsustainable hunting inevitably puts a species at risk. It was unsustainable, commercialized hunting that nearly wiped out sea otters, bison, and some whale species. It was also a primary factor in the decline of the most endangered subspecies in the world, the giant Abingdon Island tortoise, of which there's only one left— none other than Lonesome George.

When you first meet Lonesome George, he slowly extends his leathery neck, giving you a good look at his web of wrinkles and his big, wet eyes. Then, if you happen to be standing next to a succulent green plant, as I was when we were introduced, he may move his legs slowly and robotically in your direction, timid but emboldened by hunger. And even as he feasts on his dinner with his ancient maw, he may open wide at the other end and rid himself of the *last* succulent he ate, doing his part for seed dispersal and the life cycle of the planet in general.

George is the last living member of a subspecies of giant tortoises called the Abingdon Island tortoise (*Geochelone nigra abingdoni*). This gentle giant was discovered in 1971 on the island of Pinta (also called Abingdon), one of the Galápagos Islands, and quickly became a symbol for world wildlife conservation. Now, at age 90-plus and weighing about 650 pounds, George is in the prime of his life, as these huge island dwellers are thought to live more than 150 years. Charles Darwin first noted these creatures as he was traveling through the islands in the 1830s. In fact, some of the giant tortoises on the islands today may have once spied Darwin themselves.

One of the world's most prestigious national parks, the Galápagos are the laboratory of evolution, a crazy place inhabited not only by penguins and sea lions, but also by iguanas that graze on sea kelp and birds that have lost their ability to fly because they've spent so much time in the water. But the Galápagos have also been a place of terrible extinction because of humankind, and there's no better symbol of this than Lonesome George—the ultimate representation of the Hundred Heartbeat Club. When Darwin visited in 1835, there were about 250,000 giant tortoises of 14 subspecies on the 19 islands. Today, there are 11 subspecies and about 15,000 giant tortoises.[17] Starting in the 17th century, the tortoises were extensively hunted by sailors who came through the islands looking for portable food. From there, the tortoises' numbers were further reduced by museum collectors, poachers, and starvation as a result of competition for food with feral pigs and goats originally introduced to the island by settlers as livestock. The toll was especially high for the Abingdon Island tortoise. Around the world, populations of similar species of island tortoise have been wiped out or reduced to near extinction.

George was relocated to the Charles Darwin Research Station on the island of Santa Cruz in the 1970s and lived there with two females of another subspecies for many years. Attempts to mate him were unsuccessful until recently, when a mate managed to produce a clutch of eggs. Suddenly, there was hope for repopulating George's subspecies, but that hope was dashed in November 2008, when all the eggs turned out to be sterile. Still, George's keepers are undaunted. They've found females on nearby Isabella Island that have closer DNA matches than the mate that produced the first eggs with George. So one of George's future mates may yet bear fertile eggs. In the meantime, he remains a poignant image of the last of his kind, a solitary sentinel of extinction.

Unfortunately, another subspecies saw its last light flicker out in the 1930s, and by that point, there was nothing anyone could do but watch.

# EXTINCTION IS FOREVER

The marsh grass, glazed with the morning dew and a golden light, created a sparkling blanket of earthbound stars. Suddenly, the silent chill of the New England dawn was broken by the chitter and trill of a young heath hen cock in search of a mate. At about 17 inches from head to tail and approximately 2 pounds, the heath hen's head was anointed with two clusters of pointed, brownish red feathers that looked like horns. This distinctive red-hued subspecies of the greater prairie chicken boomed out its mating call in the scrubby heathland barrens of coastal New England, as it had every spring for eons.

The *heath* in *heath hen* refers to the uncultivated open space covered with low-growing shrubs and plants that sustained the bird's large population in 1700s New England. As a New Englander, I can attest that much of that coastal vegetation is gone now, supplanted by residential and commercial development. But a few hundred years ago, an incredible variety of plants thrived in the acidic coastal soil—cranberry, heather, huckleberry, rhododendron—and covered the heath with every color found in autumn. And the birds drawn to this landscape reflected the same diversity—loons, sandpipers, jays, mockingbirds, tanagers, owls, bald eagles, larks, pheasants. Heath hens (*Tympanuchus cupido cupido*) were so plentiful that they became a staple food for indentured laborers and servants. They weren't reputed to be very tasty, though, so labor contracts often stipulated that the workers couldn't be served heath hen more than three times a week.

Despite its plentiful numbers and unpopularity with the human palate, the heath hen faced tough odds. It preferred to both perch and fly close to the ground, making it an easy target. And every spring, the hens made themselves even more visible in their leks, the wide-open fields of cropped grass where they played out their courtship rituals. The cocks would dance, fight for dominance, and boom out their mating calls with a volume that belied their stature.

Year after year, the abundant subspecies was harvested without limit. By 1870, only 300 heath hens remained—all of them on Martha's Vineyard. Unfortunately for the heath hens, the island was also home to a large population of feral cats that, unlike the laborers and servants, had a keen taste for the birds. Twenty years later, between the efforts of the cats and the hunters, the heath hen population had been reduced by half. And by the end of the 19th century, only 70 hens remained.

The dawn of the 20th century brought hope: A hunting ban was enacted and the Heath Hen Reserve was established in 1908. Over the next 8 years, the population rapidly grew to nearly 2,000. Assuming that the birds were no longer in danger, their caretakers relaxed their vigilance.

But in the face of severe winters, inbreeding, disease, and a fire that struck during the 1916 nesting season, the population withered as quickly as it had blossomed. In 1927, only a dozen heath hens survived, and just two of them were females. The following year, only one male danced in the lek. He boomed out his mating call again and again, unaware that there were no others of his kind to hear him. Known as Booming Ben, he heralded the spring for 4 more years as locals hoped against hope that perhaps a female would present herself. But she never did. And on March 11, 1932, the last living heath hen made his final appearance.

Thus the heath hen followed the passenger pigeon into the ranks of North American birds driven to extinction by exploitation—a lineup that also includes the ivory-billed woodpecker, the Carolina parakeet, the Labrador duck, and the great auk.

To our credit, heath hens were one of the first birds that Americans tried to save from extinction. In 1791, the New York legislature passed a law aimed at its preservation. Though it didn't save the heath hen, it raised awareness of the issue of extinction and helped pave the way for future conservation efforts.

———

Today the rate of extinctions affecting our planet's wildlife is exceeded only by the mass extinction of the dinosaurs, which scientists think occurred when an asteroid struck Earth nearly 70 million years ago. While the dinosaurs disappeared as the result of a natural but catastrophic event, the current causes of extinction are largely the result of human behavior. Every 20 minutes, another unique animal species becomes extinct. Every year, more than 20,000 species tragically disappear from our planet. If the rate of extinctions isn't slowed, by the end of the century, more than half the animal species alive today will be lost forever.

We're not powerless, though. As demonstrated by the success story of the American bald eagle, great strides can be made through compassion and dedication.

# WINGS OF HOPE

The sky was a cloudless deep blue, and the temperature was hovering around 60°F as I stood at the edge of a rock outcropping overlooking the Gulf of Alaska. Below me, giant sea stars—fiery orange and fluorescent pink—were clinging to the rocks. I was in southeastern Alaska to film Kodiak bears, monster-size grizzlies unique to the island of Kodiak. They're some of the most successful predators on the planet, and seeing them provokes its share of awe. But on that excursion, the moment that stood out for me more than any other—the one that really inspired my inner naturalist—was when I looked out across the ravine and saw a majestic American bald eagle (*Haliaeetus leucocephalus*). There, beneath a great Sitka spruce tree with its exposed roots clinging to lichen-covered rocks, stood a powerful, noble bald eagle clenching a freshly caught salmon in its talons.

For me, it was a moment of real hope. Seeing that eagle in the wild with my own eyes drove home the fact that this stunningly beautiful bird is no longer on the verge of extinction—because its caretakers have ensured its fate. The opportunity to observe an eagle in its element, living free and fully as it was born to do, is the kind of experience that feeds my soul. When I learn that other species aren't faring as well as the eagle, I summon the intensity I felt that day and turn it toward those less fortunate animals at risk for extinction.

Believe it or not, there was another strong contender for the symbol of America. Benjamin Franklin actually wanted to make the turkey our national bird—and as it turned out, the founding fathers might as well have chosen it for all the care our nation would show the bald eagle. In 1782, when the eagle was adopted as our national symbol, there were as many as 75,000 nesting pairs in the lower 48 states. But over the next 2 centuries, we treated the eagle with little more regard than we would a bird destined for our dinner tables. By the early 1960s, there were no more than 450 bald eagle pairs in existence. After prospering on the planet for at least 5 million years, this bird of prey had been reduced to near extinction in less than 180 years. Vast acres of its natural habitat had been cleared to build towns, farms, and houses. Millions of acres of virgin forest had been clear-cut for building materials and fuel or simply burned. As civilization steadily crawled and then raced across the New World, the eagles lost much of their habitat. The quiet, isolated forests where they prefer to nest were steadily destroyed.

If you've never seen an eagle's nest, by the way, you're missing one of nature's most stunning structures. The first time I climbed inside one, I felt like I was Alice in Wonderland after eating the mushroom that made her very small. The nest, constructed of large sticks, twigs, and leaves, was about 7 feet across and almost as deep. Securely braided into the limbs of a tall white pine, it had to weigh 300 pounds, and its size was evidence that the eagle pair that lived there had been making additions to their home for many years. Once eagles mate, they typically keep the same nest for life. With life spans of up to 30 years or longer in the wild, an eagle's nest can eventually weigh 1,000 pounds.

But by the 1960s, biologists and bird-watchers were seeing fewer and fewer nests. The clean waterways the eagles depend upon were being polluted by industrial chemicals, reducing the numbers and quality of the fish—the eagle's staple prey. And the eagles themselves had been hunted, primarily out of ignorance. Under the impression that eagles killed lambs, calves, and other small animals, people considered them a threat to their livestock. In fairness to the farmers, eagles can easily kill a free-ranging chicken or a young fawn, but they bring down cattle only in tall tales. In addition to fish and carrion, the eagles had plenty of wildlife to eat, such as ducks and other waterfowl and small animals like rodents. But the shootings continued, and at one time bounties were even placed on our national symbol. Then, in 1940, Congress passed the Bald Eagle Protection Act, making it illegal to harass, kill, possess without a permit, or sell bald eagles. The prospect of losing the nation's symbol of freedom, strength, and independence to human-induced extinction was unthinkable.

Even with this protection, bald eagles continued to disappear from the skies of North America. For the most part, people had stopped shooting them, but the DDT sprayed on America's farmlands turned out to be the greatest killer of all. Used on food crops, DDT kills insects by attacking their nervous systems, and it bioaccumulates, which means that it lingers and amasses in fat cells and is passed up the food chain.

But DDT has been banned in the United States since 1973, so where is it coming from? While it's illegal to *use* DDT in this country, it's perfectly legal to manufacture and export it. Eventually, it finds its way back to us in foods grown abroad that have been treated with the chemical. So in addition to endangering animals around the world, we're also poisoning ourselves.

DDT levels become more concentrated as they travel up the food chain, and by the time apex predators like bald eagles ingest such chemicals by eating fish, other birds, and small mammals, the dose is potent. DDT isn't lethal to adult eagles, but it did pose a lethal threat to the survival of the species as a whole. By disrupting the way their bodies process calcium, it caused sterility and weakened fragile eggshells. The shells were so thin that no matter how careful the parents were, it was almost impossible not to break them. And they were extremely careful.

As paradoxical as it sounds, these ultimate predators with 8-foot wingspans and the strength to carry prey half their weight are also model parents. After preparing for their chicks' arrival by building fortresslike nests with an architect's eye for detail, eagles spend about 35 days protecting their eggs. In a humbling display of self-sacrifice, these 6- to 15-pound birds curl their talons under as they sit, allowing the sharp ends to dig painfully into their palms rather than take the chance of puncturing their eggs. Despite their devotion and self-lessness, however, the eagles couldn't sidestep the effects of DDT. The eggs broke under even the slightest pressure—literally, the pressure of a feather. The bald eagle population was in a treacherous spiral when it was declared endangered in 1967.

But as it turned out, the foundation for their salvation had been laid in 1962, and it came in the form of a book. Rachel Carson, an American biologist, had documented the environmental effects of unrestricted DDT use in *Silent Spring*. Her book also suggested that DDT and other "persistent" toxic pesticides—pesticides that "persist" in the body—may cause cancer and put wildlife in danger, especially birds. *Silent Spring* became a bestseller and inspired a public outcry so loud that President John F. Kennedy ordered an investigation into its effects. The verdict: Carson's information was accurate, and DDT and other persistent pesticides should be phased out. Ultimately, the use of DDT as a pesticide was banned in 1972, taking effect in 1973.

A year later, with Americans' awareness of the threats to wildlife and the environment at what may have been an all-time high, President Richard M. Nixon called for a higher level of species-conservation efforts. The result was the Endangered Species Act of 1973, and with a stroke of Nixon's pen, the bald eagle's struggle for survival no longer looked like a losing battle.

Within a decade of the DDT ban, their numbers had risen to about 100,000 individuals,[18] and the eagles had some breathing room to live their lives. They were once again seen across North America performing their death-defying aerial mating act. It's a courtship that's thrilling to observe. The mates fly to a great height, grab one another's talons, and, locked together, tumble through the sky, fearlessly falling hundreds of feet and sometimes somersaulting several times before letting go and finally spreading their wings.

Once this whirlwind romance has been completed, these monogamous couples begin building their nest together.

Nesting and parenting are among eagles' greatest skills, so when DDT prevented them from carrying out these tasks, it was heart-wrenching to watch. In New York, where there was only one eagle pair during the species' struggle with the pesticide's effects, empty-nest syndrome took on a different meaning. Like a human couple trying to conceive but failing the pregnancy test over and over, the eagle couple conceived egg after egg, only to watch it eventually collapse during incubation. But in 1976, after the pair had been conceiving in vain for 10 years, wildlife biologists came to the rescue. They planted a plastic egg in the nest, which the pair proceeded to "incubate" until the biologists returned with a chick from a captive-breeding program. Accepting the gift, the pair cared for the chick and went on to fledge more captive-bred chicks in the seasons that followed. And New York's eagle population went on to rebound to its current count of 145 pairs, largely through biologists' efforts to hand-rear young eagles obtained from Alaska until they're independent enough to be released.

In addition to serving as our national symbol, the bald eagle serves as a symbol of the burden shared by all the planet's inhabitants. Because of its position at the top of the ecological pyramid, the bald eagle could be considered an *indicator species*—a predictor of the fate that may await an ecosystem as a whole. When an indicator species' numbers drop sharply, it may be a sign that the ecosystem is unbalanced or under stress or has become seriously degraded. In the eagle's case, it was a sign that we were sharing a toxic burden—DDT hurts us all. So when it was banned for most uses in the United States in 1972, it was a victory for *Homo sapiens* as well as *Haliaeetus leucocephalus*.

But the responsibility to preserve species and natural resources for future generations lies with all of us, not just the lawmakers. When I was filming a show at a raptor center in Alaska, I had the privilege of working with people who were caring for a bald eagle that had been hit by a car. The driver had immediately stopped, grabbed a blanket from the trunk, and, risking injury to himself, wrapped up the massive bird and rushed him to the raptor center. In short, by taking responsibility for his actions, he gave the bird a chance to survive that it otherwise wouldn't have had. As it turned out, the veterinarians and staff at the raptor center—who were volunteering their time and skills—were able to nurse the injured eagle back to health. He was ready to be reintroduced to the wild when I was there, and I had the honor of being the one to set him free.

Another injured eagle being cared for at the center was not as lucky. It had been shot in the face, and no one at the center knew if the shooting had been accidental or intentional. The eagle had a gaping hole beneath its eyes where its upper beak had once been. It was grotesque, but I couldn't stop staring at it. I was reminded of the feelings I'd experienced upon seeing a leper for the first time in India; I felt empathy, to be sure, but I was also angry with myself for wanting to look away. I was disappointed in myself for being temporarily blinded by his appearance and losing sight of the fact that behind it was a story and a message. There was value. Many people who see the disfigured eagle at the raptor center may wonder why so much time and effort has been invested in this creature. The answer is, we keep it alive because we should. We do it because we take responsibility for this bird's plight. We do it because we *are* responsible for its plight.

On June 28, 2007, the American bald eagle was removed from the endangered species list, thanks to the efforts of lawmakers and concerned citizens alike. In 2007, the estimated number of nesting American bald eagle pairs in the lower 48 states was at least 9,789.[19] That's more than 20 times the struggling 487 pairs that were alive in the early 1960s. And in Alaska, the estimated eagle population was between 50,000 and 70,000.[20]

Eagles are still protected by the Bald and Golden Eagle Protection Act and the Migratory Bird Treaty Act. It's illegal to take, possess, transport, sell, barter, trade, import, or export eagles or eagle parts, nests, or eggs without a permit. (Exceptions are made to allow Native Americans to possess eagle emblems such as feathers that are traditional in their culture.) But beyond this legislated protection, we have an ongoing responsibility as human beings—the stewards of the planet's natural resources—to ensure that the eagles retain the habitat and clean waterways they need for their full recovery. And as an indicator species, their plight truly is our plight.

CHAPTER 2

# LOSING GROUND

AS OUR VINTAGE Range Rover cuts through the dusty road, Fateh leans out the window, his sunburned face occasionally whipped by brambles or low-hanging branches. He's scouting the horizon for a Bengal tiger, or at least signs of one.

"I think we'll find that big female today," he whispers emphatically. Fateh Singh Rathore is one of the world's best-known tiger conservationists (*Singh*, incidentally, is the Hindi/Sikh for "lion"). We're in the Ranthambore National Park, near Jaipur, India. Suddenly, a member of our team sees a tiger and points to the horizon, where the sun is slowly sinking into the western sky. We move into the gnarled brush, bouncing hard as the jeep takes the rough terrain into the tiger's inner sanctum.

"Yes, there she is!" Fateh calls out. He points to a wiry tangle of thornbush.

A huge female sits in the brambles, haunches down and low to the ground, like a cat about to strike. We follow her line of vision and see a sambar buck. "Oh my God," I say under my breath as I await the ancient drama about to unfold before me, pitting predator against prey.

The cat starts to crawl, like a kitten after a ball of string, only this cat weighs more than 700 pounds. She moves silently, gaining speed, as her haunches stealthily propel her forward with spastic-looking but very deliberate movements. When she's just 20 feet from the deer, there's a sharp crack as a branch snaps under one of her massive paws.

In the blink of an eye, the stag leaps out of striking range and quickly disappears from sight altogether. The tiger never gets her chance to pounce.

While part of me is relieved that the deer was able to escape a violent death, the predator part of me—deep in the recesses of my brain—is disappointed that I didn't get to witness the tiger catch her prey. Nonetheless, observing this wild and powerful predator in her natural habitat was an unforgettable experience.

Fateh understands tigers better than anyone I know. He's lived his whole life with them. His father was the captain of the royal hunting lodge back when sport hunting was one of the biggest causes of tiger extermination, in the days when the park wasn't a conservation center but a place for Indian princes to shoot tigers. In the 1950s, when there were many more tigers in the Indian jungle, Queen Elizabeth and the Duke of Edinburgh were invited on a tiger hunt during a royal visit to India. The queen had a last-minute case of trigger-fingeritis and opted out of the festivities, but the duke took part and bagged one of the big cats. And he turned out to be one of the *last* people to do so before the park was transformed from a hunting ground into a safe haven.

Today, wild tigers are so rare that all subspecies are endangered, some critically. Globally, only about 3,500 tigers live in the wild. In India, land of the tiger, that number is about 1,660—and falling.

# A UNIVERSAL CAT'S TALE

The habitat loss afflicting tigers illustrates the struggle facing *all* of the world's big cats, as well as their smaller cousins, such as the Florida panther and the Iberian lynx.

"Tigers are territorial and require substantial land area to survive," says Mahendra Shrestha, PhD, director of the Save the Tiger Fund (STF). "The fact that human presence is getting closer and closer to tiger reserves is a problem. Habitat loss just gets worse as the human population increases."

Tigers, lions, leopards, and jaguars all share a common ancestor that lived about 5 million years ago and was probably morphologically most similar to a modern leopard. As evolution proceeded, these cats became bigger and fiercer creatures. Our ancestors hunted their ancestors, the saber-toothed tiger, or *Smilodon fatalis*, and it hunted them. The term *fatalis,* as might be guessed, signals that it's extinct—a fate that has since befallen other large cats like the Barbary lion and the Java, Caspian, and Balinese tigers.

As humankind evolved past the hunter–gatherer stage and began to encroach on their natural habitat, big cats retreated farther and farther away. Bali was home to a subspecies of small tigers until 1937, when it was declared extinct. In India, tigers roamed freely through the forests until as recently as the 1950s. The Caspian tiger—the animal often pitted against gladiators in Roman arenas—also became extinct in the 20th century. It was the third most abundant subspecies in the world and could be found throughout Iran, Iraq, and Afghanistan as well as in the Russian Caucasus Mountains.

As apex predators at the top of the food chain, the tigers' disappearance causes especially dramatic changes in the environment. With the lessened threat of these fierce predators, the animals that serve as their traditional prey are able to overbreed. Foragers—like the deer I observed escaping from the tiger—overrun the habitat and threaten to throw the natural order out of balance.

"When you save the tiger, you save the entire ecosystem beneath him," says Shrestha. "Preserving the tiger in his natural habitat means that the rest of the animals at the other end of the food chain survive, too." He's referring to the *umbrella species* phenomenon: When a species (or subspecies) that requires a large habitat is protected, the other species living in that habitat—including humans—also reap the benefits of its protection.

As I tracked tigers with Fateh while documenting the plight and natural history, I fell completely under the spell of these powerful, beautiful animals. The lion may be known as the king of beasts, but many cultures place the tiger at the top of the list when it comes to power, stealth, and sheer beauty.

The tiger (*Panthera tigris*) is the biggest of the "big cats" in the genus *Panthera*—the roaring cats. Roaring is a behavior employed by *Panthera* cats to acoustically mark territory as well as to attract mates. The other three big cats in this genus are the lion, the jaguar, and the leopard. Measuring up to 13 feet in length and weighing up to 660 pounds, tigers can jump almost twice their body length, lending them a forceful and deadly pounce. That power of attack is vital because the tiger is an obligate carnivore—it eats *only* meat. Its primary weapons for attacking prey are its powerful front paws and shoulders and lethal teeth and claws. Tigers have the strength and endurance to swim for 4 miles at a time, sometimes lugging their prey with them. The largest tigers are similar in size to extinct big cats like the saber-toothed tiger. The species historically roamed from Mesopotamia and Russia through most of Southeast Asia. Now they exist in the wild only in India, parts of Southeast Asia, and Siberia.

## SAVING THE BENGAL TIGER

Some of the last wild refuges of the tiger—specifically, the Bengal tiger (*P. t. tigris*)—are in India and Nepal, two places where I've been lucky enough to see these big cats in their element. In the early 1900s, the tiger population in India was about 45,000; in 1972, it was estimated to be 1,827. National parks like Royal Chitwan in Nepal and Ranthambore in India were opened in the 1970s to protect the lands these tigers roam.

As solitary hunters that require a vast area to pursue their prey, tigers occasionally stray outside protected reserve boundaries when searching for food. Even when the population of a local village is moved from its traditional homeland to make room for tigers—a measure Fateh has had to take at Ranthambore—conflict can ensue. Some locals who were relocated to the margins of reserves have subsequently been attacked by tigers. Faced with the loss of their homes *and* the possible loss of their lives, some of the locals who once supported tigers have themselves turned to poaching.

"As land becomes more and more scarce, the reality is that people and tigers will be living in closer proximity. We have to provide incentives for people to become their guardians rather than their executioners," says Shrestha.

Another major motivation for poaching is the economic incentive of the black market. Though most traditional Chinese medicines aren't harmful to animals or the environment, tiger whiskers, fat, skin, and bone are still considered to be effective folk remedies for ailments such as rheumatism and impotence. The demand for such prized formulas has created a lucrative market for the parts of many endangered animals and decimated the world's tiger population. But, there's no medical evidence to support the efficacy of these "cures." Ibuprofen can ease pain and inflammation. Tiger bone cannot.

I've witnessed firsthand the devastation wrought by poachers who "harvest" and sell tiger parts. In Southeast Asia, I went undercover and met a woman who was selling tiger pelts, fat, skin, and bones. Struck by her apparent indifference to the animal parts strewn around her home, I asked, "What will you do when all of the tigers are killed and there are no more left? What will you do in a world where your son will never be able to see a living tiger?"

"I'll take him to the zoo to see them there," she answered calmly.

Fighting this widespread sentiment is a massive undertaking. "The really important thing now is to get people to see tigers as worth more alive than dead," Shrestha says.

Since economic gain is a major incentive for poaching, it also needs to be a big part of the solution. On some reserves, conservationists have hired former poachers to protect tigers. Like a criminal informant for the police, these ex-poachers have proven to be very effective scouts, pointing out the tricks of this ugly trade to help conservationists save tigers and prosecute their killers. Other forms of financial incentive include donating proceeds from tiger reserves and ecotourism directly to local communities rather than to global hotel and travel corporations.

# THE FUTURE OF THE TIGER

The survival of all tigers depends on a continued infusion of the money, dedication, and raw manpower needed to maintain existing preserves, as well as the ingenuity to find new ways of balancing the interaction of man and beast.

"The future can be hopeful for tigers," Shrestha emphasizes. He refers to the success story of the Siberian tiger: "At one point there were only 50 individuals, and now there are about 500."

The Siberian tiger (*P. t. altaica*) is the largest living tiger in the world. It was hunted almost to extinction in the 1940s, before hunting was banned due to declining tiger populations, and again in the 1990s, when the collapse of the Soviet Union—and law and order—made poaching easier. But early in the 21st century, it made a hearty comeback. Through the efforts of the WWF and an organization in Russia called Inspection Tiger, poachers were trained to stop killing them, and the subspecies rebounded. Despite some glitches in the ongoing maintenance of the program, poaching rates are down from an annual average of 70 to 80 tigers killed in the mid-1990s to an average of 30.[1]

Now the leading threat to the Siberian tiger is logging, which cuts into more and more of its pristine forest habitat, leaving it with little or no land in which to hunt. And with humans increasingly hunting the tiger's natural prey—deer, moose, and wild boar—for food and hides, there's little game left for the tigers.

But good news came in June 2007, when Russia, working with the WWF and the STF, opened the 200,000-acre Zov Tigra National Park, the world's first national park dedicated to this rare animal. While Russian conservation efforts have, in the past, been plagued by scandal and uneven efforts, it's at least a step in the right direction. The Siberian tiger continues to maintain its fragile clawhold on survival.

———

Saving the tigers—and many other endangered species—requires collaboration across national boundaries and borders. In the summer of 2008, the World Bank announced a new global effort, the Global Tiger Initiative, a coalition program involving the bank, global leaders, and worldwide conservation experts. Celebrities such as Harrison Ford (a tiger fanatic, like me) also lent their names to the effort and filmed commercials to be shown around the world to raise awareness of tigers' struggle to survive.

Shrestha sees a lot to be gained from this initiative. "There are important connections to world leaders through the World Bank," he says. "Those connections will now be put to work for tigers."

"Wild tigers now have a chance," John Seidensticker, PhD, a biologist at the Smithsonian Institution's National Zoological Park, said upon the announcement of the new initiative. "A world without tigers would be a world without hope."

Still worse would be a world without *any* wild cats.

# THE MISSING LYNX?

My first encounter with the critically endangered Iberian lynx (*Lynx pardinus*) was in Andalusia, Spain, where I visited the Jerez Zoo to see the results of a new breeding program. Like a father visiting a premature baby, I slipped on the requisite sterile paper booties and hairnet to keep my germs to myself. The instant I stepped into the nursery, both of the kittens turned to look at me, the distinctive pointy tufts of fur on their ears standing straight up. Once they'd checked me out, they returned to playing, eager to learn the valuable skills that would one day aid them in the wild. These kittens wouldn't become independent until they were 7 to 10 months old, but they were already showing off their strong spirits. This breeding program is part of a national effort to reintroduce the Iberian lynx into some viable areas of its old habitat starting in 2009.

A native of Spain and Portugal, this gorgeous, bobcatlike feline with long "sideburns" is the world's most threatened cat species. In 2005, studies estimated the population of Iberian lynx to be as low as 100, down from an estimated 400 in 2000. While a few big cat subspecies have become extinct, if the Iberian lynx loses its battle, it would be the first big cat species to become extinct since the saber-toothed tiger.

The main threats to the Iberian lynx are loss of habitat and loss of prey. In the region of Andalusia, one of its last remaining habitats, the lynx was hunted both as game and as vermin that supposedly depleted the populations of *other* game. The government granted it protection in 1973, but its battle for survival still raged on another front. A deadly disease, *poxvirus myxomatosis*, was introduced from South America in the 1950s, and the lynx's main prey—the wild European rabbit—had no natural immunity to it. Rabbits make up 90 percent of the lynx's diet. An adult male eats a rabbit per day, and a mother with young mouths to feed needs three. In some areas, up to 95 percent of the rabbit population was wiped out by the virus, and the lynx population, in turn, was tragically decimated by starvation.

Just when the rabbit population began to show some genetic resistance to myxomatosis and recover in the 1980s, it was blindsided by another disease—viral hemorrhagic pneumonia—that wiped out 70 to 90 percent of Spain's adult rabbits. Though the death rate has since dropped to 30 percent, lynxes have had to supplement their diet with young western roe deer, fallow deer, and wild sheep, making survival much more difficult.

The most critical threat faced by the lynx now, however, is the rapid loss of the cork forests they have called home for centuries. The cork forests in Spain date back to the 13th century and support some of the greatest plant and animal biodiversity in the world. But the farmers who maintain these cork forests and sell the cork for use in wine bottles are starting to see their profits dwindle. The growing popularity of plastic and metal wine "corks" has slashed their profits, so now many of these ancient and vital forests are being systematically bulldozed to make way for more profitable farming, such as growing pine, eucalyptus, and cereal grains. And as a result, the Iberian lynx has lost much of its natural habitat. The only breeding populations left inhabit three distinct regions of Spain, one of which is a protected national park.

Fortunately, an organization called Fauna and Flora International (FFI) is constructing a corridor of habitat suitable for the lynx across southern Spain and Portugal. Besides protecting the existing lynx population—which had turned the corner to number 200 to 250 as of 2007[2]—FFI is implementing a plan to reconnect isolated populations and provide a secure place for introducing captive-bred animals into the wild. The release site will also be suitable for rabbits that are currently being bred.

As the world's most endangered feline, the Iberian lynx's survival is a test case for saving the rest of the world's amazing wild cats—and letting them continue to be wild.

# A WHOLE DIFFERENT ANIMAL?

Much closer to home, another big cat in the Hundred Heartbeat Club is suffering the inevitable effects of booming human population growth and land development.

I almost didn't have the opportunity to witness the Florida panther (*Puma concolor coryi*) in the flesh because this critically endangered subspecies is incredibly elusive. Though they're Florida's second largest mammalian predator, behind the black bear, you can easily stand within 60 feet of a 100-pound male panther in Florida's swampland and *still* not see him. Or, at least, that was my experience while tracking a radio-collared panther with a biologist in Big Cypress National Preserve during taping for a television show. When our transmitter began to beep faster and faster, we knew he couldn't be more than 60 feet away. But this big cat hid from us among the palmetto, kudzu, and poison oak, shielding himself so completely that we never did see him. The panther is beautifully designed for the twisted, nearly impenetrable vegetation of the wilds of Florida. It can move through the forest soundlessly, without snapping a twig, or quickly climb 60 vertical feet up a tree to pounce on its prey. And, of course, it can expertly evade a film crew of four.

Disappointed by our near miss, I halfheartedly explored the preserve. It was encouraging to see the underpasses, or culverts, that have been built under some highways to connect panther habitats and reduce the number of panthers killed by cars. But I couldn't shake my desire to see one of these sleek creatures up close. After finally giving up on our search, we wrapped filming for the day.

A year later, I was in south-central Florida filming a spot on snapping turtles, and during a break I went for a walk by myself. As I made my way along a sandy trail through swamp and stands of palmetto, I caught a slightly musky scent, and my first thought was that an armadillo must be nearby. Within the shadows of the branches of an old scrub oak, about 20 feet off the ground, I could see something moving. Before I could even venture a guess as to what it was, it broke through the leaves and, seemingly in slow motion, floated to the ground. When it landed, I could see a long tail with a crook in it, and I realized it was the very animal I'd been longing to catch a glimpse of for so long. It was darker than the panthers I'd seen in photos, more charcoal than sage, and it weighed only about 60 pounds. But each of those 60 pounds seemed to be all muscle. It turned its head my way for a split second—just long enough for me to wonder whether I should shout for the crew—and then lithely, silently sauntered into the brush.

For a moment, I regretted that the crew hadn't been able to document the sighting of this incredible animal. But then it struck me that this experience may only have occurred *because* I was alone, not at the center of a busy filming session. I couldn't stop thinking about the way the panther had seamlessly, effortlessly disappeared without so much as disturbing a leaf. It seemed sadly symbolic of the way this entire subspecies is quietly slipping away before our eyes.

The critically endangered Florida panther is the sole member of the cougar species in the eastern United States, and although it's protected by law, Florida's growing human population and resultant land development are constant threats. As wetlands continue to disappear, panthers have been forced into dangerous terrain fragmented by busy highways. From 1978 to 1994, 20 panthers were killed by cars; in 2007 alone, 14 panthers met the same fate. With only an estimated 80 to 100 panthers left in the wild, that's a significant number of deaths. Though the highway culverts have somewhat alleviated the problem by providing a safe alternative to crossing congested roads, this safety measure doesn't restore habitat continuity. Female panthers have proved reluctant both to use the culverts and to cross major roads. And an adult male panther needs an average of 200 square miles of habitat to survive.

Inhabiting just 5 percent of their historical range, these big cats live mainly within a region that includes Everglades National Park, Big Cypress National Preserve, and the Florida Panther National Wildlife Refuge.

Unfortunately, controversy has made the protection of these animals even more challenging. Traditionally, the Florida panther has been considered one of the 32 unique subspecies of cougar, classi-fied under the name *Puma concolor coryi* (*Felis concolor coryi* in older listings), but now there's disagreement over whether it really is a subspecies unto itself. The US Fish and Wildlife Service (USFWS) had listed it as endangered in 1967 based on its cougar classifica-tion, so now its protected status is in question as well. A genetic study conducted in 2000 concluded that there's insufficient basis for the existence of 32 cougar subspecies—there aren't enough differ-ences among them—and suggested that they be reclassified into 6 subspecies. Such a designation could remove the Florida panther from the critically endangered list and classify it with cougars that have been assigned a less-than-critical preservation status.

And it's not just the panthers that will suffer. Because the pan-ther is an umbrella subspecies, animals such as the endangered gopher tortoise and indigo snake would also be threatened by the lack of habitat protection, as would animals that aren't currently endangered but could become so. As members of the *Puma* genus rather than the *Panthera* genus, these powerful cats can't roar, much less advocate for themselves. It's up to us to speak up on their behalf. If the Florida panther loses its critically endangered status, the question will be not whether they constitute their own subspecies, but how we can ensure that those 100 heartbeats become no weaker.

Like people, animals simply need their space—they require ade-quate habitat to survive. Once they had all the space they needed, but humans have steadily encroached on this finite resource. As long as people continue to claim animals' natural habitat as their own, even our best conservation efforts face an uphill battle. We need to draw boundaries and to honor them: This side is ours, that side belongs to the panthers. That's the approach China has imple-mented with the giant panda—and it's showing promise.

# 1,829 GIANTS STILL ROAM EARTH

The giant panda (*Ailuropoda melanoleuca*) lived in the bountiful valleys of China and Tibet for 22 million years, roaming from one bamboo-rich forest to the next. When humans began to settle in the same areas, however, many of the trees that make up these forests were cut down. The pandas were forced to seek higher and higher ground, and today their home is a group of cloud-enshrouded mountaintops, "islands" in the sky.

Often referred to as the roof of the world, the Tibetan Valley is the highest and largest plateau on Earth. While giant pandas once lived both in the mountains and on the eastern edge of the plateau, their habitat has been reduced to about 30 patches of forest high in the Minshan, Qinling, Qionglai, Liangshan, Daxiangling, and Xiaoxiangling mountain ranges of southwestern China. In such remote, fragmented environs, survival is challenging. Today, there are an estimated 1,590 Chinese pandas in the wild, and in 2007 there were 239 living in captivity.[3]

Compounding the challenge is the fact that bamboo—the main component of the panda's diet—undergoes a natural cycle of flowering and dying off to produce seedlings for the next batch of bamboo. Once it dies, it can take a full year for bamboo to regenerate from seed and as long as 20 years before the new plants are plentiful enough to support a giant panda population. Because all the plants in a given bamboo species go through the stages of a life cycle at the same time, a bamboo forest must have at least two species of bamboo to support a voracious panda population. That way, if one species is undergoing a die-off, there will be at least one other species in the active stages of a cycle. In 1983, a massive bamboo flowering and subsequent die-off occurred. It created a biologic catastrophe for the giant panda, claiming about 40 percent of its population. If such an event were to happen again, there would be 636 fewer pandas in the world.

A hundred years ago, when bamboo die-offs struck in the broadleaf and coniferous forests that pandas prefer to inhabit, it wasn't a disaster—they could simply move to adjacent forests to find food. Pandas are born wanderers, eschewing permanent dens in favor of spots under tree stumps protruding from the mountainside or under rock ledges, and "following" the bamboo was a way of life. But as China's population raced toward its current figure of more than 1.3 billion—17 percent of the world's population—and humans pushed into panda habitat with agricultural and other development, pandas were forced to higher and higher elevations. While more than 50 panda reserves have been established in these mountains, the food sources there are severely limited. Pandas eat 25 species of bamboo, but only a few of those species are found at the 5,000- to 10,000-foot elevations where they now live.

What we refer to collectively as *bamboo* is one variety of a group of woody perennial evergreen plants in the true grass family. The fastest-growing woody plant in the world, bamboo can grow as much as 2 inches an hour—or 2 *feet* in a day. This is convenient for the panda, which has to eat almost constantly during waking hours because bamboo offers very little in the way of nutrition. And though pandas have broad, flat molars and powerful jaws that can easily crush bamboo, they also have the digestive system of a carnivore (despite the fact that they eat a primarily vegetarian diet) and aren't able to digest cellulose from the bamboo efficiently. As a result, they eat up to 84 pounds of it a day. (Incidentally, the amount of cyanide in that much bamboo could kill a human.) While they eat other foods such as flowers, vines, honey, eggs, fish, shrub leaves, and oranges (when available), bamboo accounts for 99 percent of their diet. Why pandas eat so much of something that has so little nutritional value is just one of many things that scientists don't understand about them, another being their distinctively patterned black-and-white coats. One theory is that this color scheme allows them to stand out to prospective mates, while another posits just the opposite: The coloring serves as camouflage in their shade-dappled and often snow-covered environment.

Pandas don't hibernate like other bears, and this is largely because of the dearth of fat in their diet—they can't build up the reserves needed for a long winter's nap. Their nutrient-deficient diet is also a reason that pandas lead largely solitary lives. They simply don't have the energy for much social interaction. As such, pandas are often observed in a state of Zenlike stillness, sitting in the trees they're able to climb because the pads of skin that cover their wrist bones serve as opposable thumbs. Panda expert Russell Ciochon, PhD, professor of anthropology at the University of Iowa, has suggested that the giant panda's low ratio of body surface area to body volume indicates that it has a low metabolic rate, much like the gorilla (which is also a vegetarian). Their 6-foot, 220- to 330-pound bodies have adapted to their low-calorie diet.

Tending to the panda's needs is an uphill battle when you consider how much of China's resources are devoted to sustaining the country's population of *people*. The panda's indigenous habitat, China's Yangtze Basin, is home to more than 400 million people and countless animal and plant species, many of which are rare or endangered (including the red panda, takin, golden monkey, and golden pheasant). This region is also the geographic and economic epicenter for much of the country—it supports subsistence fisheries, agriculture, energy plants, and tourism on a mass scale. According to a 2008 ecological footprint report, it would take an area of land and sea more than 250 times the size of Hong Kong to produce the natural resources consumed by the residents of Hong Kong and to absorb the carbon dioxide the city emits.[4] China's ecological footprint is more than twice the sustainable level, and its carbon component continues to increase. With a metropolis of such huge size to feed and fuel, preserving panda habitat in the Yangtze Basin is a formidable challenge.

# HELPING NATURE ALONG

Fortunately, China has come a long way in protecting the giant panda. In the 1970s, with only an estimated 2,400 pandas remaining in the wild due to habitat loss and centuries of poaching, the Chinese government built a field camp for studying pandas—the Wolong Panda Reserve—in Sichuan. It also began to enforce the death penalty for poaching pandas (the punishment was scaled back to a 20-year prison term in 1997). China intensified its efforts at "panda diplomacy" as well, offering pandas as gifts to other countries, most famously giving the National Zoo in Washington, DC, panda cubs Ling-Ling and Hsing-Hsing in 1972. From 1957 to 1983, China gave 24 pandas to zoos in different nations as goodwill gestures.

Since 1984, though, goodwill has come at a high price: Hosts must pay up to $1 million a year for the privilege of a 10-year panda loan, and any cubs born during the term of the loan also become the property of China. In 1998, the USFWS wisely added its own clause to the arrangement: A US zoo may adopt a panda only if it can supply documentation that China will allocate more than half of the loan fee toward the conservation of wild pandas and their habitat. It's probably not coincidental that by 2005, the number of Chinese reserves for these refugees of human encroachment more than quadrupled, protecting more than 4,000 square miles and more than 45 percent of the remaining giant panda habitat. More important, provincial forestry departments are reestablishing and protecting migration corridors between preserves, giving these solitary wanderers room to roam and a means of escaping their isolated homes in the clouds in the event of a bamboo die-off.

One of the problems with habitat fragmentation, which breaks up the population of a species into separate geographic zones, is that smaller habitats necessarily mean smaller panda populations, making them more susceptible to extinction. The magnitude-8 earthquake that struck the southern Sichuan region in May 2008, for example, could very well have killed most of the wild pandas. Although Sichuan is home to 75 percent of the wild panda population, only one panda died in the earthquake, which killed more than 69,000 people. Chinese officials estimate that the quake affected up to 80 percent of the pandas' mountainside habitat in Sichuan, sending rocks, soil, and vegetation crashing into the river valleys below. The Wolong reserve was damaged beyond repair, and its 53 pandas had to be transported to other areas. A new breeding center is planned for a site 12 miles south of the original Wolong site.

Recovering the panda's natural habitat is critical to the survival of the species; pandas seem to lose interest in mating once they're in captivity, so captive breeding has been slow going. And it's no wonder, really—captive pandas have traditionally had few opportunities for socialization with other bears. So when a male and a female suddenly become "roommates," they're typically as uncomfortable with the arrangement as humans might be. Males sometimes even attack females if they don't have rival males to fight with, which is how they win a female in the wild, says JoGayle Howard, DVM, an animal-reproduction specialist with the Smithsonian Institution.

But captivity conditions are improving as scientists learn more about pandas' habits; their enclosures are now bigger, and they live with groups of adults rather than just one potential mate.

Adding to the difficulty of mating pandas is an immutable fact of life: Female pandas are fertile for only 3 consecutive days each year. So if things don't work out during the brief window of time they have to successfully mate, another year will go by before the opportunity arises again. Luckily, science has come to the rescue. China has been artificially inseminating pandas for almost 50 years. In recent years, the program has been able to produce more than 10 cubs annually, with the record standing at a whopping 34 born in 2006, 30 of which survived. Zhang Zhihe, PhD, director of the Chengdu Research Base of Giant Panda Breeding, says that it's no coincidence that it's the same year he began showing "panda porn"—footage of pandas mating—to inexperienced males.[5]

In addition to this unusual DVD collection, scientists at Chengdu have the largest panda sperm bank in the world. Samples from 17 bears are held there, including one from a bear who died in 1991. Panda cells frozen in liquid nitrogen are also stored in a genomic data bank, which allows scientists to track genetic lines and ensure diversity among future populations. Lack of genetic diversity is a problem that many species face when their populations are fragmented by habitat loss.

Breeding is only half the battle, though. Pandas have been as unenthusiastic about parenting in captivity as they've been about mating, though some progress has been made. Veterinarians at Chengdu and the Wolong Panda Reserve have begun "swap-raising" pairs of panda cubs. Pandas can give birth to one or two cubs at a time, but one is all the mother can feed because each helpless, 6-ounce baby—born pink, furless, and blind—nurses 6 to 14 times a day for up to 30 minutes at a time. So when two cubs are born, the mother usually abandons one of them. (Males don't participate in parenting and usually associate with females for no more than 4 days after mating.) But at the Chengdu and Wolong panda centers, veterinarians put one of the cubs in an incubator and bottle-feed it with formula. Then, when the mother goes to sleep, they swap that cub for the other cub, ensuring that both get a full measure of mothering and giving the panda population a better chance than it would have under Mother Nature's plan.

When humankind corners a species in a tract of land that isn't sufficient to ensure its survival, we need to compensate for its losses. In the panda's case, that means giving back crucial stretches of land we've taken and intervening in a 22-million-year-old parenting practice. We can't fall back on letting nature take its course when we've changed the land and its inhabitants in ways that nature never intended.

# PRIMATES LOSING THEIR GRIP

In 2008, the IUCN reported that nearly half of the world's primates now face extinction after 65 million years on the planet. The primary cause is habitat loss, though poaching for their meat and body parts also contributes significantly to the problem. The biggest devastation is being seen among primates like gibbons, spider, capuchin, and red colobus monkeys, and great apes.

"We've raised concerns for years about primates being in peril, but now we have solid data to show the situation is far more severe than we imagined," Russell Mittermeier, PhD, chairman of the IUCN Species Survival Commission's Primate Specialist Group and president of Conservation International, said upon the IUCN report's release.

The study found that of 634 recognized primate species and subspecies worldwide, 11 percent are critically endangered, 22 percent are endangered, and 15 percent are vulnerable. Asia has the greatest proportion of threatened primates, with 71 percent considered to be at risk for extinction.

Scientists classify primates as *generalist* mammals, which means they have an extensive range of specialized characteristics that have evolved out of the need to survive. Though some primates, such as baboons, don't live in trees, all primates are able to climb them. And all of them can swing and leap from branch to branch and walk on just two feet. It's hard to imagine what new characteristics primates could develop that would help them escape or adapt to the massive problems now confronting them.

# THE ORANGUTAN FREEDOM JOURNEY

Orangutans are losing their rainforest homes at an alarming rate, and poachers are adding insult to injury. My own experience with primates came to an emotional climax in Indonesia, where I'd gone to film Biruté M. F. Galdikas, PhD, one of the world's leading experts on the orangutan. She has rehabilitated, raised, and released more than 400 orangutan orphans back into the wild and has been studying these creatures in their natural habitat at her camp in Indonesian Borneo for more than 3 decades.

Nearly all of the endangered Bornean orangutans (*Pongo pygmaeus*) that Galdikas and her staff care for and rehabilitate have been orphaned as a result of poaching. Poachers capture and kill orangutans both to sell body parts on the black market and to sell as *bushmeat*—a term used to describe the edible meat of animals poached in sub-Saharan Africa. The newest addition to Camp Leakey when I arrived was a baby orangutan that was in such bad shape that he was being administered intravenous fluids. It would have been traumatic enough had this infant been orphaned by an accident, but, as with most of these orphans, it's likely that his mother was slaughtered before his eyes and he was ripped from her arms by poachers.

While humans and orangutans are distinctly different primates, we still share much in common, which was painfully evident as I held this baby orangutan. As I cradled him gently in my arms, I couldn't imagine the horror he had endured, and I hoped he felt some sense of safety now that he was at this sanctuary. With his eyes fixed on mine, he occasionally reached up to touch my face—a familiar gesture that reminded me of my daughters when they were babies. Within just a few minutes, he fell asleep in my arms.

This 9-pound orangutan would need to spend 6 to 8 years mastering the necessary skills to live in the wild. Until an orangutan is 3 years old or so, it's completely dependent on its mother and clings to her as she swings through the trees. When its motor skills and confidence have developed enough, it follows her like a shadow as she forages for fruit. Because orangutans have such a long "childhood"—and raising them is a full-time job—orangutans in the wild have only one infant every 7 or 8 years.

It was an honor to meet Galdikas, and I soon saw that she had a constitution to match her iron will. To illustrate the process of rescue, rehab, and rewilding for our television viewers, she'd chosen Moktar, an adult orangutan who had completed extensive forest training with the staff and other orangutans. Now able to swing with characteristic grace through the high canopy of the forest trees, he was ready to go it alone. So I joined Galdikas and her colleagues (some of whom were local Dyaks tribesmen, indigenous people known more than 50 years ago as the Wild Men of Borneo for their head-hunting rituals) on a journey rowing down a remote river with the freedom-bound orang in a catch-and-release cage. As the hellish midday heat beat down on us, I became increasingly awed by this woman who'd spent more than 30 years of her life in the jungle, wading through leech- and malarial-mosquito–infested waters to search for signs of the elusive orangutan in the wild.

We arrived at our stopping point and carried the cage the remainder of the distance to a safe place in a protected area, where we unburdened our aching arms and backs of the 140-pound ape. A blanket of wet heat hung heavily around me, but I felt a thrill course down my back.

Moktar shifted in his cage, looking into my eyes and waiting for what I sensed he knew was coming. We said a short prayer of blessing in Indonesian, and the cage door flew open. I can honestly say it was one of the richest and most meaningful moments of my life as a naturalist to watch this creature with the strength of eight men—the largest of the tree-living primates—find his way back into his own wild world. One branch at a time, he mounted into the forest canopy and finally sailed through the trees on his elegantly long, red-furred arms, his grunting cries growing fainter as he made his way deep into the jungle.

Orangutans are highly intelligent, and I couldn't shake the feeling that Moktar knew we humans were to blame for his species' demise. In fact, according to recent research by psychologist Robert Deaner, PhD, orangutans are the world's most intelligent animals after humans. And fieldwork led by Carel van Schaik, PhD, a Dutch primatologist at Duke University, seems to confirm it. He found orangutans capable of mastering tasks that far exceed chimpanzees' abilities and of teaching these skills to their offspring. For example, orangutans in parts of Sumatra make seat cushions with stacked leaves and use leaves to protect their hands when they harvest and eat fruit that has sharp spines. And in parts of Borneo, mealtime includes using a fistful of leaves as a napkin. *Planet of the Apes* fans will remember that those movies depicted orangutans as the intellectuals and scientists of the ape world, a classification based on the real pecking order of primate intelligence. And theirs is an intelligence you can *feel* when you look in their eyes. Maybe that's why *orangutan* means "person of the forest" in Indonesian and Malay.

But those forests—and the world of primates in general—are losing ground, with orangutans clinging to survival on the forest fringes of what used to be vast habitats ranging from Borneo to Sumatra and the mountain gorillas numbering fewer than 700 in Uganda, Rwanda, and the war-torn Democratic Republic of the Congo (DRC). In South America and Madagascar, some smaller species of primates such as the golden lion tamarin are *relative* success stories, with the golden lion tamarin having been downgraded by the IUCN to endangered from critically endangered in 2003. But it's the exception.

The great apes that Galdikas works with are losing their habitat due to deforestation that's clearing the way for palm oil plantations, mining, farming, and illegal logging. In addition, forest fires have dramatically altered or destroyed more than 75 percent of the orangutan's rainforest habitat. Galdikas believes that if these forests continue to be wiped out at this rate, orangutans could cease to exist in the wild in as few as 5 years. Orangutans are also poached and captured for the international pet trade, both of which appear to happen when orangutans venture past the edge of their forest habitat to forage fruit crops planted by farmers, according to the IUCN.

Galdikas's passion for primates was sparked when she checked out her first library book at the age of 6: *Curious George*. The man in the yellow hat and his primate pal inspired her, and by the second grade she'd made up her mind to be an explorer. When Galdikas was studying the natural sciences at UCLA as a graduate student, she met anthropologist Louis Leakey, PhD, and told him of her aspirations to study orangutans. As it turned out, it was a fateful meeting—she would go on to become one of "Leakey's angels," along with Dian Fossey, PhD, and Jane Goodall, PhD. Galdikas, who named her own daughter Jane after Goodall, fondly recalls the two older women treating her like a younger sister.

While Fossey turned to gorillas and Goodall to chimps, Galdikas chose to explore the mysteries of orangutan behavior and ecology. She and her husband at the time, photographer Rod Brindamour, arrived at the Tanjung Puting Reserve in Indonesian Borneo in 1971. One of the last wild places in the world, the reserve had no telephones, roads, electricity, or other modern conveniences. Her first home there was a rat-infested ranger's station that hadn't been inhabited for years, but Galdikas forged ahead. She created "Camp Leakey" before a year had gone by and began to record and write about the behavior and ecology of orangutans.

Over 32 years in Tanjung Puting, now a national park, Galdikas has conducted the longest-ever continuous study of a wild mammal by a single principal researcher. To this day, her efforts continue to make a major difference in the conservation of this species.

Rehabilitating orangutans for release into the wild is no easy feat. Before an orangutan can be reintroduced, he must learn to identify hundreds of edible plants. An orangutan orphan also needs to learn to live independently, and part of that education is learning the rules of territoriality, which are different for males and females. With creatures this complex, rehabilitation requires a staggering investment of time and money.

Orangutans prefer lowland tropical rainforests because of their abundance and variety of fruit, which makes up 61 percent of these omnivores' diet. Galdikas says there are 317 food items in Bornean orangutans' diet, including leaves, bark, insects, honey, small vines, and fungi. But the forests that provide them with this massive buffet also provide timber for the logging industry and the right type of soil for raising palm plants.

When I talked with Galdikas about her hopes for the orangs that she and her colleagues have saved, she said in her characteristically soft, Canadian-inflected accent that their future hinges in large part on the palm oil industry, which has transformed the orangutan's forests into danger zones.

The rising demand for palm oil, derived from the fruit of the *Arecaceae elaeis* oil palm, is resulting in the destruction of tropical forests in Sumatra and Borneo, which are fast being cleared to establish new plantations. Palm oil is used in packaged food products like cookies, crackers, frozen dinners, low-fat dairy products, and candies as well as in toiletries like soap and cosmetics. Incredibly, 1 out of 10 products available at the average US or European supermarket contains palm oil. And it's one of the region's most abundant and lucrative resources. In 2006, the total land area of palm oil plantations was approximately 11 million hectares (almost 42,500 square miles). In 2005, the Malaysian Palm Oil Association, whose members produce about half the world's crop, reported that it manages about 500 million perennial palm trees.[6] According to the World Resources Institute, Indonesia lost 40 percent of its forest habitat from 1950 to 2000.[7] It continues to lose 5.4 million acres a year, and Galdikas says that the rate is accelerating. Indonesia contains 10 percent of our planet's precious and biologically rich rainforests, according to the WWF, and it's predicted that by 2012 the country will have lost 98 percent of its remaining forests.

When workers slash and burn forests for palm oil production, they often kill, maim, or entrap orangutans. When the mothers are caught in traps, their babies are ripped from their arms to be sold and the mothers are typically killed. It's a common problem with habitat fragmentation: As "civilization" closes in, it creates more "edge" lands, where animals' habitats are back-to-back with humans' converted land. Many species just aren't cut out for life on the edge and require the protection of a habitat's interior in one way or another.

In addition to the spread of palm oil plantations, the capacity for pulp and paper production has expanded in Indonesia by nearly 700 percent since the 1980s.[8] And as much as 40 percent of the wood used by pulp producers from 1995 to 1999 came from illegal logging.[9] The Indonesia–United Kingdom Tropical Forest Management Programme estimated in 2000 that 73 percent of the logging in Indonesia is being done surreptitiously on land where logging is outlawed.[10]

According to Galdikas, the Indonesian government has put a stop to most illegal logging, but palm oil concessions continue to rip apart the forest at a rate that will leave Bornean orangutans, critically endangered Sumatran orangutans, and other species without any wild habitat at all by 2012. A female orangutan needs a home range of about 2,100 acres, and a male needs 6,100 acres or more.

Galdikas hopes the current economic chaos might ultimately slow the encroaching destruction. "If the money isn't there to back it," she said, "maybe the palm oil industry will slow down a little." In the meantime, she urges consumers to boycott products that contain palm oil.

I ask Galdikas what it is that continues to draw her to this primate that is at once so much like and so different from humankind.

"Its gentleness," she says. "There's a gentleness there that surpasses anything that humans are capable of. You can turn your back on an orangutan. Their friendship can span species. You gaze into their eyes and you know you are dealing with an intelligence equal to your own."

# The Golden Lion Tamarin— A Brazilian Rainforest Success Story

Half a world away, in the coastal Atlantic canopy forests of Brazil, a small monkey called the golden lion tamarin is a success story. This species has been the subject of one of the most fruitful conservation programs in the wild, one that began only about 20 years ago but has already helped to stabilize the population of these creatures.

"We can now sustain them in perpetuity," says University of Maryland biology professor James Dietz, PhD, a researcher with the Golden Lion Tamarin Conservation Program. "The species has a good prognosis for survival." Dietz and his wife, Lou Ann, have been working to save the golden lion tamarin since the 1980s.

Among the 35 species of small monkeys in the family of Callitrichidae, there are 4 species of lion tamarins: the golden lion tamarin (*Leontopithecus rosalia*), the golden-headed lion tamarin (*L. chrysomelas*), the black or golden-rumped lion tamarin (*L. chrysopygus*), and the black-faced lion tamarin (*L. caissara*). All of these

species live exclusively in the Atlantic coastal forests in eastern and southeastern Brazil, near heavily populated cities like Rio de Janeiro and São Paulo. They're also all endangered, but three species have been downgraded from critically endangered because of intensive conservation programs.

Deforestation, hunting, and capture for the illegal pet trade had caused the numbers of these small primates to decline drastically. Current population estimates in the wild are 1,200 for the golden lion tamarin, 6,000 to 15,500 for the golden-headed lion tamarin, 1,000 for the black lion tamarin, and as few as 400 for the black-faced lion tamarin, according to the National Zoo.

Golden lion tamarins have been popular pets since the 1700s, no doubt because of their striking, exotic appearance and small stature, weighing a maximum of about 1½ pounds and measuring just 13 inches, not counting a 16-inch tail. With golden "lion's manes" framing their faces, the tamarins were described by the Italian scholar Antonio Pigafetta, who accompanied Magellan on his voyage to the Maluku islands, as "beautiful simian-like cats similar to a small lion." It was said that Madame de Pompadour, one of the official mistresses of Louis XV, kept this small monkey as a pet and strolled the grounds of Versailles with it perched on her shoulder.

"People didn't see their value except on the illegal pet market," says Dietz. "There was no effort to conserve them, and their habitat shrank to a few 'forest islands' where they've clung to survival."

That survival is due, in part, to education and public outreach, an enforced ban on the sale of tamarins as pets, a halt to deforestation, and successful reintroduction of captured tamarins into the wild. Now the golden lion tamarin's major challenge is maintaining genetic diversity. "There aren't currently enough animals to

ensure a healthy population," explains Dietz. So the Golden Lion Tamarin Conservation Program is now embarking on a process called *metapopulation management,* in which individual animals will be moved from island to island, creating greater genetic diversity and a healthier population overall.

When Dietz and his colleagues began studying the tamarins in the '80s, there were only "a few hundred monkeys out there," he says. "We didn't really know exactly how many. We started doing a census and then reintroducing individuals from captivity. Most golden lion tamarins today in the wild are the progeny of those released captives."

Another challenge, along with metapopulation management, will be building forest corridors to link the small "island" habitats of this species, which are high in the trees. Dietz explains that the Atlantic forest of Brazil is near some of the most populous areas of the country and that, in the '90s, less than 7 percent of it remained. So simple corridors, even just a few trees wide, can be literal lifesavers for a tamarin, connecting it to vital pockets of protected forest.

As far as the pet trade goes, it's now illegal to own or trade a golden lion tamarin, and even the captive population of the species around the world is controlled by the Brazilian government in accordance with a treaty signed by almost all zoos. In essence, Dietz says, a zoo doesn't "own" a golden lion tamarin, nor may it sell one. The tamarins are on loan from the government of Brazil.

Wealthy landowners in the area have also begun to value the golden lion tamarin in a different way. It's now considered a status symbol to own a piece of the wild land that the tamarins inhabit, and these areas will form part of the tamarin's future forest corridors. "The golden lion tamarin went from a pet and a food item

to a conservation icon here in Brazil," says Dietz. "It's even featured on Brazilian currency. And deforestation where we work now is almost zero."

The golden lion tamarin was the first primate ever to be downgraded from critically endangered to endangered status. "It takes more than a village to conserve this species. It takes a whole community, and we've been very fortunate," Dietz says. "Many towns and lots of people have worked on this. It's a team effort."

It takes a *planet* to save all its species, and the conservation efforts that have benefited the golden lion tamarin have made an invaluable contribution to that larger cause. "I think that what we've learned about golden lion tamarins will serve as a stepping-stone for the conservation of other species," Dietz says.

## Bamboo Lemurs: Madagascar's Gentle Primates Bounce Back

On the island of Madagascar, off the southeastern coast of Africa, conservation scientist Pat Chapple Wright, PhD, has spearheaded the effort to save another primate species from the brink of oblivion and restore healthy populations. A soft-spoken woman whose modesty belies her formidable achievements, Wright is a professor of anthropology at the State University of New York, Stony Brook, and one of the world's leading conservationists and primatologists. And she's passionate about lemurs.

Lemurs are primates native only to Madagascar, though they are also found on some smaller surrounding islands. Fossil evidence indicates that they traveled to Madagascar after it broke away from the mainland, possibly by "rafting" on clumps of

vegetation. Isolated from competition with other primates, lemurs differentiated into more than 100 species that capitalized on different food sources, a phenomenon that has also occurred among bats in the tropics and finches in the Galápagos. The surviving 85 species range in size from the tiny, 1-ounce pygmy mouse lemur to the 22-pound indri.

One of the larger surviving species, the greater bamboo lemur (*Prolemur simus*) is also one of the rarest mammals in the world. Once thought to be extinct, it was spotted by two French scientists in the 1970s but was not seen again for more than 10 years. When Wright went to Madagascar in the 1980s looking for the elusive species, she found the only living bamboo lemurs (75 are now known to be alive in Madagascar) and also discovered a new species, the golden bamboo lemur (*Hapalemur aureus*). Both species' diets consist almost exclusively of bamboo. Like the giant pandas, these animals are able to consume quantities of cyanide—found in some species of bamboo—that would be fatal to humans.

The golden bamboo lemur is now critically endangered, with fewer than 1,000 individuals in the wild. In 1991, the Malagasy (as the people of Madagascar are known) government agreed to Wright's request to set aside more than 40,000 hectares (154 square miles) as Ranomafana National Park. Today, Ranomafana is a conservation model for parks and reserves around the world. It's also the world's last refuge for the bamboo lemurs and other related species that cling to this fringe of forest, with much of Madagascar's forests having been slashed and burned for logging and charcoal production.

Ninety percent of the forests of Madagascar, the world's fourth-largest island, have been destroyed. We're talking about a place that's home to 10,000 plant species, 316 reptile species, and 109

bird species in addition to the lemurs.[11] When you consider that 95 percent of the species that live there aren't found anywhere else in the world, this amounts to an ecological disaster.

Bamboo lemurs in particular need wide ranges of habitat to survive, and "they get into trouble with all the splitting and fragmenting of the forest," Wright says. "I'm worried for them, but I'm also optimistic for their survival in the wild, especially because the Malagasy people, led by the new president, are aware and concerned and want to save these animals."

The good news, Wright explains, is that enhancement of protected areas was decreed in 2008 and a social network of awareness that also accounts for the welfare of local residents is enduring. For example, residents are being paid to help reforest large areas, she says.

"Part of our job as conservationists is to talk to the local residents. They once thought of lemurs as we do squirrels, as common pests, and if they got hard up for food, they would eat them. But we've gone into remote areas to tell them how special these animals are, especially with the bamboo lemurs. We are showing them how rare and unique these animals are, and they are becoming more valuable to locals alive than dead."

In more than 20 years of working with the lemurs, what keeps Wright spending more than half her time in the forest is the saucer-eyed lemurs themselves, whose name means *spirit of the night* or *ghost*—probably an allusion to the bansheelike wailing of some species, particularly the indri.

"Lemurs are more laid back than other primates," she says. "They don't squabble like chimps and have all kinds of social systems that are quite fascinating. Females are dominant over males, for instance, which might be one reason why they are not as aggressive as other primates."

# GORILLAS IN THE MIDST— OF WAR AND STRIFE

As I've mentioned, I try to avoid anthropomorphizing—assigning animals qualities and characteristics that are unique to humans. Animals are animals, they are not a reflection of us. But the truth is, when you look at a gorilla, you're looking at your cousin (several times removed). Behind those lucid eyes lies a highly developed mind, one that employs many of the same survival tools that we do. And if humans have souls, I find it very hard to believe that great apes don't have them, too. They experience the same things we do—play, passion, war, grief—and they have individual, personal flaws just like we do.

While orangutans will look a human in the eye, adult gorillas are guarded about making eye contact. But younger gorillas are very open and will look you right in the eye, as I learned during a 2005 trip to the Bwindi Impenetrable Forest in Uganda. My crew and I had to hike through a misty, soggy cloud forest—a tropical forest with low-level cloud cover—to find the mountain gorillas (*Gorilla beringei beringei*). The slopes of the mossy broadleaf forest dissolved beneath our feet as we made our way along, but there was nothing soft about the Jurassic-scale nettles that scarred my legs for life. I'd been warned—by everyone—to wear long pants for this trek, but I'd insisted on wearing shorts, never imagining I might fall victim to the stinging nettle with rhubarb-size leaves and finger-length spines. But several miles into our hike, all I could do was suck it up and soldier on. As it would turn out, I was also suffering the combined effects of the early stages of African tick fever and malaria. Suffice it to say, it was a challenging experience, but then, all the best ones are. It was a small price to pay for the opportunity to visit with the ghosts of the forest.

With clouds hovering in the treetops, we finally came upon a gorilla family in a clearing. I sat at the base of a hagenia tree and watched in awe, my heart raging in my chest as an adolescent gorilla made his way toward me under the watchful eyes of a massive adult male, called a silverback, and three adult females. Twice the size of a female, silverbacks are the largest of all gorillas. They can be incredibly intimidating; weighing between 350 and 500 pounds and standing up to 6 feet tall, a silverback can spread his arms to a span of $7\frac{1}{2}$ feet. Though mountain gorillas are covered in fur that's longer than that of other gorilla subspecies—allowing them to thrive in these wet cloud forests, where temperatures can drop below freezing—there was no hiding the strength of the long, thick arms the silverback was leaning on.

When the young gorilla—probably 5 or 6 years old—boldly sat down next to me, he nearly made contact, letting his fingers "walk" to within inches of my shoelace and looking me right in the eye. In that incredible moment, it was very easy to understand the allegiance that had driven Dian Fossey to bring the plight of the mountain gorilla to the world's attention more than 20 years ago in the small mountain outpost of Karisoke, Rwanda. "When you realize the value of all life, you dwell less on what is past and concentrate more on the preservation of the future" were the last words written in her journal before she was murdered with a poacher's confiscated machete that hung on her wall. She'd placed it there as a testament to her work protecting these gentle giants that today clutch at survival, numbering only about 700. No one ever confessed or was found guilty of her murder, but suspects as diverse as poachers, government officials, and her own coworkers were considered for years. All that was certain was that at the time of her death, Fossey had given her life to protect an animal she loved.

There are two groups of mountain gorillas (one of two subspecies of the Eastern gorilla), one found in the Impenetrable Forest and the other in the Virunga volcanic mountains of central Africa that lie within four national parks. And with only about 700 mountain gorillas left in the world, their survival is caught in a complicated net of social problems, poaching, and habitat destruction that plague the three countries where they remain.

Mountain gorillas aren't commonly killed for bushmeat, although they do sometimes get caught in poachers' snares. Gorillas are usually killed to harvest their hands and feet, which are sold on the black market as ashtrays and other souvenirs. They are also captured to be sold illegally as pets. As with orangutans, when an infant is taken, the adults in the extended family are often also slain for their parts or simply because their attempts to defend the young ones hinder the poaching process.

Apart from deforestation and poaching, another challenge to the mountain gorilla's survival has been the constant warfare, social strife, and famine that have assaulted its habitat for more than 20 years. Guerrilla warfare in the DRC threatens the animals—and their protectors—in Virunga National Park, which straddles the boundary of Rwanda and the DRC. Many rangers have given their lives to protect the gorilla, and those on the Rwandan side of the park have worked for years at great risk and sometimes for little or no pay. The guerrilla factions are also trying to cash in on the country's small but lucrative tourism market by leading unofficial visits to local gorilla populations. These excursions put the gorillas at risk because the warlords who conduct them rarely observe basic conservation methods, such as keeping tourists at least 12 feet from the gorillas at all times. Mountain gorillas are one of the few primates that live primarily on the ground, only occasionally climbing fruiting trees that will support their bulk, and their humanlike genetic makeup means that close contact with humans often results in the transmission of viruses that could make them very ill. Within a population so isolated, a virus or other contagious disease could literally wipe them out.

But as controversial as it is, *responsible* mountain gorilla ecotourism may be one of the only weapons the gorillas have against extinction. Benjamin Beck, PhD, director of conservation for the Great Ape Trust of Iowa, points to tourism as an "incredibly valuable source of foreign exchange between Rwanda and Uganda and, to some extent now, the Democratic Republic of the Congo.

"It's a high-end business that brings in tremendous revenue, and right now in Rwanda and Uganda, at least, the gorillas are paying their own way," he says.

The mountain gorilla exists "on islands in oceans of poor humanity who are desperate to feed their families," Beck says. "The forest is seen as much-needed revenue. The odds the gorilla is facing are astonishing, but there is hope for their conservation so long as the tourism industry exists."

The fact that people continue to be fascinated by gorillas doesn't hurt, either. "We share 97 percent of their DNA," says Beck. "We are astonishingly similar and yet so different. When I look an ape in the eye, I think, 'Why is this being so like me and yet so dissimilar?' It's a feeling that gives me a shiver down my spine."

The steady stream of tourists has made the gorillas more tolerant of, or habituated to, the presence of humans. While an "unhabituated" male will have a certain level of nervousness and discomfort around humans, the females in the group will generally sit relaxed, eating and grooming. But for all the chest pounding that males do as a warning to protect their groups, the mountain gorilla's demeanor is essentially peaceful.

Gorillas know that humans' presence can be deadly or benign, and they're very sensitive to the differences—they seem to be able to distinguish whether a human is approaching them with good or bad motives. And for now, tourism might be a source of benign contact necessary for the species' survival. "It's crucial for the three governments that jointly hold the species' fate in their hands to continue to see gorillas as a cash cow," Beck says.

The International Gorilla Conservation Programme (IGCP), an organization composed of the African Wildlife Foundation, FFI, and WWF, says ecotourism is a success, with annual tourist visits sometimes exceeding 10,000. "The income from tourism to gorillas has probably been the single most important factor in ensuring . . . that the parks have continued to be supported and conservation activities continued," notes the IGCP. "The income from gorilla tourism is one of the main sources of foreign revenue for the three host countries."[12]

"Without the ecotourism industry, the prospects for the species are dim," Beck says. "But I still see the glass as half full, and I definitely feel optimistic about the mountain gorilla. There is just too much at stake for these governments to fail in their conservation efforts. And while that's the case, the mountain gorilla is safe."

# Part II

# INTRODUCED SPECIES, POLLUTION, DISEASE

# CHAPTER 3

# WHEN WORLDS COLLIDE

I N   S P R I N G   1 9 9 8 , I flew to Hawaii with a film crew to tape a segment on a critically endangered songbird, the puaiohi (*Myadestes palmeri*), a member of the thrush family. When we landed in Hawaii, I knew I'd arrived on an island that was home to—among other magnificent wildlife—some of the most endangered birds in the world. In fact, if you were to make a list of the 10 most endangered birds in our 50 states, 7 would be native to Hawaii—which is why the National Audubon Society (NAS) gives Hawaiian birds their own endangered list. These incredibly rare, ancient birds merit special attention and protection.[1]

The number of puaiohi in existence dropped to between 200 and 300 by the 1970s, and I knew that the population had declined even further by the late 1990s, when I was there. The puaiohi population faced a number of threats from *nonnative species*, or animals that are not native to a specified habitat. The puaiohi had to compete for food and habitat with nonnative birds, became infected with malaria borne by mosquitoes, and was losing parts of its habitat due to the destruction of vegetation by nonnative pigs and goats.

When my crew and I arrived at the Keauhou Bird Conservation Center, which is part of the San Diego Zoo's Conservation and Research for Endangered Species department, we were met by Alan Lieberman, an enthusiastic biologist who was not only this species' caretaker but also clearly its biggest fan. He ushered us to the field station and proceeded to give us a list of the dos and don'ts regarding our contact with the extraordinary bird we were about to meet. After a lengthy orientation, we were finally given permission to take our film equipment to the aviary.

It was beginning to feel like we were visiting a prison rather than an animal preserve. After making our way through the gate of an electrified fence, we encountered a 6-foot-tall concrete perimeter wall. These barriers had been constructed to keep out the puaiohi's predators—feral cats and the Indian mongoose. Like cats, mongooses aren't native to the Hawaiian Islands, but they're both adept at hunting thrushes and other Hawaiian birds. Without the electric fence and concrete barrier, the puaiohi wouldn't have stood a chance.

Once we were allowed through the concrete perimeter, we stood outside a wire-mesh enclosure with yet another set of security doors. Before unlocking them, we slipped into sterile surgical jumpsuits and stepped onto a spongy pad saturated with antiseptic solution. With a finger to his lips, our somewhat anxious guide reminded us to keep quiet—one of the do's on the list.

After traveling a great distance to arrive at this island sanctuary, this was the moment I'd been waiting for. I was trembling with excitement—I was finally about to set eyes on an extremely rare creature that few others have seen, which is always an incredible thrill for a wildlife biologist. Standing before the small hatch door concealing this endangered species, Lieberman whispered, "Okay, guys, here's the scoop. I can only give you about 20 minutes in here, so you'll have to be quick about it." Twenty minutes was barely enough time to get our equipment set up, but it was a privilege to be there, and we'd known before arriving that there would be strict limitations on our visit.

When the moment arrived for me to step in front of the camera and take a look at the bird for the first time, I did a double take. It was one of the most ordinary-looking birds I'd ever seen. I'd intended to deliver a few witty remarks and avian factoids, but what came out was, "This is it? I came all the way from Massachusetts to see this?" I had to admit that I was expecting something a little more interesting. This ordinary-looking creature wasn't much bigger than a sparrow, and its plumage was a dull brownish gray—the same dull shades worn by any number of birds I'd seen in my own backyard.

In the puaiohi's defense, it could carry an interesting tune. It varied from a squawk to a warble to a labored wheezing sound to a metal-on-metal screech. And with breeding season approaching, this male was singing nonstop. So I remarked on the song and expounded on the biology of this particular thrush on camera for about 10 minutes before I ran out of words. Then I looked at Lieberman and, unable to entirely keep the sarcasm out of my voice, asked, "So tell me, what makes the puaiohi different from any other species of thrush? What's the big deal about this bird, I mean?"

He paused for a moment, and when he spoke, the words were simple but astonishing: "He may be one of the last of his species."

I looked at the puaiohi again, and it had transformed into the most vivid bird I'd ever seen. Every little feather, every twitch of its head seemed as vital an expression of life force as I'd ever witnessed.

Lieberman explained, "There are only about 15 in captivity. We collected 10 eggs in the wild, and these are the survivors and their offspring. If these birds don't breed, they will be no more."

It was stupefying. I struggled for an appropriate response. What was there to say about the fact that, by destroying its habitat and introducing nonnative species, man had forced the puaiohi into its twilight on Earth—and very possibly into extinction. Paralyzed by our sense of helplessness, we watched as the cheerful bird eagerly hopped through the branches, oblivious to his potential doom. He was even proudly singing out an invitation for a mate, an invitation that could well go unanswered.

Our crew was quiet as we made our way back to the pier for our return trip to Maui. Although the little thrush was ignorant of his prospects, I could think of little else. As the sky and the sea glowed orange under the weight of the setting sun, I found myself hoping against hope that the puaiohi wouldn't meet the same fate that the po'ouli, a fellow island bird, had met just 31 years after its discovery.

The po'ouli (*Melamprosops phaeosoma*) had gone unrecorded until University of Hawaii students discovered it in 1973. It was the last native Hawaiian bird to be scientifically classified. The students first spotted this relatively brawny honeycreeper—a small, tropical bird in the finch family—in the rainforest wilderness of Haleakala Volcano on Maui. Because the likelihood of discovering a new animal species on a relatively small island that's been populated by humans for more than 14 centuries is incredibly low, the discovery was big news. It turned out that this newly listed species—which the students named *po'ouli,* or "dark head," for the black ski mask it seemed to wear—was very rare, with an estimated population of fewer than 200.

Sightings of the bird had declined steadily since 1976, and by 1997, there were just three known birds remaining. The population had struggled against the same threats posed by nonnative species that currently imperil the puaiohi. Ultimately, the po'ouli population of three was simply too tiny to prevail against such a daunting challenge.

What finally sealed the fate of the po'ouli? Consider this scenario: The small bird is sleeping soundly on a twisted forest branch when a furtive assassin, drawn to the gaseous beacon of carbon dioxide and heat continuously radiating from the bird's body, lands softly on it. Driven by an innate hunger for blood, the killer robs its unsuspecting victim of its future in a matter of seconds. The bird doesn't even put up a struggle.

The assassin in this scenario is nature's most resilient vampire, a creature with a miraculous ability to adapt to the ecological challenges of diverse habitats, from the Arctic tundra to the humid rainforests of the tropics: the tiny and sometimes-deadly mosquito. As the insect siphons an insignificant droplet of the bird's blood, it simultaneously passes a microscopic creature into its blood- stream. That microorganism, a plasmodium parasite, effortlessly squeezes through the mosquito's proboscis on its way into the wel- coming corporeal fluid of its new avian host. The parasite multi- plies exponentially, and within just a few days, millions of its kind are thriving in the warm, viscous habitat of the bird's bloodstream. As the colony of plasmodium microorganisms prospers, the health of its host rapidly declines. Ultimately, the bird succumbs to a dis- ease that, over the course of 30 million years, has infected count- less vertebrates, including humans: malaria.

The last surviving po'ouli died of complications related to advanced age at the Maui Bird Conservation Center. While the case of malaria it was carrying at the time was benign, the dis- ease had no doubt played a large role in the events that decimated the species. That's what happens when worlds that nature never intended to meet collide. The po'ouli was native to the Hawaiian Islands; the mosquito is not. How, then, did this bird become the target of an alien parasite? The answer can be traced back to what was probably the first nonnative species to arrive in the Hawaiian Islands, more than 1,300 years ago: *Homo sapiens*.

# PARADISE FOUND . . . AND DESTROYED

The impact of humankind on the pristine environment of a new frontier has almost always been catastrophic for indigenous life. The ecological impact that results from the human colonization of an unspoiled habitat isn't unlike the pathological damage that a parasite imparts on its unwitting host. For the Hawaiian Islands, human colonization represents the definitive story of paradise found and, ultimately, destroyed.

Hawaiian wildlife began to feel the effects of colonization soon after the Polynesians arrived, between the 3rd and 7th centuries, and began cutting down trees and clearing large areas of forest for agriculture, logging, and the building of homes and villages. By the time Europeans colonized the islands in the 18th century, more than half of the archipelago's avian life had been hunted to extinction, including a massive species of flightless duck, the moa-nalo, which weighed up to 16 pounds. For 3 million years, these had been the islands' principal browsers, or animals that feed on high-growing plants (as opposed to grazers, which feed on low-growing vegetation). Still, when Captain James Cook took his first steps on the black sands of Hawaii in 1778, he encountered an extraordinary array of birds found nowhere else on Earth; today, only 25 percent of those species remain. Of the 32 species of native Hawaiian birds that have survived, 24 are critically endangered. Most of these birds have less than a 20 percent chance of surviving beyond the next decade.

Many of Hawaii's bird species were hunted to extinction by animals such as the mongoose, as well as by cats that were introduced by the Europeans to hunt rodents that ate seeds and crops. One such rodent was the Norway rat—which, ironically, had been accidentally introduced after stowing away on ships sailing from European ports. Historically, nonnative species introductions have often been poorly conceived attempts to control a native pest. Like the children's rhyme about the old woman swallowing a spider to catch the fly, introducing one species to deal with the undesirable effects of another species lower on the food chain can lead to disaster. Historically, little thought was given to the impact that nonnative plants and animals would have on the ecosystem as a whole.

The term *introduced species* refers to plants or animals that are released into a foreign habitat. Many introduced species don't survive in a new habitat, and those that do don't always pose problems for the native flora or fauna. But typically, if a highly adaptable species is introduced into a new environment that's similar to its previous home, some native species will be challenged, while others may actually benefit. For instance, after the brown tree snake found its way from the South Pacific to Guam sometime around 1950, possibly by hiding in the wheel wells of cargo planes, it ravaged the island's native bird populations but enhanced the insect populations the birds had preyed on. The snake has even been known to snatch chickens and pets from yards and attack babies in their cribs. Because its prey is so abundant on Guam, this voracious predator has grown to nearly 10 feet in length there—4 feet longer than the average length in its native habitats. If there had been enough natural predators in Guam to keep the brown tree snake in check, the native birds would have had a better chance. But in the absence of such predators, the snake effectively silenced the forest. It's not uncommon for an introduced species to live in a new habitat for many years before it gains the competitive edge, but once it establishes a firm foothold, it can become extremely aggressive. Animals and plants that outcompete the natives for food and other limited resources and those that prey on the native animals or lay waste to the plant life are referred to as *invasive species,* and they cause an estimated $1.4 trillion in environmental and economic damage each year.[2]

While less common, a native species can also become "invasive" if a change occurs that causes or allows it to spread widely or exponentially increase its population. This change can be brought about by a natural event such as a long-term drought or a flood, or by a human-induced change, such as overhunting of a native species' predators. In almost all instances in which introduced species become invasive, humans have already disturbed the habitat.

Such was the case for the 'alala (*Corvus hawaiiensis*), Hawaii's only native crow. Ravaged by loss of habitat and many of the same introduced and native predators faced by the po'ouli, the 'alala no longer exists in the wild. While the captive-breeding program in Maui, run by the Zoological Society of San Diego, reintroduced 27 young crows into the wild in 1993, 21 of those birds had disappeared or died by 1999. The remaining six were recaptured in 1999 and placed back in captivity. For this Hundred Heartbeat Club member to survive in the wild again, we would essentially have to turn back time on the Hawaiian Islands and reclaim the natural habitat lost to agriculture, replant the trees that have been cut down, bulldoze the houses and hotels, unpave the parking lots and roads, and reintroduce the vegetation that once thrived there. We would also have to round up all the nonnative species that exist in addition to the feral cats, mongooses, mosquitoes, rats, and feral pigs. The pigs have destroyed much of Hawaii's native plant life and, in so doing, radically reduced the number of native trees and shrubs that produce fruit for the crows. The USFWS acquired and set aside 5,300 acres of land as the Kona Forest Unit of the Hakalalau Forest National Wildlife Refuge in 1997 in an effort to preserve the crow's remaining habitat. While the refuge is a safe haven for many species, sadly it's no longer home to the 'alalas. As of 2008, the last 50 native Hawaiian crows were living in captivity.

The demise of the po'ouli and the Hawaiian crow illustrate a story that's unfolding all too frequently around the world. Introduced species rarely improve a habitat and more often than not disrupt or destroy it for the native plants and animals. One powerful threat is enough to devastate a species, but when an endangered species faces two or more threats simultaneously, its odds of extinction increase significantly.

# Two Threats Prove One Too Many

How did the two-pronged assault by humankind and introduced species result in the extinction of the po'ouli? Let's back up to man's arrival in the Hawaiian archipelago. While there are no written records about these islands before the 14th century, historians believe Polynesians were the first people to live there, arriving sometime between the 3rd and 7th centuries. They came from the Marquesas and Society islands, navigating their way by the stars through the uncharted Pacific in double-hulled dugout canoes heavy with supplies from their old world. Unaware of what animals they might find in their discovered lands, they brought hearty pigs and domesticated fowl with them. After the Polynesians spotted the group of islands and landed on its shores, they were awestruck by the natural splendor. In Polynesian mythology, the realm where people are rewarded after death is called Hawai'iki, translated as "the old homeland," and so the Polynesians set about making the old homeland their new home.

Virgin habitat was compromised for the needs of agriculture as the forests were burned and the rich, volcanic earth was sown with taro, coconuts, yams, ginger, breadfruit, and other crops. The nonnative life spread quickly: Pigs escaped captivity, and wind and water dispersed seeds from the plantations. Within the confines of such an isolated ecosystem, the native Hawaiian flora and fauna were ill equipped to deal with the aggressive nature of these invasive species.

Then there was the added stress of predation by humans and animals alike. Whether for the collection of ornamental feathers or for the consumption of flesh, the Polynesians hunted many of the native birds. And the damage to the endemic wildlife was made even worse by the ravenous feral pigs that devoured many of the native plants, insects, and ground-nesting birds and their eggs. The Europeans' arrival in the 18th century brought an even greater disregard for nature as well as many more new creatures, including dogs, cats, rats, mongooses, goats, deer, and pigeons. Some of these animals were brought intentionally to enhance the settlers' quality of life and improve their odds of survival, while others were accidentally transported as stowaways. For the European colonists, Hawaii represented a new beginning, but for many native species of wildlife, this alien invasion was the beginning of the end. Of the 40 mammalian species in Hawaii today, only the hoary bat and the monk seal are native, and both are critically endangered.

As for the introduction of the pesky mosquito, its journey to paradise followed a more sinister path—at least according to one legend. As the story goes, in the mid-19th century, the crew of a merchant ship requested permission to visit a convent located on one of the islands. Perhaps they tried to make the case that they were in sore need of prayer, but the authorities thought otherwise and denied permission. This enraged the crew, and they allegedly dumped water contaminated with mosquito larvae into the pristine water of a nearby well. That in itself wasn't enough to loose a plague of mosquitoes on the Hawaiian Islands, but burrowing pigs—descendants of those brought by the Polynesians—had excavated wallows that filled with stagnant water. So, rather than remaining a local irritant, the mosquitoes found these breeding spots and proceeded to build a population. One introduced species helped another to spread at the expense of all, including the pigs themselves. And with the spread of the mosquitoes came the spread of avian malaria, itself introduced to Hawaii, probably by birds from continental America that carried the plasmodium parasite. The result? Within just a century and a half, 14 species of honeycreepers have been consumed by extinction, the po'ouli among them.

————

Birds are important indicators of the health of an environment. They're one of the first animals to react to climate change, and the state of their health gives us important information about the quality of the air and water in their habitat. Judging from the population declines that have occurred so far, their natural habitats leave much to be desired. About 10,000 species of birds are alive today, more than 1,200 of which are threatened with extinction, many of them because of human activities. Since the 17th century, about 130 species of bird have become extinct, and there were hundreds more before that. Agriculture poses the biggest threat, affecting the habitat of 65 percent of species. Invasive species prey on 52 percent of bird species.

The populations of many common birds found in the United States, such as the meadowlarks and boreal chickadees, are declining, too. According to the NAS, the average populations of the 20 common bird species that are in the steepest decline have dropped by 68 percent since 1967. And the causes are distressingly wide ranging: suburban sprawl, expanded agricultural operations, industrial development, logging, mining, drilling, and deforestation resulting from insect epidemics and fire.

Currently, the IUCN lists 190 bird species as critically endangered. At least 23 species of bird are members of the Hundred Heartbeat Club, and there may be as many as 72 others with populations of fewer than 100 that haven't yet been quantified. But while the varied threats may seem unstoppable, conservation efforts do make a difference. In the past 3 decades in the United States, such efforts have kept 99 percent of endangered bird species from disappearing.

And happily, the puaiohi is among them. Thanks to the Keauhou Bird Conservation Center's breeding program that began with those 10 eggs, the Hawaii Endangered Bird Conservation Program has released 137 birds over the past 10 years, and now the wild population is estimated at 500. As dire as the situation appeared during my visit in 1998, the puaiohi may be on the way to recovery.

In recent years, several other bird species that were teetering on the brink of extinction have also made impressive comebacks thanks to the efforts of wildlife conservationists. The population of the rarest falcon in the world, the Mauritius kestrel, had been reduced to an estimated 10 birds when Carl Jones, founder and scientific director of the Mauritian Wildlife Foundation and a fellow with the Durrell Wildlife Conservation Trust, took over the conservation efforts. Today, more than 500 of these falcons are living in the wild again. Other species that have graduated from the Hundred Heartbeat Club include the black robin (native to the Chatham Islands of New Zealand), the Mauritius parakeet, the Rarotonga monarch (native to the Cook Islands), the Seychelles magpie-robin, the Laysan duck (endemic to Hawaii), the whooping crane, and the California condor. These conservation stories demonstrate that species can recover if appropriate and timely action is taken. And it doesn't always take legions of conservationists—some species have been saved by just a handful of dedicated people.

# RESCUING THE MAURITIUS KESTREL

In 1974, the Mauritius kestrel (*Falco punctatus*) was the most endangered bird of prey in the world, with only four birds existing on the same southwestern Indian Ocean island where the extinct dodo bird once made its home (a third pair lived in captivity). The birds suffered their greatest decline in the 1950s and '60s as a result of habitat destruction, unregulated use of DDT, and the introduction of nonnative predators.

During the 1974 nesting season, one of the two remaining pairs in the wild built a home in a tree cavity as usual. But after a macaque—a nonnative monkey and predator—raided the nest, the future of this species rested on the wings of the other wild pair.

In a departure from tradition, that pair had decided to build that season's nest not in a tree, but in a niche on a sheer, monkey-proof cliff. The result: three fledglings. After they'd matured, those three likewise set up housekeeping in the cliffs, and, by 1976, the Mauritius kestrels had increased their numbers in the wild to 11— a 175 percent increase in only 2 years.

The problem was, the kestrels couldn't maintain that growth rate on their own. The captive-breeding efforts that began when

Stanley A. Temple, a Cornell University postdoctoral researcher associated with the Peregrine Fund, took a pair into captivity in 1973, weren't immediately successful. By 1979, the population still showed no signs of growth, and the International Council for Bird Preservation (ICBP) pulled the plug on a long-running project to save the species. Conservation funding was tough to come by, and the ICBP could no longer justify the expense of saving the 8-ounce, short-winged falcon.

So the organization sent a scientist named Carl Jones to the island 500 miles east of Madagascar with instructions to shut down the program. When he got there, though, he couldn't go through with it. Instead, he did just the opposite: He *salvaged* the program. Heeding a calling higher than the command to follow orders, he set up predator-proof nesting boxes and spent countless hours persuading the kestrels to eat dead mice and birds—not traditionally part of their diet—from his hand. And he didn't stop there. He also climbed trees to snatch eggs from kestrel nests and used incubators to coax them into hatching. In the meantime, their nests empty, the females laid second sets of eggs.

Incredibly, this "double-clutching" strategy was a raving success. In 1985, Jones reported the 50th "assisted birth," and his Mauritian Wildlife Foundation developed a captive-breeding program that, with help from falcon breeder Willard Heck, boosted the kestrel population to 200 by 1993. When the falcons were released, the program continued to help the birds by providing supplementary food, nest guarding, and other predator controls. And the birds helped themselves by continuing to nest in cliffs like the pair that had helped to save the species back in 1974. Twenty years after that first important step, in 1994, the kestrel population had become self-sustaining, and the captive breeding program was no longer necessary.

More than 500 mature kestrels now call Mauritius home—50 times more than were there when Jones arrived. The Mauritius kestrel is officially listed as vulnerable, not endangered, and it will *always* be vulnerable, given its relatively small population. But this is a success story of epic proportions, complete with a species that learned to adapt to adversity and a genuine, real-life hero.

Unfortunately, there's no shortage of species in need of heroes.

# ATTACK OF THE GIANT TOADS

In a scenario very much like something from a horror movie, the Puerto Rican crested toad (*Bufo lemur*) has had to contend with an invader that originates from a place where toads grow to gigantic proportions and have appetites to match. Compared with the crested toad—whose males average 1¾ ounces and whose females range from 3½ to 5¼ ounces—the invasive cane toad (*Bufo marinus*) averages about 1 pound in size, with some weighing in at more than 2 pounds. That's an average of four times as large as a female crested toad and *nine* times as large as a male. Imagine if a species of Martians nine times the size of humans landed on Earth and proceeded to feed their hulking bodies with the same food we eat. We're already pushing the planet toward the point of exhaustion to feed our rapidly expanding population—not only would a rival alien species speed our progress toward that point, but many humans would also starve to death along the way.

And when these giant toads are preyed upon, the poison-filled parotid glands in their skin have the power to kill many of the native predators unfortunate enough to have chosen them for dinner. Even their tadpoles are poisonous enough to kill most animals when eaten.

That's the horror story that the tiny, pebbly skinned Puerto Rican crested toad is living. The cane toad—aka the giant marine toad—feeds on the same insects, insect larvae, worms, and other invertebrates as the crested toad, and it's the warty, dry-skinned giant that's winning this contest for survival, according to the Wildlife Conservation Society. It's also taken over many of the crested toad's breeding sites and much of its habitat. This comes in conjunction with habitat loss due to urbanization, drainage of wetlands, and deforestation. Crested toads were believed to be extinct until 1967, when they turned up in a seasonally flooded parking lot in the Guánica Forest Preserve. At that point, they had no protected or natural breeding areas and bred only in concrete cattle troughs or tanks. So the crested toad has been living at the edge of extinction for decades, and the IUCN lists it as critically endangered, with a population of about 250 and dropping.

The cane toad's impact on the crested toad's habitat is an especially grim example of the dangers posed by invasive species. And the cane toad threatens species around the world. It was introduced in Puerto Rico in 1920 to control white grubs that were attacking sugarcane crops. It was also taken to Florida, the Philippines, Japan, Papua New Guinea, most Caribbean islands, many Pacific islands, and Australia.

Cane toads were introduced to Australia in 1935 as a means of controlling the cane beetle, another sugarcane pest. While they failed to do the job because they were unable to jump to the tops of the sugarcane stalks where the beetles lived, the prolific breeders did succeed in building a population estimated to surpass 200 million today. They've reached densities of 2,000 per hectare in newly colonized areas. Graeme Sawyer, coordinator of the Northern Australian Frogs Database System, says the cane toads' march across the continent could be complete within 2 years, which is when they could reach Western Australia if there's sufficient rainfall between now and then.

Incidentally, some of the greatest destruction inflicted by invasive species has taken place in Australia. European colonization and the Industrial Revolution in the 18th and 19th centuries led to a significant rise in the importation of new species to this formerly isolated continent. Many of these nonnative animals had no natural predators in their new home and therefore easily preyed upon or outcompeted the indigenous species. This inundation has impacted not only native plants and animals, but also the soil and waterways. When invasive species such as rabbits eat and degrade the vegetation upon which many animals are dependent for food and shelter, it threatens the survival of vulnerable or endangered species such as the rabbit-eared bandicoot, also called a *bilby*, a long-eared, long-nosed marsupial that doesn't need water but very much needs carbohydrate-rich seeds and roots. Plant degradation like that inflicted by rabbits can also cause soil erosion, which creates wide-ranging problems. In addition, invasive cats and foxes threaten the survival of native birds, mammals, reptiles, and insects. And because invaders might carry diseases from domestic animals, they tend to keep those diseases circulating among both wildlife and livestock. Australian brush-tailed possums, for example, can pass tuberculosis to cattle and deer herds.

In the case of the cane toads, the severity of their impact is probably due to the fact that they outcompete so *many* species. And the vast expanses of open grassland—where the toads feel at home—make it easy for them to find habitat.

While in some cases of species decline it's impossible to definitively point a finger at the poisonous toad, the circumstantial evidence is piling up. Sharp drop-offs in populations of Northern quoll, a carnivorous marsupial related to the Tasmanian devil (an endangered marsupial featured in Chapter 5), have been detected after the toads have made their debut in an area, and declines in the numbers of snakes and the monitor lizards known as *goannas* (medium to large lizards in the same family as Komodo dragons) have also been reported in the wake of toad invasions.

The toads' poisonous skin could also be playing a role in the declining populations of their would-be predators. Because the cane toad is a new arrival on the scene, other species haven't had adequate time to adapt to its presence—they haven't figured out how to safely eat it. There is one exception, though. Like a one-bird bomb squad, the crafty, industrious kookaburra skins the toad before eating it, defusing a potentially deadly meal.

When it comes to inspiring invention, adversity is right up there with necessity, and Australia's cane toad onslaught has produced an intriguing counterattack strategy. Peter Koopman, PhD, of the University of Queensland's Institute for Molecular Bioscience, is genetically engineering a strain of cane toads that can give birth only to males, a tactic that, if successful, would cause the toad population to die off eventually. He's confident that his lab can produce the "daughterless" strain within 2 years. At that point, his team will need to make sure that these new toads are capable of mating competitively in the wild and, if so, manage their release.

But with a remaining population of only 250, the Puerto Rican crested toad can't afford to wait for such indirect conservation measures to take effect. So, since 1982, the Association of Zoos and Aquariums (AZA) has been breeding the golden-eyed beauties with the turned-up snouts at 20 zoos and aquariums and reintroducing them to their natural habitat in Puerto Rico. It's part of the AZA's Species Survival Plan (SSP), a conservation initiative that develops breeding programs, raises awareness, and develops new technologies to aid conservation. It's an impressive program that entails "master plans" aimed at achieving maximum genetic diversity and demographic stability for threatened wildlife.

In the case of the crested toad, its SSP researchers and the USFWS merged their recovery plans, and the partnership has led to the construction of ponds for releasing captive-bred toads into their traditional habitat, public education programs, and population and distribution surveys. Twenty-two zoos and aquariums are working with the USFWS.

Humans are responsible for introducing many of the nonnative plant and animal species that have thrown entire ecosystems off-kilter. It's only fair that we now step in with our advanced knowledge and technology to protect the natural resources of today for generations to come.

# CHAPTER 4

# TOXIC SOUP

I'VE HELPED CAPTURE cheetahs and lions, assisted in lifting a 700-pound anesthetized polar bear into a harness, immobilized an elephant, and *been* immobilized and almost killed by an elephant, but I've never had a more unnerving hands-on experience than restraining a full-grown California condor (*Gymnogyps californianus*). I was working with senior wildlife biologist Joe Burnett at the Ventana Wildlife Society in Big Sur, California, and we were about to release a rehabilitated condor. It was a picture-perfect day, with clear, cobalt blue skies, bright sunshine, and a sweet, salty, breeze, and there I was—standing on a hillside and using all my might to clasp to my chest one of only 321 California condors in existence.

Imagine holding a bird with a beak so powerful, it can easily rip through the bloated hide of an elk carcass, slashing through flesh and tendons. It's *your* job to make sure he doesn't hurt himself or the other two biologists who are restraining his head and feet. Yes, it's a three-person job—one wrong move, and the bird could tear out an eye or shred the skin off a finger. Now imagine holding that bird with the knowledge that if he *does* get hurt, the world loses a precious member of an endangered species. Losing this bird would be the human equivalent of scraping the entire populations of Vermont and Rhode Island right off the US map. Imagine the pressure of knowing that this creature you're releasing, this commanding presence that stands nearly as tall as you do, needs to survive and breed or his species may not survive. Think of the months of effort and the thousands of dollars that have gone into nursing this particular bird back from a near-deadly case of lead poisoning. Think of the *years* of effort and the *millions* of dollars that have been invested to pull this species back from the precipice of extinction. The mighty bird I'm attempting to wrangle has an awful lot riding on his glorious black wings.

It's been a few months since the condor has had a chance to stretch those wings and take flight, and it's up to us to provide perfect takeoff conditions. Anything less could cause injury, and there are far too few of these beauties left to let that happen. By the time we get to the launch spot, located a few yards from the top of a steeply sloped hill, the vertebrae in my lower back are starting to buckle from the exertion. This enormously powerful bird is palpably aching to spread his wings, and it takes every bit of force my muscles can generate to restrain his.

When the condor and his three handlers are all in position, the moment arrives, and it's an incredible one. With talons as substantial as the roots of an old tree, the 3-foot-tall, 25-pound bird takes a running start toward the drop-off and falls from our sight. But just as quickly, he reappears on a trajectory toward that cobalt sky. It's a stunning sight, but it's what you hear that leaves you speechless—the beating of those wings, like the sound of sheets flapping on a clothesline in an angry gale. At such close range, I can hear exactly why Native Americans nicknamed the condor *thunderbird*. When it gains its desired altitude, the condor simply catches an air current and glides across the sky with astonishing grace. And it may glide like that for miles—at speeds of up to 85 miles per hour—before it needs to flap its massive, aerodynamically perfect wings again.

When you see a condor for the first time, it's as if you've been transported back to a time when pterodactyls owned the sky. A member of the vulture family, the California condor is North America's largest flighted bird, with a wingspan of up to 10 feet and weighing from 20 to 25 pounds. "People can't believe an animal that looks like this still exists," Burnett says. "Condors were almost gone by the time we really became aware of them, and people tend to have this mysterious preconception about them. When they finally see one, it really lives up to their expectations, or even surpasses them."

These noble, somewhat intimidating birds aren't just physically powerful, they're also fascinating communicators. In a form of visual communication, the skin on their mostly bald heads changes color depending on their mood, ranging from a pale yellow when they're under stress or agitated to a vibrant red when they're feeling amorous. To attract a mate, the sexually mature male flushes red with passion while puffing out the ruffle of black feathers at the nape of his neck. Then he slowly walks toward the female with his wings spread wide. If she dips her head, indicating that she accepts his proposal, they become mates for life, right then and there.

Their courtship takes place on the ground, but condors spend a good part of their lives airborne, searching for food, sometimes traveling 150 miles in a single day. As scavengers, they favor the rotting flesh—called *carrion*—of large-bodied animals such as deer, sea lions, and whales, but as they circle the skies on empty stomachs, it's not those animals they're looking for. Instead, they look for groups of other scavengers, such as turkey vultures, that they can attempt to bully and chase away from their feasts. Lacking a strong sense of smell and hunting from heights of up to 10,000 feet, condors rely entirely on their keen vision to spy the other scavengers. When carrion is plentiful, condors capitalize on the abundance and greedily gobble as much as 3 pounds of flesh in one sitting. Incredibly, this can sustain them for up to 2 weeks, which is how far off their next meal could be if feast suddenly turns to famine.

Tragically, the carrion they're so dependent upon can harbor a formidable threat: lead. When an animal has been shot with ammunition that is made of lead, condors and other animals that feast on the carrion ingest the lead, which is absorbed into their bloodstreams. Over time, their lead levels can become life threatening. Lead poisoning has played a major role in the struggles of a number of other bird species as well, including the American bald eagle. For our national bird, the source was waterfowl that had been hit by or ingested lead shot. Many eagles that fed on killed or crippled birds were gradually poisoned to death. After the problem was recognized in 1991, the USFWS initiated a 5-year program to phase out the use of lead shot for waterfowl hunting. This measure radically reduced the number of bald eagle deaths from lead poisoning.

Biologists with the Ventana Wildlife Society capture condors and test their blood for lead. If they don't find much, the birds are released. But if their lead levels are life threatening, they're sent to zoo veterinarians for a medical treatment called *chelation,* a process also used in humans that flushes heavy metals from the body. It may take several weeks of treatment for a condor to be detoxified.

In December 2007, a law was enacted that could help the condor, like the bald eagle, make it off the endangered species list. The Ridley-Tree Condor Preservation Act, which bans the use of lead ammunition within the condor's geographic range, became effective in the middle of California's hunting season. While its effectiveness was uncertain at the time of this book's publication, Burnett is optimistic that condors' lead levels will decrease by the end of the 2009 hunting season.

Compliance, of course, is key. Fortunately, the condor has thousands of people on its side. The successful release and awe-inspiring flight I witnessed at Ventana is symbolic of the species' recovery. As a whole, the efforts to save the California condor have been outstanding, including a $35 million conservation project—the most expensive for any species in US history. Still, it's much less expensive to preserve a species than to attempt to bring one back from the brink of extinction.

Just a few hundred years ago, the condor's range extended along the Pacific coast all the way from British Columbia to Baja California, Mexico. Prehistorically, they'd soared over Arizona, Nevada, New Mexico, and even Texas, but when settlers arrived in the American West, it was the same old story: Somehow, the great wide-open just wasn't big enough for both man and beast, and the numbers of these regal creatures soon dropped precipitously. Like the bald eagle, condors were victims of false accusation, unfairly condemned for preying on calves and lambs. In response to this myth, ranchers wiped out condors in parts of the West. Condors are naturally susceptible to population declines as it is, given their low reproduction rate (couples produce just one egg every other year) and late onset of sexual maturity (at age 6). Add to that the decades of poaching and habitat loss, and their fight for survival is like flying into the wind. By the mid-1980s, fewer than 30 birds had survived. The California condor seemed to be on an inexorable flight path toward extinction.

But in the 1980s, the Zoological Society of San Diego and the Los Angeles Zoo received approval from the federal government to begin a captive-breeding program. The two organizations rounded up the 27 remaining condors, capturing the last one on Easter Sunday, 1987. The turnaround was under way.

At the San Diego Zoo and the Oregon Zoo, which also participated in the effort, the program's breeders used the same double-clutching technique employed by Carl Jones with the Mauritius kestrel—removing a condor couple's biennial egg and securing it in an incubator while the couple went about producing a second egg. This effectively doubled the condors' birth rate. After the incubated eggs had hatched, breeders raised the chicks and fed them using puppets that resembled adult condors so that the chicks wouldn't "imprint" on their human keepers. Imprinting is a learning process by which captive birds and other mammals can develop a dependent relationship with their human caretakers. If the chicks identified more closely with humans than their fellow condors, they would be unlikely to survive in the wild. To increase their odds of success, the recorded sounds of wild adult condors were even piped into the incubators. When possible, the parents were allowed to raise their second hatchlings themselves.

In 1992 condors raised in captivity were released into the wild. In 2005, a nestling fledged in the wild for the first time in 24 years. In 2006, a pair of condors nested in a hollow redwood tree near Big Sur—the first time in more than a *century* that a couple had been known to nest in northern California. And in 2007, a condor egg was laid in Mexico for the first time in at least 80 years. Today, there are more than 321 California condors in the wild—and the figure is rising steadily, albeit slowly.

The Ventana Wildlife Society is doing an exemplary job of keeping tabs on the birds and protecting their welfare. This non-profit organization operates on a tight budget, but it's a model of environmental stewardship. Besides capturing condors and testing their lead levels, members of the society monitor the birds with radio transmitters and, when funding allows, a global positioning system (GPS). While radio transmitters each cost about $200, the GPS units are closer to $4,000 apiece—and that difference in price reflects the differences in monitoring capability. With GPS, signals aren't lost when a bird flies behind a mountain, and locations are revealed with pinpoint accuracy. The information they're able to gather from GPS tracking gives the Ventana crew an invaluable advantage. In fact, in May 2007, it led them to a cliff-side nest, where they found and vaccinated a chick against West Nile virus.

In addition to lead poisoning, electrical power lines are another human-imposed threat to condors. Because their wingspan is so expansive, a bird perching on a pole can touch two power lines at once when it spreads its wings—causing a short circuit—or touch both the pole and a line simultaneously, turning the bird into an electrical pathway. Both scenarios are lethal. While little can be done to prevent condors from flying into power lines so thin that they can't be detected by the birds' powerful vision, Ventana has been successful in teaching the birds not to perch on the poles. Mock power poles constructed in the condors' prerelease pens give the birds a mild shock when they land on them. It usually only takes one unpleasant jolt for the lesson to be learned—they never perch there again. Before they're released and have the opportunity to encounter the real thing, the condors have learned to steer clear of poles, increasing their chance of survival in the wild.

Ventana's devotion to the condors was put to its biggest test in June 2008, when a dry lightning storm set a patch of Big Sur's grass ablaze 5 miles south of the release site and sent a raging wildfire straight toward the facility. By the end of the day, the fire had cut off access to the area's only road. The staff had evacuated, but the next day it was imperative to get back to save the birds, as firefighters hadn't yet been able to bring the blaze under control. It became clear to Burnett that the only way in would have to be by helicopter, but private helicopters were too small to carry the cages that house these massive birds. In a brainstorm born out of desperation, he called the Coast Guard. Though its helicopters are designed for ocean rescue (and condor evacuation certainly isn't within typical Coast Guard purview), Lieutenant Harry Greene accepted the mission and incorporated it into his unit's training exercises for the day.

As Greene and the Ventana crew, which also included biologist Mike Tyner and field assistant Henry Bonifas, made their way down the coast to Big Sur, the magnitude of their undertaking suddenly became clear. After 24 hours, the fire had moved 3 miles—halfway to Ventana. As they skirted the flames, Burnett's mind was consumed with troubling math problems. Physics also turned out to be a tricky subject: After covering the 30 miles from Monterey to Ventana, the helicopter proved too big to land at the condor release site, and Greene had to put down on a pad almost 3 miles away. By the time the Ventana crew hiked in, it was almost 6:00 p.m. and a new layer of complication was settling over them like a net: It would be dark by 8:30, and the Coast Guard isn't permitted to fly after dark for training exercises. They had 2½ hours to shuttle eight birds to the helicopter using an all-terrain vehicle (ATV) that had a history of overheating and could carry only two kenneled birds at a time. Teamwork would be absolutely critical. "As a crew, we had to work together seamlessly," Burnett said. "We almost had to finish each other's sentences."

The road that stretches between the facility and the helicopter pad is treacherous, hugging cliff sides much of the way, so it was slow going, and each round-trip took about 40 minutes. It was a little after 7:30 by the time the fifth and sixth birds were brought to the helicopter, and five of them were squeezed aboard. With the precious cargo secured, the Ventana crew watched as the helicopter lifted off into the smoky sky.

But time was running out, and they still had to return to the pen to grab the last two birds. As usually happens when there's just one animal in a pen and lots of room to maneuver, this one proved especially elusive. They finally caught it and secured the kennels in the vehicle, but then they encountered yet another obstacle: The ATV had overheated. Their only option was to push it up a hill so that it could roll down the other side—and hope Tyner could pop the clutch. So that's what they did. When it reached the bottom of the hill, Burnett and Bonifas heard the engine spring to life. The ATV had given them a second chance, and Tyner raced to the helicopter pad. Now all the other two had to do was hike the 3 miles and 2,000 vertical feet to the pad—through a canyon that was steadily filling with smoke. About halfway there, the smoke became so thick that they lost sight of their destination. Finally, after another half mile, they saw a beacon: the ATV's headlights cutting through the smoke at the top of the ridge. A moment later, they could see the helicopter's fog lights a mile away, and Burnett radioed to let the crew know they were a mile off course. The smoke was so thick that it seemed unlikely Greene would be able to find the pad. In fact, Burnett would later learn that getting through the smoke required the use of night-vision goggles and every other technological advantage at the Coast Guard crew's disposal. When the helicopter finally landed, the Ventana crew crowded aboard with the last condors and made their way out from under the blanket of smoke. When they could see stars and clear sky once again, they looked back and were astonished to see just how close they'd come to being swallowed by an inferno.

The heroic devotion of these people saved 2½ percent of the world's condor population. It's frightening to think how close we came to losing that 2½ percent, though. When you consider the potential impact of just one natural event, as well as the many impacts of *un*natural threats such as lead poisoning, it becomes clear just how precarious the existence of this incredible bird is. The ban on lead ammunition and the use of aversion conditioning to keep the birds away from power poles do help to protect condors, but power lines will crowd the sky for as long as suburbia continues to sprawl, and hunters will need to honor the ban for the threat of lead poisoning to cease. Will the condor rise from the ashes like the phoenix, or will it meet the same fate as the heath hen? The answer lies largely in our hands. It's likely that while the condor may survive into the future, it will always be a species that needs our attention and care.

## THE PERILS OF POLLUTION

Pollution is one of the many means by which people have drastically modified wildlife habitat. Many animal species are attracted to trash and litter, and some animals, such as polar bears, will attempt to eat almost anything, including plastic, Styrofoam, car batteries, antifreeze, and motor oil. These polar bear habits were documented at a dump in Churchill, Manitoba, and in 2006 the dump was closed to protect the bears. While the threats posed by trash dumps and man-made debris are obvious, in many cases, it's the unseen pollutants—pesticides and toxic chemicals—that pose the greater risk.

Wildlife is negatively affected by air, soil, and water pollution, as well as by acid rain, in most parts of the world. In the United

States alone, we now use more than 18,000 different pesticides, a dramatic jump from the 200 that were used in the early 1960s.[1] Astonishing as that increase is, consider that 50 years ago we were using 400 million pounds of pesticides a year, and today we're using more than 4.5 *billion* pounds a year. In that same time span, the industrial chemical business has grown from a $2 billion industry to a $635 billion industry.

In the Arctic, because polar bears are apex predators, their bodies accumulate the pollution that many other animals have absorbed or ingested. Halocarbons, for example, which are found in pesticides, refrigerants, solvents, and plastics, lurk in the blubber of seals, a major staple of the bears' diet.

As we've seen so many times, theirs is a shared plight. "To think that polar bears are going to be affected as the top of their food chain, the top organism in their environment, you have to sort of make the leap that if polar bears can be affected by these profound changes in the ecosystem, humans are also likely to be affected," says Steve Amstrup, the senior polar bear scientist at the US Geological Survey Alaska Science Center who led me on my expedition into the Arctic (see Chapter 1). "Although many people would like to think of humans as observers of ecology, we are really participants in it, and the changes in the ecosystem are going to affect us."

# THE YANGTZE, RIVER OF TEARS

Toxins come in a distressing multitude of forms, from small fragments of lead shot to the pollution that permeates one of the world's longest rivers: the Yangtze, a 3,700-mile-long stretch of water that reaches from central China's Qinghai region to Shanghai on the eastern coast. Scientists believe pollution is a major reason the Yangtze River dolphin (*Lipotes vexillifer*), also known as the *baiji,* was steadily pushed to extinction. Judging by fossil records, the dolphin surfaced 25 million years ago in the Pacific Ocean and migrated to the Yangtze River, which became its sole habitat 5 million years later. When it was first described in the 3rd century in the Erya (thought to be the oldest Chinese dictionary or encyclopedia in existence), the baiji's future appeared to be bright. It's estimated that 5,000 dolphins lived in the river at that time; by 1950, the count had actually climbed to approximately 6,000.

In a popular folk story, the baiji is depicted as the reincarnation of a princess who was drowned for refusing to marry a man she didn't love. As such, the dolphin became emblematic of peace and good fortune in Chinese culture. But despite the reverence that the "goddess of the Yangtze" commanded, its population fell from 6,000 to zero in just 50 years—a blink of history's eye. How did an animal that thrived for millions of years disappear so rapidly? As with most modern-day extinction stories, a number of culprits played roles, but the primary offender was the pollution that accompanied progress on the Yangtze.

———

It began in 1958, when Mao Tse-tung, leader of the People's Republic of China, launched the Great Leap Forward, a plan to swiftly convert mainland China from a farming-based economy into an industrialized nation. Transportation on the Yangtze soared, and the baiji was forced to share more and more of its habitat with ships and commercial fishing boats. Adding insult to injury, Mao officially stripped the baiji of its venerated status and opened it to unrestricted fishing.

The baiji also had to contend with deadly noise pollution.

Because these sleek dolphins had poor eyesight, they relied on sonar to navigate the river, but noise from the heavy river traffic hampered their ability to detect individual boats, and they often swam into propellers. In the 1970s and '80s, entanglement in fishing nets and other gear was the direct cause of about half of baiji deaths. In 1979, the People's Republic of China declared the baiji endangered, and 4 years later, the government banned intentional killing and imposed limits on fishing operations in an attempt to protect the dolphin from nets and gear. Despite that, the population had slipped to just 300 by 1986.

Making matters even worse for the baiji was the Gezhouba Dam, completed in 1988. The already-dirty water of the Yangtze became even more contaminated when the sediment suspended near the dam transported additional pollutants into the river. By 1990, only 200 dolphins remained.

Scientists at the Chinese Academy of Sciences' Freshwater Dolphin Research Centre tried to capture dolphins in hopes of establishing a breeding program and providing a safe habitat for them until conditions improved in the Yangtze. But the baiji proved elusive to those attempting to capture them, and the few that were trapped died only months later.

The last straw for this freshwater dolphin appears to have come in the form of another dam. Despite the toll already taken on the river and its wildlife by the Gezhouba Dam, construction of the Three Gorges began in 1994. When it was completed in 2003, ship traffic increased and the dolphins' habitat shrank even further. The last baiji was seen in 2004. By 2007, the IUCN classified the Yangtze River dolphin as critically endangered and possibly extinct.

As the Yangtze becomes further degraded, scientific expeditions have found indications that the finless porpoise (*Neophocaena phocaenoides*) is facing extinction as well. It's a data-deficient species, meaning that we don't have enough reliable information to know exactly how its population has been affected, so it can't be put on the endangered list. But scientists believe its population has been greatly reduced after decades of decline. In 2006, there were estimated to be 1,400 porpoises, 700 to 900 of which lived in the polluted Yangtze. Fortunately, the porpoises are easier to capture than baijis, and 28 are now living and reproducing in a national reserve in Oxbow Lake, near Shishou City. But there's a catch: The water quality of Oxbow Lake has been declining over the past decade. Fortunately, a sluice gate built to ease flooding can carry necessary nutrients to the porpoises' habitat.

When a river is as toxic as the Yangtze, the casualties are bound to be numerous. Another species that has been affected is the Chinese alligator (*Alligator sinensis*). This smaller cousin of the American alligator originally flourished throughout much of China, but in recent years, it has retreated to the last viable wetlands connected to the Yangtze. Unlike its American cousin, whose dorsal surface is covered with bony protective plates known as *scutes,* this alligator bears armor on both its dorsal surface and its belly. Unfortunately, that's not the kind of protection that can ward off extinction, even for a formidable creature whose local name (*Yow-Lung* or *T'o*) means "dragon." The defense it really needs is an ironclad commitment to conserving its remaining habitat along the Yangtze from further development.

Fewer than 200 Chinese alligators—only about 50 of which are mature—exist in an area consisting of little more than a handful of ponds. The Three Gorges Dam has disturbed the ecology of the river for miles in every direction, and despite captive-breeding efforts, this alligator's survival is far from assured.

In 2003, the first captive-reared alligators were released in China's Anhui Province in a collaborative effort between the Wildlife Conservation Society and East China Normal University. The results: All three animals have survived, and at least one of the females nested in 2004 and 2005. But releases and reintroduction efforts don't always go this well, and when you consider that 40 more dams are planned for the Yangtze, it's hard to imagine that *any* species living along this polluted expanse won't face greater and greater challenges to its survival.

Besides evading the troubles afloat in the Yangtze, the Chinese alligator must contend with the folk medicine–based belief that its meat is both the cure for the common cold and an elixir that prevents cancer. Consequently, alligators can be spotted outside of restaurants and markets with their mouths taped shut, awaiting the butcher.

All in all, the future doesn't look promising for the Chinese alligator, a species I've always wanted to see firsthand. If I don't see it soon, I may never have such an opportunity.

## Gharials in Troubled Waters

In India's prime reptile habitat, a similar problem exists: A massively polluted river runs through it. And another unique creature is in danger.

The gharial looks as if it could have come straight from the pages of Dr. Seuss. It is one of the largest members of the crocodilian species, measuring up to 23 feet in length and weighing as much as 2,200 pounds. The gharial is one of two surviving members of the Gavialidae family, a long-established group of crocodile-like reptiles. Lined with razor-sharp teeth, its long jaws are much narrower than a crocodile's or an alligator's and are designed to catch small, fast-moving fish, the main component of its diet. The large, pronounced knob at the end of its snout resembles an Indian clay pot called a *ghara*—inspiring its name.

Though the species has endured for 80 million years, gharials are now critically endangered and barely eking out an existence. Native to India, Southeast Asia, and Nepal, they are thought to be nearly extinct in Pakistan, Myanmar (formerly Burma), Bhutan, and Bangladesh. In India, the gharial is facing a new threat. While the country is traditionally home to one of the world's healthiest gharial populations, researchers believe an unidentified pollutant is seeping into the Chambal River at its confluence with the Yamuna River—considered to be one of the world's dirtiest—and affecting the gharials' food supply. Experts suspect the unknown substance is either an industrial chemical that's being released into the Yamuna River by a new manufacturing facility or one that was used by a plant that shut down and illegally dumped waste into the river. Animal autopsies, known as *necropsies*, have revealed that the gharials are dying from gout, a painful metabolic disease, after ingesting polluted fish. Elevated levels of lead and cadmium have also been found in these bodies, which may have suppressed the gharials' immune systems and left them vulnerable to infection.

In addition to the threats posed by water pollution, the gharial was also a victim of poaching—which was perfectly legal. By the 1970s, the gharial teetered on the brink of extinction. The Indian government responded to the crisis and extended full protection to the species, which significantly reduced the poaching losses. In addition, there are now nine protected areas where captive-breeding and ranching operations are centered. Eggs are collected in the wild, and hatchlings are raised in captivity for 3 to 4 years to protect them from predators before being released into the wild. With the release of more than 3,000 gharials, these programs have helped to bring the wild population in India to an estimated 1,500.

But this ancient creature is dangerously close to extinction all over again. Along with the Chinese alligator, it's one of the world's most endangered reptiles. Take a moment to think about that: A creature that has existed for 80 million years may be near the end of its time on Earth. What kind of future does that signal for the *Homo sapiens,* who has had only 250,000 years of evolution[2] to fortify its defenses against extinction? When it comes to the poisons in our land, rivers, ponds, and lakes, we're all in the same toxic soup.

# CHAPTER 5

# THEIR HEALTH
# IS AT STAKE

THE NATURAL WORLD sprang to life for me one sunny New England afternoon as I lay on my bare belly on the damp, mossy bank of Vinal Pond. Hidden deep within the woods behind our family home, cradled by acres of quaking bogs, this is the place where I explored, discovered, and found peace during my childhood. Amid the clouds reflected on the still water as black as slate were creatures so strange that I felt as if I'd stumbled onto another planet: dragonfly nymphs with enormous eyes, six legs, and extendable jaws; water bugs with their sickle-shaped appendages; and the incredibly bizarre caddis fly larvae. In their grublike aquatic stage, some types of caddis fly build "cases" out of tiny twigs and pebbles to spend their pupal stage in. When it's time to emerge, they chew their way out and swim to shore, where they become adults. The miracle of life played out before my 8-year-old eyes in astonishing ways.

A school of tadpoles was also hatching at the pond, wriggling out of translucent eggs that appeared to be glued to an emerald green lily pad. I studied the tadpoles all season, watching them metamorphose—sprout limbs, absorb their tails, and swim to the surface for their first breaths of air. I observed as they shape-shifted and grew. At the same time, I watched last year's tadpoles, which were now small bullfrogs, begin to emerge from the water. I didn't want to miss a minute of the action, and my mother had to drag me away from the pond when dusk set in and it was time to go home.

Watching this life cycle play out as a child left an indelible mark on my life. I had no idea then that my blossoming interest in frogs would one day lead me to a career studying amphibians and reptiles as a herpetologist. I also didn't know that the entire pond's biodiversity and survival lay upon the fragile backs of those amazing creatures. And I certainly didn't know that amphibians are absolutely crucial to the health of wetland habitats everywhere. I just knew that I loved frogs.

Amphibians are a diverse class of cold-blooded, vertebrate creatures. This fascinating group of species includes frogs, newts, salamanders, toads, and shy creatures called caecilians (seh-SILL-yuns) that resemble worms and spend most of their lives burrowing underground. Amphibians have been abundant for the past 350 million years, and they roamed Earth even before the dinosaurs. One of the ancient members of this family is the Chinese giant salamander, which can grow to nearly 6 feet in length. It preceded the mighty *Tyrannosaurus rex* by more than 100 million years but is critically endangered today. Other unique amphibians include a purple-pigmented frog that wasn't discovered until 2003 because it spends most of the year buried more than 10 feet underground; a blind salamander called an olm that has transparent skin, lives underground, uses its sensitivity to electromagnetic fields to hunt for prey, and can survive for 10 years without food; the Malagasy rainbow frog, which can climb vertical rock surfaces; and the lungless salamanders of Mexico, which breathe through their skin and mouth linings.

Though many amphibians are now endangered, they have weathered the Ice Age, undergone millions of years of evolution, and, until recently, thrived around most of the globe (Antarctica is the only continent that isn't home to native amphibians). One reason amphibians have been able to survive throughout the ages is that they are incredibly adaptable. Although they need water or moisture for egg laying and development, amphibians can survive in a variety of habitats, from high mountaintops to parched deserts to humid rainforests.

But to me, one of their most amazing qualities is the metamorphosis they undergo. Many amphibians are born as gilled, water-breathing tadpoles before they develop lungs and transform into air-breathing adults. This versatility has helped them survive for millions of years. Early amphibians were the first animals to hop, wriggle, or crawl from the aquatic world onto land, a crucial step in the evolution from aquatic to terrestrial vertebrates.

It's no wonder that their transformative "powers" have long been revered. In ancient Egypt, frogs were seen as symbols of life and fertility, as millions were born every year after the annual flooding of the Nile, which left fertile silt, or sediment, in its wake. Some Egyptian art depicts the goddess Heqet, whose priestesses were trained midwives, as having a frog's head.

And in the Mayan world—deep in the forests where clouds cling to the canopy of trees even as deforestation chips away at them— shamans worshipped the rain god Chac, whose companions were frogs and who sometimes appeared as a frog himself. The Mayans prayed for rain to keep their crops alive in rituals that posted young boys beneath a sacred canopy. The boys would "croak," calling upon Chac to bring moisture to their parched patch of earth.

Throughout history, frogs have played a central and often mystical role in popular culture, folklore, and religion. In medieval Europe, toads were considered powerful and sometimes demonic spirits that could lead travelers to treasure or give housewives warts. In Christian literature, an army of frogs descended upon Egypt during one of the plagues. And in a familiar fairy tale, a princess's kiss transforms a frog into a prince (and, depending on your interpretation, the frog isn't the only one reborn). These stories are testaments to our enduring fascination with amphibians and their ability to morph into other forms.

Mythology has also bestowed powers upon the salamander—powers it hasn't always used for good. Seen scurrying from lit campfire pits, possibly after hitching rides in cool, damp bundles of wood, salamanders have long been blamed for extinguishing fires (even though the dampness of the wood was the likely culprit). They were believed to be immune to fire and to draw nourishment from it, and they're even named for this: In Greek, *salamander* means "fire lizard." In a bit of linguistic redundancy, the species *Salamandra salamandra* has been nicknamed the "fire salamander."

While their powers may be exaggerated in popular myths and legends, amphibians do possess some very real—if incredible—attributes. The phantasmal poison frog (*Epipedobates tricolor*), a species of poison dart frog, is a dramatic example of frogs' power to both heal and kill. On one hand, its toxin has the power to kill an animal as large as a water buffalo, and on the other, that same toxin has the potential to be used as a painkiller that is 200 times stronger than morphine. While it may prove to be too powerful for use in humans, studies of this frog have provided scientists with valuable information.

There are numerous frogs whose skin secretions contain antimicrobial peptides—molecules consisting of two or more amino acids—that do have medicinal uses for humans. Among many others, there's the Oriental fire-bellied toad, a brilliantly colored frog whose peptides can lower blood pressure by dilating blood vessels;

the Australian green tree frog, a strapping, long-lived species that secretes peptides that block HIV infection without harming vital white blood cells; the African clawed frog, which can escape stretches of dry weather by digging deeply into mud and whose skin secretions can cure foot ulcers resulting from diabetes; and the waxy monkey tree frog, an especially slippery species whose peptides have antifungal properties and can be used to treat antibiotic-resistant staph (*Staphylococcus*) infections. There's also the crucifix toad, a baseball-size species whose sticky proteins serve as a glue to hold it and a partner together during mating. This same glue is also used as a medical adhesive that can bind together human cartilage.

The more we learn, the more we realize that there's much we haven't yet discovered about amphibians and the many ways that keeping them alive—and well—can benefit the world. If we allow them to vanish forever, the ramifications will be profound for the planet's ecology and, quite possibly, the survival of the human species.

## AMPHIBIANS: THE CANARIES IN OUR COAL MINE

The silence was deafening. As I trekked through the hot Panamanian rainforest, my T-shirt clung to my back; there was so much moisture in the air that the perspiration on my skin couldn't evaporate. The humidity made it feel as if we were in a sauna, but for a biologist, this was nirvana—I was surrounded by wriggling snakes as thin as pencils, monkeys howling in the canopy above, gorgeous butterflies moving so slowly through the thick air that they appeared to be floating. The scent of dark, fertile earth and orchids filled my lungs—all familiar from years of searching for unique and mysterious animals in the emerald forests of South and Central America. What wasn't familiar was the eerie quiet. This is biologically the richest habitat on Earth, teeming with life, but there was no chirruping, no trilling. Only the sounds of the monkeys, a lone bird winging through a nearby thicket of trees, and the crisp leaves and twigs crackling beneath my footsteps. Where was that familiar chorus of croaking I'd heard in this same rainforest just a few years earlier? Everything *looked* picture-perfect, but the air above my head, normally booming with the cacophony of life, just hung there, empty. My heart sank, and I felt a sickening cramp balling up in my stomach. I knew something was terribly wrong.

What was wrong was that the frogs had vanished. Amphibians are referred to as ecological canaries in a coal mine because they're among the most sensitive of the planet's indicator species. Functioning as an early warning system, the fate of these animals may indicate the fate that awaits an entire ecosystem. There are few more accurate barometers of water quality, air quality, climate change, and environmental degradation than amphibians. So when amphibians die off in massive numbers, as they've been doing all over the world since the 1980s, there is cause for grave concern.

The IUCN's 2008 Global Amphibian Assessment lists 489 amphibian species as critically endangered; 32 percent of amphibian species are threatened (which includes the IUCN categories of vulnerable, endangered, and critically endangered); and at least 42 percent are suffering population loss. Thirty-eight species are known to be extinct, and one species is extinct in the wild but still alive in captivity. Another 120 species of amphibians are listed as being undetectable in recent years and possibly extinct.[1] At the time of this book's publication, there were an estimated 6,443 amphibian species remaining.[2] Based on the rate at which their environments are changing, we could lose half of them in our lifetime.

How does the loss of a frog touch the lives of humans thousands of miles away? One word: *biodiversity,* or the variety of life-forms present in a particular ecosystem. While there's disagreement about how much we should intervene to keep a habitat sustainable—is it more important to preserve the greatest possible variety of genes, or does that hinder the process of orderly natural change in an ecosystem?—it's safe to say that when human *interference* causes a species' demise, we aren't serving the cause of global sustainability.

It's taken 3 billion to 4 billion years of evolution for Earth to achieve the biodiversity that now exists, and the devastating declines in amphibian populations pose a clear threat to this crucial element of our planet's health.

Though the IUCN lists 32 percent of frog species as threatened or extinct, the numbers are actually even more distressing. When you take data-deficient species out of the equation, the number rises to 49 percent. Surviving species in the Panamanian cloud forests have experienced average population declines of 80 percent. Even Panama's national animal, the Panamanian golden frog, once believed by indigenous tribes to turn to solid gold when it dies, is most likely extinct.

Fortunately, because of the dedication of countless scientists and volunteers, some critically endangered frogs are being protected and preserved. One of these, the Veragoa stubfoot toad (*Atelopus varius*), commonly grouped with harlequin frogs, is what brought me to the hot Panamanian rainforest in April 2008. Discovered in 1995, this orange and black harlequin frog is now threatened by climate change and a deadly fungus. We were searching for a sign that the species might be clinging to survival somewhere beneath a rock or in the form of a clutch of jelly eggs.

As I climbed up rocks made treacherous by a layer of wet leaves and tangles of moss, I was accompanied by Edgardo Griffith, director of Panama's El Valle Amphibian Conservation Center (EVACC), and Bill Konstant, director of conservation and science at the Houston Zoo. Our mission was to find a male harlequin to mate with a female back at the El Valle lab. She was gravid (bearing eggs) and in desperate need of a form of mating called *amplexus*. In amplexus, the male mounts the female and generally hangs on for dear life. This action stimulates the female to release her eggs, which the male then fertilizes. She's simply not capable of laying her eggs without a mate's intimate contact—and without that connection, she can become "egg bound" and die. Her species' life-giving process can actually *take* her life.

Harlequin frogs, which once leapt in great multitudes throughout the forests of Ecuador, Colombia, and Panama, lost two-thirds of their population in the 1980s and '90s. Scientists are racing to protect them from the fate that befell the now-extinct golden toad (*Bufo periglenes*) of Costa Rica. The golden toad had lived in an 18-square-mile tropical forest in the mountains above the city of Monteverde and was utterly dependent on the region's humidity. Its disappearance in 1989 came after 2 decades of increasingly severe dry seasons, pointing to the drastic effects that climate change can have on a *specialist species*, animals that require a very particular environment to thrive. And in this case, the species had only a tiny habitat and no higher ground to which it could escape. Even 2 or 3 days of arid conditions can wipe out such an animal.

As Edgardo and I scrambled through jungle vines in tropical heat and humidity that took our breath away, we hoped to see the telltale orange-and-black harlequin pattern in the underbrush. What happened next really took my breath away. I'd just climbed up one of those giant, slippery rocks when I saw something moving in the leaf litter at the foot of a decayed tree hollow. "Edgardo!" I yelled. "I think I've found something!" Delicately cupping my hand over the wet, porous body of this fragile creature, I could feel it breathing rapidly, perhaps fearing I was a predator rather than someone dedicated to its salvation. Peeking between my fingers, I could see its vivid trademark pattern: a young harlequin. After dashing over to see what I'd found, Edgardo stooped, looked closely at what I was holding in place in the mud, and grinned. Although he's been conducting amphibian surveys throughout Panama for a decade, this was the first young *Atelopus varius* he'd ever laid eyes on in the wild. While we didn't know whether it was male or female, where there's one young, healthy toad, there are others of its kind. Suddenly, we'd found a source of hope for a sustainable breeding colony.

As luck would have it, the toad was male—we had found a mate for the female back at the lab, and he was recruited for EVACC's mission to rescue Panama's rapidly disappearing amphibian species. So, there *is* new hope, but it's still an uphill battle. The fungus that's at least partly responsible for the harlequin frog's plight has escalated into a frightening global onslaught against amphibians—and, ultimately, against us.

# CHYTRID AND GLOBAL WARMING: A DEADLY STORM FOR AMPHIBIANS

When biologists first noticed the sudden disappearance of frogs in the late 1980s, no one could understand what was happening. The primary suspects were habitat destruction and the use of pesticides such as atrazine (which disrupts hormone production and may be linked to certain cancers[3]) and malathion and carbaryl (which have been linked to surges in tadpole mortality in waters where frogs spawn). As it turned out, degradation of the frogs' aquatic habitat was definitely taking a toll, but that didn't explain the abrupt die-off that was occurring worldwide. Something else was happening. Something horrifying. Something scientists couldn't understand.

The first hint had come in 1979, when a one-of-a-kind amphibian could no longer be found in its protected range in Queensland, Australia. The gastric-brooding frogs, also known as platypus frogs, were the only genus of frogs whose offspring were incubated in the mother's stomach. Many photos of the platypus frog depict tiny frogs situated in the mouths of those bigger, identical-looking frogs, like Russian nesting dolls. Those little guys in the photos were fully developed and ready to set their slimy, webbed feet on terra firma for the first time.

The circumstances that brought them to this jumping-off point read more like science fiction than biology. After a male externally fertilized a female's eggs, she swallowed them. Incredibly, she didn't digest the eggs because they were encased in a protective jelly that contained a substance called prostaglandin E. This jelly guarded the eggs from the stomach's digestive enzymes. And when they hatched, the tadpoles also created prostaglandin in mucus excreted through their gills. The mother carried about 25 eggs at a time—so once those eggs became 25 tadpoles, her body had a lot of accommodating to do. Her stomach expanded until it had nearly taken over her entire body cavity. Her lungs collapsed, creating more space for the tadpoles and necessitating that she acquire most of her oxygen through her skin. And in addition to all of these extraordinary accommodations, she didn't eat from the time she swallowed the eggs until the time her babies emerged—6 or 7 weeks later.

Naturally, I'd wanted to see the gastric-brooding frog with my own eyes, but both species disappeared nearly as soon as they were discovered. The southern gastric-brooding frog (*Rheobatrachus silus*) was identified in 1973 in the Blackall and Conondale mountain ranges of Queensland, and the last reported sighting of one living in the wild came in 1981; the last one in captivity died in 1983. The northern gastric-brooding frog (*Rheobatrachus vitellinus*), meanwhile, was discovered in 1984 and was gone just 18 months later.

Scientists were stunned by the swiftness of their disappearance and disturbed to learn that other species were also being hit hard by an unknown killer. Fourteen more species of high-elevation aquatic frogs lost 90 to 100 percent of their populations across Queensland during the early '90s. That's the information that Lee Berger, then a doctoral student at Australia's James Cook University in Townsville, Queensland, had to work with when she set out to crack the mystery: Frogs that lived in or near streams at high elevations were dying, while species living closer to sea level and far from streams continued to thrive.

After ruling out viruses as the cause of death, Berger focused on the superficial cysts that were often found on the frogs' carcasses, which were sometimes discolored and marked by rough or peeling skin. The cysts turned out to be the waterborne *Batrachochytrium dendrobatidis*, a chytrid fungus, which wouldn't be scientifically described and proved to be an agent of disease until 1999 by scientists at the National Zoo and the University of Maine. What made the discovery so unusual is that this chytrid fungus is *saprophytic*, which means that its role in nature is to help the decomposition process along by feeding on decaying organic matter. A few of these fungi kill plants and insects, but this was the first one known to attack a vertebrate. For scientists, "firsts" serve as red alerts, and now every herpetologist was paying attention.

After the findings were published, scientists began seeing the fungus in frogs at research facilities around the world. It wasn't always fatal, though—just in moist environments, like the streams in Australian rainforests and eucalyptus forests that the gastric-brooding frog had called home.

Young chytrid spores—reproductive cells capable of motion and found in streams and puddles—seek out frog flesh, burrow in, and wreak havoc on the vital outer layer of skin by breaking it down and producing more zoospores. That layer of skin is nothing less than a breathing apparatus, an avenue by which water, oxygen, and carbon dioxide enter and exit the frog's body. It's not known how, but the chytrid cells block this pathway. The result is chytridomycosis, which, besides the skin damage, causes increasing sluggishness and leads—or at least contributes—to the frog's death. The frog literally chokes to death.

Exactly how the fungus spreads isn't clear. Karen Lips, PhD, who studies Central American frogs at Southern Illinois University in Carbondale, believes it started in one spot and recently spread around the world, possibly through the commercial sale and export of amphibians. But one known source of spread is the African clawed frog (*Xenopus laevis*), which has been referred to as the Typhoid Mary of the epidemic. These hardy and adaptable aquatic frogs are found throughout much of Africa and especially thrive in the ponds and rivers of the southeastern sub-Saharan region, eating voraciously and reproducing quickly. In its native habitat, predators keep it in check, but when it's introduced to new habitats, all bets are off. Lacking any natural predators, its presence can be devastating, as it eats native fish, tadpoles, and insects and damages ecosystems in turn.

And, unfortunately, the African clawed frogs were very well traveled. In the 1940s and '50s, they were shipped around the world for use in human pregnancy test kits (it seemed that injections of pregnant women's urine prompted females frogs to become pregnant themselves). The African clawed frog is also the frog most commonly used in biological research. And what made the frogs appealing to scientists—they readily breed in captivity, don't require much care, and have strong immunity to disease—made them irresistible to the parents of kids like me who begged for a pet frog. So a booming pet trade in the species also took hold in the 1950s.

With a significant number of this introduced species suddenly living in new habitats, a significant number of *roaming* frogs was inevitable. In short, African clawed frogs have been escaping and breeding all over the world for decades—and bringing with them the deadly chytrid fungus, to which they're immune.

Some scientists doubt that there's a link among the chytrid outbreaks around the world. The fungus has been around for thousands of years, but it had never annihilated frog populations as it has over the past 20 years. Biology professor Ross Alford, PhD, of James Cook University, for one, thinks the fungus may have been present but dormant before emerging in the affected areas. Or perhaps an environmental change, such as the effects of global warming (the fungus thrives at temperatures of 63° to 77°F), weakened either frogs' immune systems or the parasitic microbes that would normally overpower the fungus.[4]

Capturing the attention of scientists—putting great minds to work debating theories, sharing ideas, and collaborating in their efforts—is the best-case scenario for an endangered animal. This level of mind melding is taking place all over the world as scientists and conservationists race to save endangered species. In this case, initially, the researchers weren't even certain what they were saving it *from*. To preserve as many amphibian species as possible, we must act wisely and at warp speed. When chytrid strikes, 50 percent of an amphibian species on average can be expected to disappear within a year. Amphibian Ark (AArk) was formed in Panama to respond to the dire circumstances. A joint effort of the World Association of Zoos and Aquariums and the IUCN, AArk promotes, develops, and coordinates captive-breeding programs at zoos around the world. It declared 2008 the Year of the Frog and embarked on a global campaign to raise awareness and funds for conservation.

Meanwhile, at the Amphibian Research Centre in Melbourne, Australia, they're breeding hope with the offspring of individual frogs that have survived chytrid outbreaks among their particular species. The hope is that if they were resistant enough to survive, their offspring will be, too, and that safeguarding their eggs in captivity will help populations recover. This type of recovery strategy is now being widely practiced wherever species are in or are slipping toward the Hundred Heartbeat Club.

In 2008, more hope was inspired by the good news that a particular bacterium seemed to boost a frog's immunity to chytrid. Biology professor Reid Harris, PhD, and other scientists at James Madison University in Harrisonburg, Virginia, discovered that *Janthinobacterium lividum*, a bacterium normally occurring in the skin of lungless redback salamanders, has an immune-boosting effect on frogs exposed to chytrid. This discovery is one of the first major breakthroughs we've had in the battle against this frog-killing fungus. Scientists will need to conduct a trial among infected populations in the wild before we'll know whether this process is working, but it appears to be an encouraging new beginning.

It's a new beginning that I wish the gastric-brooding frog had been able to benefit from. The powerful maternal instinct that led these Australian frogs to protect their eggs by swallowing them couldn't protect their young from extinction. I never had the chance to meet that extraordinary, singular frog, but knowing that it existed is cause for wonder in its own right. In a glaring example of how the loss of biodiversity affects all of us, scientists believe that the prostaglandin that prevented the tadpoles from being digested in their mothers' stomachs might also have been able to stop the oversecretion of stomach acid, helping to treat gastric ulcers in humans.

Sadly, disease is ravaging another creature in Australia, one that occupies a special place on the evolutionary ladder. As the largest surviving carnivorous marsupial, it's a living link to an ancient group of mammals.

# THE DEVIL'S OWN PRIVATE HELL

Though the croaking of frogs is elusive, there's another sound that still rides the night breeze in Australia, though not as resoundingly as it used to. As I trek through a quickly darkening primordial Australian forest of ferns, eucalyptus, and acacia trees well after sunset, I feel as if I've stepped back in time, and the sensation is a little eerie. The sweep of my headlamp illuminates the occasional brushtail possum scurrying up a tree as I follow a terrifying, unmistakable, almost indescribable sound that's a cross between a vicious growl and a piercing shriek. The only sound I can compare it to is the wavering squeal of a buzz saw struggling to cut through knotted wood.

The sound is faint at first, but after I've walked about a half mile, I know I'm close to the source because the volume has intensified and I can almost feel the growl in my own throat.

My steps become more cautious, and I can hear myself breathing as I make my way toward the noise that only the Tasmanian devil (*Sarcophilus harrisii*) emits. Another half mile later, I swivel my headlamp to the right and see what looks like a mass of black fur throbbing in a bed of ferns. As I make my way toward it—slowly and quietly—the mass separates into individual parts, and I can make out three Tasmanian devils the size of small poodles feeding on what looks like a wallaby. (Wallabies are in the Macropod family and look like small kangaroos.) The shrieking that made it possible for me to track them is the warning they use with one another—a warning that some especially juicy wallaby bits have been spoken for. But that doesn't prevent the occasional tug-of-war over glistening tendons and intestines. And bones and fur. A Tasmanian devil is like a little Pac-Man—all mouth. Pound for pound, it may be the fiercest animal on the planet. Factor in that these miniature saber-toothed tigers can also emit a strong, offensive odor (like a skunk) when they're in stressful situations, and it becomes clear that this is one well-armed species.

Recluses by day, the devils emerge at night to scavenge for carrion. Tasmanian devils are observed in groups only when nature has arranged a feast. They occasionally take down prey such as small mammals and birds, but they primarily eat whatever is already available, using their long whiskers like antennae to locate carcasses in the dark. When pickings are especially good, they'll eat up to 40 percent of their body weight in one sitting. The devil stores fat from the food it consumes in its tail, so when researchers spot a devil with a spindly tail, they know it hasn't been eating well.

Discovering the Tasmanian devil in action is a peak experience for an adventure naturalist, even if you do need to constantly watch your back (and your ankles) because this bold creature isn't afraid to investigate humans' meal potential by scampering in for a bite. The Tasmanian devil is the last remaining member of the *Sarcophilus* genus, and it's no wonder they're survivors. *Sarcophilus* means "flesh lover," and fittingly, Tasmanian devils are designed primarily to breed and eat. With tiny back legs, a relatively massive, anvil-shaped head, and most of its strength in its upper body, this squat, stocky, 13- to 18-pound animal looks like it evolved mainly to carry around a set of jaws that are more powerful than those of a pit bull. Further aiding its carnivorous cause, the devil is equipped with a nose that can catch the faintest whiff of a fresh kill up to a mile away.

These marsupials also have an edge in reproduction. Females give birth to an average of 20 to 30 pups, also called joeys, at a time. But then these quarter-gram babies have to race the 3 inches from the birth canal to their mother's pouch, where they stay for *4 months*. But only 4 of these pups will survive. The Tasmanian devil has only four teats, and competition for them is steep as the pups make their way out of the birth canal—competitive from the get-go. When the first 4 to get there, they clamp down and don't let go until it's time to be weaned. The mother usually consumes the others when she cleans the birth area.

During this nursing period, there's no other interaction between mother and babies, since her pouch opens to the rear. These 6 weeks are the only time she has to herself all year. Once the pups emerge from her pouch—sometimes scarred from the battle to reach the teats—they will require her undivided attention and care for the next 8 months.

With such well-protected pups and a hardy constitution, the Tasmanian devil certainly appears to be built to last. And it has in fact endured where another marsupial, the thylacine—also referred to as the Tasmanian tiger—couldn't. (Sightings of the "tiger" continue to be reported, but it was declared extinct in 1936. See Chapter 7.) The devil had the advantage of being smaller and more adaptable than the tiger. Though it roamed the Australian mainland until about 600 years ago, it's believed that hunting by both humans and dingoes—a nonnative species introduced by the Aboriginal people—eradicated it there, effectively confining its remaining population to dingo-free Tasmania's 26,400 square miles off Australia's southeastern coast.

Though the devils have made themselves at home here, taking up residence in all habitats, from the urban areas to the coastal regions to the mountains, Tasmania hasn't provided a perfect habitat. The Europeans who settled here about 200 years ago had a taste for Tasmanian devil meat, which they described as similar in flavor to veal. They weren't very impressed with the other native game, though, and brought rabbits and foxes to breed, which became invasive to the native animals. According to the Tasmanian state government, 25 native Australian mammal species have become extinct since then, making Australia the country with the worst extinction record to date.

Around 1830, Australian ranchers established a bounty system for Tasmanian devils because they feared that the devils preyed on livestock. The ensuing trapping and poisoning nudged the devils toward the precipice of extinction over the next century. Finally, a law to protect them was enacted in 1941—4 years after the last known Tasmanian tiger died in captivity. Demonstrating their ability to survive and thrive under their new protection, the devils' numbers gradually rebounded to the point where estimates of its population today range anywhere from 10,000 to 100,000. Farmers now consider the diminutive eating machine an ally, thanks to its ability to strip a carcass so quickly that livestock-threatening insects never even catch a whiff, let alone a taste. The devils are also credited with keeping the population of the illegally introduced red fox in check. This is a critically important job, and the devils are the only wild creatures that can do it.

But the devils are fighting a new battle: A contagious cancer is threatening them with extinction. Sadly, the devil's tenacity, the trait that has kept it alive for centuries, seems to be the very quality that may cause its demise. It seems that if a species endures long enough, it can nurture into existence its very own fatal disease. In this case, it's called *devil facial tumor disease* (DFTD), and the theory is that this cancer has evolved. First detected in 1995, the cancer forms tumors and lesions in eye sockets and in and around the mouth, causing the devils' cheeks to swell. This interferes with the animals' voracious feeding and leads to starvation. But how does a cancerous tumor spread to another animal? The main vehicle appears to be the wounds that males inflict on one another while fighting over potential mates. Which would explain why mature adults—4 and 5 years old—have been dying in the greatest numbers (the devil's life expectancy in the wild is 6 years).

But that still doesn't answer the question of *how* cancer can be contagious. How can a parasitic organism moving quickly from animal to animal develop the strength and staying power of the Tasmanian devil itself?

In 1976, leukemia researcher Peter Nowell, MD, suggested that what happens when normal cells become cancerous amounts to natural selection—survival-of-the-fittest cells in a pool teeming with mutations. They develop adaptive traits that give them an edge over normal cells, and they're able to dig themselves in and colonize an area of the body. And now scientists believe that DFTD cells have drawn on this evolutionary capacity to develop a way to become transmissible.

This fierce competitor known as the Tasmanian devil—this creature that competes for every bit of wallaby carcass it can devour—is locked in an evolutionary battle with an equally fierce form of cancer. And at the moment, the devil is losing that battle. The cancer has spread within more than 65 percent of Tasmania's land area and has killed an estimated 20 to 50 percent of the devil population. In May 2008, the devil was declared endangered, and scientists fear that if a cure or a preventive measure isn't found, it will be extinct in 20 years.

Twenty years is very little time, and scientists know it. Many approaches to saving the devil have been debated, including the approach of simply letting nature take its course, which would hopefully produce an even hardier species. The devils have been confined to a small island and have a small gene pool, and this lack of genetic diversity means that their immune systems don't work as well as they were intended to. This is the primary reason they're so vulnerable to DFTD, and the hope is that a hands-off conservation approach will result in a band of survivors that are immune to the disease. In the meantime, the establishment of captive-breeding programs in disease-free settings and long-term monitoring programs have been promising steps toward saving this species. In fact, Australian zoos have bred more than 170 devils in the past several years. One of the latest conservation plans is to erect a double fence in an attempt to stop the cancer from spreading toward the west side of the island, where devils are still disease free. The challenge with this plan, says Hamish McCallum, PhD, senior scientist with Tasmania's DFTD program, is that the fences will have to be in place within 2 years if they're going to have any chance of success.

But for now at least, the group of devils I'm observing seems to be very healthy. Leaving not so much as a patch of wallaby fur uneaten, they go their separate ways once again. As I watch, it occurs to me that this is a creature whose fate probably would have been sealed if conservation efforts were based on an animal's popularity. But this species isn't the unpredictable, unhinged Tasmanian devil of cartoons. It's just an animal that happens to emit the same menacing-sounding growl when it expresses affection as it does when it competes for food. Ironically, the very company that helped make the devil an infamous character in American pop culture is now aiding these threatened creatures. Ted Turner and Warner Brothers contribute to the Australian and Tasmanian governments' efforts to save the devil.

One of the foreseeable changes that may occur if conservation efforts fail is a surge in the population of the red foxes that the British introduced to Tasmania 200 years ago. Devils and foxes are the apex predators there, and until recently the tens of thousands of devils had kept the fox population from expanding by feasting on their litters and competing for the same food sources. But as the devil population has declined and the fox population has risen, a chain of events has been put into play that affects an entire ecosystem. If the fox gains the upper hand, it could ensure that the devil is never able to rebound. Native penguins and bettongs (sometimes referred to as *rat kangaroos*) would also be threatened by the fox.

In the midst of a climate crisis and at a time when natural habitat is disappearing by the minute, fish and wildlife can't afford the energy to fight the additional threats of a toppling ecosystem.

# TROUBLE AT SEA

Closer to home, another mysterious disease is targeting a beloved species: the sea otter (*Enhydra lutris*). Since April 2004, when 62 southern sea otters were found dead or stranded along the Morro Bay area of California's coast—about three times the average of the previous 10 years—scientists have been on the trail of the killer. To help search for answers, I joined a research and rescue team made up of members of the California Department of Fish and Game, the US Geological Survey, and the Monterey Bay Aquarium for a day on the water off the coast of Monterey. Our mission was to capture a few otters in order to take measurements and samples that could be examined for chemical contaminants and disease. Then we'd radio-tag them so that biologists could monitor the otters remotely.

Gregarious by nature, sea otters often gather in groups called *rafts* when they're resting, lying on their backs in a tight cluster within the surface canopy of a kelp forest to gain protection from waves and currents. As we approached the nearest raft, I could see through the Zodiac's spray of saltwater more than a dozen otters bobbing in the gentle waves. Mothers and their young were holding each other's paws, and others had wrapped themselves in kelp to keep from floating out to sea while they slept.

Sea otters are one of an estimated 1,930 species of threatened marine mammals. It's estimated that there are about 91,000 sea otters worldwide, but the southern subspecies in California numbers only about 2,800, and the multitude of threats they face puts them at constant risk for extinction. While their threatened status protects them from unsustainable hunting, it can't shield them from disease, parasitic infections, pollution, collisions with boats, or entanglement in fishing gear.

In the boat, we kept a safe distance as we drifted to a stop less than 200 feet from the perimeter of the raft. We were so close that I could see the slick hair on their chocolate-colored bodies and their gray, bristly faces. With almost a million strands per square inch, the sea otter has the densest and most luxurious fur in the animal kingdom. Unlike other sea mammals, such as whales, sea lions, and seals, otters don't have blubber for insulation and must rely on their fur coats for warmth. For those coats to insulate them as they should, otters need to devote hours each day to vigorous grooming; this replenishes the natural oils and maintains a layer of air against their skin that keeps their bodies warm and dry while they're under water, functioning much like a scuba diver's dry suit. The otter nearest to me was skillfully grooming the thick coat of the young pup she had balanced on her chest.

Sea otters are considered a *keystone species*—one that has a greater stabilizing effect on its ecosystem than the size of its population would suggest. When sea otters are present, the coastal environment is three times more diverse, making it a more stable and productive ecosystem than those with less diversity. This is particularly important during times of environmental change or imbalance.

The members of this raft were already awake and alert and thus were not candidates for easy capture. So we maneuvered around them, keeping enough distance that, except for a few curious glances cast our way, they mainly ignored us. Equipped with all the latest diving gear and gadgets and clad in our wet suits, we felt like Navy SEALs on a top-secret mission. Had marine biology and conservation given way to espionage? As a matter of fact, yes. That's what it takes to catch a sea otter.

We were searching for a sleeping otter that we could sneak up on, and when we spotted one, we cut the engines and quietly paddled toward it until we were about a quarter mile away. When we were in position, we slipped into the water in teams of two, stealthily swimming through the forest of kelp and getting into position.

Instead of using scuba tanks, we were equipped with rebreathers, which are 21st-century scuba devices that recycle air by scrubbing out carbon dioxide and don't produce bubbles. Sea otters have an excellent sense of smell, and the bubbles emitted by standard scuba gear will quickly alert them to the presence of divers below. With rebreathers, you also have zero buoyancy issues, which means we didn't have to carry weights to offset the effects of an emptying tank. So maneuvering in the water was much easier—an advantage we would need.

As cute and approachable as sea otters appear to be, make no mistake: At 4 to 5 feet long and 40 to 100 pounds in weight, they are formidable creatures. Each otter capture must be carried out with extreme caution and total team coordination to prevent injury to the otter as well as the human capturing it. The last thing you want is for your hand or arm to fall victim to the jaw pressure and fangs that otters use to rip open octopus and leather-hard abalone. Besides the unspeakable pain, an otter bite to the hand can give you an infection called *seal finger* that causes debilitating joint inflammation. Today, it can be treated with antibiotics, but for fishermen and curious sea travelers a century ago, the only treatment was amputation.

When we were about 20 feet below the otter, we silently swam to the surface, keeping the opening of the large net trap aligned with its long body. My heart raced as we swiftly swallowed her up in the net and drew the opening shut. By now, the otter was wide-awake and not at all pleased about her capture. Very carefully, we scooped her into the Zodiac and whisked her off to a mobile medical van that transported her to the aquarium within minutes. Working quickly so that the otter would be sedated for as short a time as possible, the veterinarian took blood and tissue samples and inserted a small VHF radio transmitter and a passive integrated transponder (PIT) tag the size of a grain of rice under her skin. The VHF transmitter allows biologists to track an otter's movements and monitor its vital signals; a PIT tag allows them to identify an animal many years after its capture (female sea otters can live up to 20 years—much longer than the transmitter's 2 to 3 years of battery life).

Many of the animal missions I've taken part in, whether with otters, elephants, lions, or leopards, have had elements of the alien abduction stories you read about in tabloids. And that's what it must have seemed like for this otter. She was sleeping peacefully on the water's surface, when suddenly, she was captured, transported to a strange place, put under a bright light, and probed. If she could communicate it, she'd have quite a story to tell her friends back at the raft.

# TO THE BRINK OF EXTINCTION AND BACK

While otters aren't fond of being abducted, it's the only way for biologists to gather the information that's crucial to their conservation management, provide medical intervention, and assess their overall health. It's taken nearly 100 years and an extraordinary amount of scientific research and intervention to bring the sea otter back from near extinction to its current abundance, which is still less than a third of the population of a few hundred years ago. Unfortunately, as successful as the recovery has been, many sea otter populations are still at risk for extinction. The common sea otter, which has a range from the Kuril Islands to the Komandorski Islands, is listed as endangered. The IUCN classifies the northern sea otter, native to the Aleutian Islands, mainland Alaska, and living as an introduced species in locations from Alaska to Oregon, as threatened in southwestern Alaska. The southern sea otter, also known as the California sea otter, lives off the coast of central California and is also listed as threatened; in 2008, the population was estimated at 2,826.

Although the Aleutian Islands were teeming with 55,000 to 100,000 sea otters in 1980, the number plummeted to just 6,000 by the year 2000. Of the tens of thousands gone, at least 5,000 were killed when the *Exxon Valdez* hit Bligh Reef in 1989 and spilled more than 10 million gallons of oil into Prince William Sound, Alaska. One of the worst environmental disasters in US history, it also killed close to half a million sea birds, 24 orcas, and millions of salmon and herring eggs. Although it's been 2 decades since that catastrophe, damage to the marine ecosystem in that area is still evident. In 1994, Exxon was ordered to pay $287 million in actual damages and $5 billion in punitive damages to nearly 33,000 commercial fishermen and other plaintiffs whose livelihoods were hobbled by the spill. But after a 14-year court battle, the US Supreme Court limited the damages to $507.5 million in 2008—just more than $15,000 per plaintiff.

The southern sea otter population began declining in the late 1990s, and although the numbers are now generally stable, many otters off the coast of California are now dying from disease and parasites. In fact, almost half of sea otter deaths are caused by infectious disease. One of the worst offenders is toxoplasmosis. Often fatal to otters, this infection is caused by the protozoan parasite *Toxoplasma gondii,* which is carried by feral and domestic cats as well as bobcats and mountain lions. It's not yet known how this land-based parasite is getting into the ocean. One possibility is that parasite eggs may pass through storm sewers and even be spread by domestic cat droppings flushed into sewage systems. (*T. gondii* can also cause birth defects when pregnant women are exposed to it through cat feces in litter boxes.) The sick otters often suffer seizures, demonstrating signs of brain damage. Their eyes become dilated, they can't hunt or eat, and they can no longer care for their high-maintenance fur. Identifying this illness was a victory for sea otters, but now we need to find a way to stop the infection, and that answer continues to elude us.

Another prevalent disease that afflicts the otters is acanthocephalan peritonitis. When an otter is infected, this parasite irritates the lining of the otter's abdomen, causing distention, pain, and fever. Eventually, the otter goes into shock and dies. Otters are infected by eating crabs and other crustaceans that have consumed coastal birds' droppings containing the parasite.

And now, according to Tim Tinker, PhD, a biologist at the US Geological Survey's Western Ecological Research Center, a pathogen called *Sarcocystis neurona* is causing even more otter deaths than *T. gondii*. Carried by opossums introduced to the West Coast in the late 19th century, the parasite's eggs get passed on to sea otters through the food chain. The eggs remain inert when an invertebrate or cold-blooded animal ingests them, but once they are in a warm-blooded animal such as a mouse, the eggs hatch and form tissue cysts. The parasite doesn't reproduce until the mouse is eaten by the definitive host—the only host in which it can reproduce—in this case, the opossum. When an opossum eats the mouse, the cysts break open, releasing thousands of little zooids, which are organic cells or organized bodies that have independent movement within a living organism. These reproduce in the opossum and start the cycle all over again. When this pathogen makes it into the marine system, it can cause brain and other tissue damage—and death—for the otter.

Tinker is working with a team of scientists that includes parasitologists and pathologists from the University of California at Davis and geneticists from the National Institutes of Health who are examining the diseases' genetic constitutions. "There definitely doesn't seem to be a single silver bullet to handle all the assaults on the otter population," Tinker says. "Since a suite of different diseases is killing them, we suspect that there are underlying factors. One theory is that loss of genetic diversity has compromised the otters' immune function, making them less resistant to disease. Or it might be a broader environmental problem, like chemical pollutants or reduced food availability, that's weakening their immunity to certain diseases."

As we drove back to the ocean to release the captured otter into her habitat, I couldn't help but marvel at how exquisitely adapted to marine environments these mammals are. They're born in the water and can live in the ocean at all stages of life. And their beautiful, abundant fur is the thickest, richest, most insulating on the planet. Not surprisingly, this very attribute is the reason that the otters were once hunted so voraciously.

Sea otters have endured a horrific past. What's known as the Great Hunt began in 1741 when Russia expanded sea otter hunting from the Kuril Islands off the coast of Japan to the Komandorski Islands in the southwest Bering Sea. During one of his missions, Russian naval captain and explorer Vitus Bering and his crew were shipwrecked off the coast of the land now named for him, Bering Island. Those who survived the frigid winter they spent there made it through by hunting otters. By the time the crew members returned to Siberia, they'd killed close to 1,000 otters. The Great

Hunt would last for 100 years, bringing down the sea otter population in that area to an estimated 750.

The Russians weren't the only ones interested in sea otters. On Vancouver Island, British explorer Captain James Cook purchased several sea otter pelts in 1778 and unwittingly opened the floodgates to the sea otter's demise. When his crew displayed the pelts at the port of Macao on the Chinese coast, they sold for such a high price—$100 or more per pelt—that it nearly created a mutiny; the sailors suddenly decided they wanted to make their fortunes by going back to Vancouver for more pelts rather than returning home to Russia. Word of the luxurious pelts spread like wildfire, and within months, hunters from North America and Europe were harvesting and trading furs in the Pacific Northwest. On the west coast of Vancouver Island, sea otter pelts doubled in price from 1787 to 1792 and doubled *again* over the next 3 years. From 1790 to 1812, at least 150,000 sea otter skins were shipped from the Pacific coast to Canton, China. During the 1880s, sea otter pelts sold for as much as $165 in London; and by 1903, the price was up to $1,125. The sea otters had become so scarce, with only 1,000 to 2,000 still alive, that commercial hunting was no longer viable.

The turning point for the otters came in 1911, when the United States, Russia, Japan, and Great Britain (on behalf of Canada) signed the Treaty for the Preservation and Protection of Fur Seals and Sea Otters. The safety provided by this treaty has allowed sea otter numbers to rise slowly but steadily to the current count of 91,000. This successful population increase was further supported by the US Marine Mammal Protection Act of 1972, and today, sea otters occupy about two-thirds of their former range.

It's no wonder their coats were so highly prized. That thick veneer of cuddliness makes it possible for otters to dive 300 feet under water to capture their prey and survive frigid conditions that most mammals can't bear. In fact, otters can live in water so cold that we couldn't survive exposure to it for more than 10 minutes. They're the only marine animals that can lift and turn over cinder-block–size boulders, which they do with their front paws when they're hunting for clams, mussels, and other invertebrates on the seafloor. They're also the only marine mammals to catch fish with their paws instead of their teeth, and one of just a few species of mammals that use tools. A sea otter will use a large stone to free an abalone from its death grip on a rock surface, for instance. And an abalone's no easy catch. It can cling to a rock with a force equal to 4,000 times its body weight, so otters need to use a tremendous amount of force to free them.

Back when we were in the Zodiac, I watched as an otter, its coat sleek and shimmering, broke through the surface of the water and flipped over onto its back. I thought at first that it was empty-handed, but within seconds, it reached into the loose pouch of skin under its left foreleg and withdrew an abalone, followed by a large hammering stone. The otter balanced the stone on its chest and, firmly gripping the abalone with its forepaws, repeatedly whacked the abalone on it until the shell finally cracked open.

Otters have been vilified for cutting into commercial fishing profits by depleting populations of abalone, clams, and fish. But ironically, many of the fishing operations that bemoan the presence of sea otters actually benefit from this keystone species. Research indicates that populations of shellfish, crustaceans, and other fish actually *increase* when sea otters are present.

Sea otters also maintain the kelp-forest ecosystem by eating sea urchins and other benthic (seafloor) herbivores. When sea urchins graze on the lower stems of kelp, this alga drifts away from the ocean floor. Kelp forests provide habitat and nutrients for many marine animals, and their depletion creates a profound domino effect on the marine ecosystem. The areas along the North Pacific coast that most lack kelp forests are also the most devoid of sea otters. After the recovery of sea otter populations in California's Big Sur and their reintroduction to British Columbia, the health of these coastal ecosystems improved significantly.

Sea otters also stimulate greater diversity in an ecosystem by eating the mussels that could otherwise dominate the rocky areas and crowd out other species. So, as with amphibians, saving the sea otter is about much more than saving the animals themselves—it's also about keeping a healthy balance in the marine ecosystem.

But preserving and protecting the sea otter is proving to be a difficult task. In addition to the threats of parasites and disease, otters are victims of shark bites and human conflict. While otter hunting is rare today, many rescued sea otters living in captivity are missing limbs or are blind due to run-ins with boats and fishing nets. As for the shark attacks, researchers think they are actually unfortunate results of mistaken identity. The highest mortality rates from shark bites occur near elephant seal beaches, which white sharks patrol when the seal pups are being weaned and entering the ocean. To a shark, the young seals are irresistible treats, and otters are about the same size and shape as baby seals. Biologists suspect that otters are being mistaken for seal pups, since there's no evidence that sharks are actually eating the otters. "I think once the sharks get a bite of all that otter fur, they decide they don't want to consume it and set their sights back on the nearest seal pup," Tinker says. "We see a lot of dead otters that were bitten once and survive for a week or so before they die of internal infection." Without this geographic coincidence, the sea otter population would be growing more rapidly.

Environmental degradation also takes a toll on the otters. Pollution by toxic industrial chemicals and other sources such as pesticide runoff from agriculture can lower water quality and even deplete the supply of prey species. One large oil spill off the coast of California could eliminate the entire southern sea otter's wild population. It would also devastate the marine ecosystem. Scientists are formulating rescue plans in the event of another catastrophe like the *Valdez* oil spill, but prevention will always be the best strategy.

And believe it or not, none of these threats is as critical to the otters' survival as climate change. Increases in temperature and the resulting acidification of the ocean and shifts in coastal currents and upwelling patterns will cause enormous changes in the abundance and distribution of many marine invertebrates that make up the sea otter's diet. Because otters already live on the razor's edge in terms of the vast numbers of calories they need for energy, even small changes in their environment can have large impacts on their survival. As a result of these changes to their food supply, otters must travel greater distances to hunt and forage for the calories they need.

But despite these threats, the sea otter is prevailing, and so are the scientists championing its cause. Last year, the Monterey Bay Aquarium celebrated the birth of an otter pup "pioneer." The pup was born to a female otter that the aquarium had rescued and reared. This is the first birth for a surrogate-reared animal in the history of the aquarium's trailblazing Sea Otter Research and Conservation program.

It's true that for endangered species, every day presents a challenge. But it's also true that every day presents opportunities for us to make resounding strides.

## BACK FROM THE DEAD

Imagine that an animal thought to be extinct suddenly reappears—lifeless, in the jaws of your German shepherd.

It may sound like fiction, but that was the case in 1981 for rancher John Hogg of Meeteetse, Wyoming, when his dog, Shep, brought home a furry trophy. Hogg suspected that the animal in Shep's mouth had been eating the dog's food and that Shep had decided to put a quick end to the problem. When Hogg and his wife, Lucille, couldn't identify the lifeless creature, she was intrigued enough to take the carcass to the local taxidermist. It turned out to be an "extinct" black-footed ferret (*Mustela nigripes*), and the taxidermist notified the USFWS.

Where there's one member of an animal species, there are usually more nearby. Thus began the search for other survivors that had somehow weathered sylvatic plague and ranchers' decimation of prairie dogs—ferrets' main prey. In what seemed a modern-day miracle, 130 more ferrets were discovered.

But, just as abruptly, in 1985 disease struck this beleaguered species yet again. This time it would turn out to be both plague and canine distemper. With only 10 ferrets known to be alive—most likely making them the rarest mammals in the world—the species was clinging to life by a thread, and the USFWS and the Wyoming Game and Fish Department rushed to the rescue. Their only hope was to capture the 4 remaining wild ferrets and place them with the 6 already in a captive-breeding program. Suddenly, a remote Wyoming town with a population of 500 became ground zero for one of the United States' most significant conservation efforts.

Dean Biggins, PhD, wildlife biologist with the USFWS at the time and now with the US Geological Survey, was on hand to help find and capture the remaining ferrets. Over an 18-month period, during which the wild population increased to 12, his team and other colleagues successfully captured all but one. That one became known as Scarface, both for the many wounds he bore (probably from battles over mates) and for his skill at eluding the authorities.

"My crew and I tried to find him by spotlight, the normal technique, on numerous occasions for more than a year," Biggins says. "We would get just a glimpse of green eye shine and then it would disappear. We were never totally sure it was even a ferret."

Eventually, weary of being held off—it was February 1987 by now and all the other known ferrets had been caught by the end of summer—Biggins's crew decided to wait for snow and then look for tracks leading to a burrow. When snow arrived, they were surprised that the tracks led them a mile away from the colony where Scarface had originally been spotted, to the burrow where Biggins's crew had captured one of the last two females—and their litters. "He was undoubtedly the father," Biggins says.

They set traps outside the burrow, but the ferret proved to be so elusive that Biggins and two crew members worked 8-hour shifts around the clock for a week before finally catching him. Now they had all 18, and not a minute too soon—the captive-breeding program hadn't been much of a success, and if the ferret population were ever to rebound, this Casanova needed to start performing.

Fortunately, he accepted the challenge and immediately began breeding with the females in captivity. In fact, he did such a thorough job that he became genetically overrepresented, and breeders had to spend the next 10 years trying to balance the ferrets' population.

So it's thanks largely to a lover and a fighter that the black-footed ferret population was able to rebound successfully from the original 18 to an estimated 700 today, 400 of which are living in the wild. It's an amazing comeback for a species that was thought to have disappeared in the 1970s.

It was a thrill for me when, in July 2007, I participated in the release of 49 ferrets at Wind Cave National Park in Hot Springs, South Dakota—the culmination of 7 years of reintroduction planning. I'd first filmed a segment on ferrets at a breeding facility in New Mexico in 1997, when there were an estimated 66 ferrets in the wild. We were only able to capture fleeting images of them through the mesh of their enclosure, and the scene had the same kind of fateful feeling that had hung over our experience with the puaiohi in Hawaii. So it was deeply satisfying—and a huge relief—to be able to witness ferrets making the transition from captivity to the wild more than a decade later. The ferret in my carrier seemed to sense the weight of the occasion, too, loudly chattering away—though his response was actually a defensive behavior designed to shock predators and discourage them from carrying away their slinky, 2-pound bodies.

He was obviously prepared for the worst. I set the carrier down in front of a prairie dog burrow and opened the cage door. All he had to do was scurry into the burrow and settle in (yes, they move into the homes of their prey), crossing just a few feet of open ground. He wouldn't have to face so much as the heat of the sun, let alone contend with a coyote or a golden eagle or any other predator. But when I opened the gate, he didn't go for it. Park biologist Dan Roddy, who was accompanying me, explained that the experience is a bit of a shock for some ferrets, and they grip the walls of the carrier. In those cases, he said, you need to scratch the rear of the cage to make them nervous, forcing them to decide which perceived threat they're more afraid of. Suddenly, the brief stretch of open ground may seem less formidable. So I scratched the rear of the cage, and the next thing I knew, he sprang out of the carrier and slipped into the burrow. I didn't even get a chance to see his black-masked, raccoonlike face as he surged toward safety. What I saw looked like all neck, a furry soft brown tube with tiny ears and a black tip at the end of its tail.

Since the reintroduction of 49 ferrets bred in captivity, the park has reported an even bigger success: the discovery of 14 ferret kits born in the summer of 2008, proof that the reintroduction plan is working and the population is thriving.

"Ferrets usually have three or four kits per litter, so there were probably five or six females that had kits last year," Roddy says. "That seemed to answer the question that had been on all our minds for so long: Were they going to take hold or weren't they? And were we going to need to keep bringing ferrets in for many years?"

Only about half the ferrets at reintroduction sites make it through the winter to mating season, "and that's when we crossed our fingers," Roddy says. "We'd found tracks in the snow, so we knew they were out there, but now it was a question of whether we'd see some kit production." The answer came in October 2008, when the kits were found, and Roddy says there's already been talk at Wind Cave about the possibility of never having to bring more ferrets in to breed. In fact, the park staff hopes the group will eventually produce enough kits that it can act as a nursery colony and provide ferrets to other reintroduction sites.

———

The ferret isn't safe yet, though. Its old nemesis the plague struck a colony of 300 in South Dakota during the wet spring and early summer of 2008, killing as many as 100. The plague had spread to 9,700 of the 25,000 acres of prairie dog habitat that's federally managed for ferrets at the US Forest Service Buffalo Gap National Grassland before it was halted in August. At the time, wildlife officials expected it to begin spreading again in the fall or the following spring. The plague is spread by fleas, so the USFWS and its partners are taking a pesticide-based approach in their efforts to stop the disease, dusting prairie dog burrows with flea powder. "We've gone as far as to put insecticide down in burrows by driving across prairie dog towns with four-wheelers," says Pete Gober, USFWS black-footed ferret recovery coordinator. "There's also a vaccine on the horizon that could be delivered in bait that prairie dogs would eat. Of course, managers put *poison* in bait that prairie dogs eat, like oats, to control their spread to areas where they aren't wanted, so it would be some return of justice if we found a way to put vaccine in food to protect them from plague." Before the use of this vaccine can be approved, its effects need to be tested on wild ferrets in a lab setting. For now, ferrets raised in captivity and those captured in the wild are protected from plague by vaccines that are delivered by way of injections.

Though a remedy for the rest of the prairie dog population might be a couple of years off, the insecticide is proving to be effective at protecting them while they wait. Biggins says he's seen the plague's progress come to a halt upon encountering a prairie dog town that's been sprayed, or dusted. Whether that's a quick fix or a long-term strategy comes down to resources. It's an expensive treatment, and it may need to be done every year or two.

It can be difficult to get financing to save an animal as controversial as the prairie dog, regardless of the fact that the ferret's fate is inextricably bound with its survival. As a specialist species, the ferret is completely dependent on prairie dogs for survival. A black-footed ferret eats 125 to 150 prairie dogs a year and needs contiguous stretches of prairie dog burrows for its habitat. As Gober puts it, "For a ferret, to be above ground is to be dead." But many farmers and ranchers harbor ill will toward prairie dogs because they compete with livestock for forage and damage crops by clearing the way for the spread of weeds and stripping the areas near their burrows of most vegetation. Ranchers also want to protect their cows and horses from accidentally stepping into prairie dog holes and becoming injured.

Gober says that while we'll never be able to regenerate the prairie dog population to its historical numbers, conservation is possible. But conservation efforts must take into account the prairie dogs' impact on livestock foraging, whether real or perceived. In other words, in order to save the ferret, we need to reestablish prairie dogs in areas where they won't inconvenience ranchers and their livestock: We need protected prairie dog land.

"We're not going to get rid of cornfields, but there are places where ranching operations are less profitable," Gober says. "And then the question becomes, how do you take poor-quality ranching country and turn it into adequate prairie dog habitat, and what do you need to do that? Do you need dollar incentives paid to ranchers? Do you need someone who can control prairie dogs at the boundaries of these areas so that neighbors won't be bothered? Do you need recurring plague management? Do you need biologists to track these populations?"

It's a lot like the story of Humpty Dumpty, as Gober explains. "Once these species fall off the wall, you don't put them back together again. You take a few fragments and you hold them together, hoping they match up. It's not like we're going to put these species back and they're going to be okay without any additional management intervention. Management is forever once you take an ecosystem apart as thoroughly as we have with the prairie dogs."

And finding the resources isn't easy. "We've lost 50 percent of our wetlands, and we've lost 95 to 98 percent of the prairie dog complex," Gober says. "While wetlands have an incredible value for reasons that are easily recognizable to people, when you start talking about prairie dogs—a pest in many people's minds—it's a different story."

But there's good reason to believe the ferrets will continue to make a comeback. Since 1986, more than 6,000 ferrets have been born in captivity, Gober says. Of those, more than 2,300 have been released into the wild at 18 sites in North America. And there are plans in the works for two more release sites.

Not bad for a species we'd given up for dead.

# PART III

# EDUCATION VS. EXPLOITATION

# CHAPTER 6

# DEATH BY UNNATURAL CAUSES

I N 2 0 0 2 , I took my own journey into the heart of darkness: the black market for rare and endangered animals. I was working with professionals from the Indonesian group ProFauna and the Jakarta Animal Aid Network to film their raid on a mansion in Jakarta, where endangered animals were rumored to be held captive.

And it didn't take us long to find out that the rumors were true. As we walked toward the door, we passed a filthy cage in which an orphaned baby orangutan languished. When the owner approached us, we showed him our permits to search the compound. From his nonchalant attitude, it was clear that he felt no shame for his crimes or for the conditions in which these animals were forced to live.

After we freed the orangutan and many of his fellow prisoners and took them back to ProFauna's holding center, I found it difficult to keep my anger in check. All around me were rare animals in various stages of declining health—a macaque, Javan leaf monkeys, gibbons, eagles, yellow-crested cockatoos, and hundreds of other birds. Some of these prospective pets—or meals—were injured, some were recovering from starvation, some were in shock. And yet these were the lucky ones—at least they were in ProFauna's hands now. They would be treated and rehabilitated, in some cases for several months, and then released back into the wild if possible.

Little did we know that this facility teeming with animals in distress was about to become significantly more crowded.

Within moments of our arrival, a battalion of trucks pulled up carrying a pulsating heap of burlap bags. Hundreds of them. When we learned what was in them, my anger grew even more intense. Cobras, Asian rat snakes, banded kraits, pythons, tree vipers, and other snakes were coiled around one another in agonizing knots. These snakes had been on their way to being butchered and shipped far and wide for human consumption. Some would no doubt have been stripped of their skins and eviscerated while still alive, the bile squeezed from their gallbladders like liquid from a tea bag and drunk from shot glasses in the false belief that it offered benefits such as virility, good vision, longevity, and healthy skin.

Some of the snakes had been severely injured, either in their attempts to escape or directly at the hands of the poachers. It was one of the most disturbing sights I've ever seen. Hundreds—maybe even a thousand—stunning snakes, some of them rare, stuffed into cotton sacks and pillowcases like so much garbage, their sacrifice a monument to human greed and indifference. But as appalled as we all were, there was nothing to do but start sorting and classifying the snakes—a task that took hours and required much mopping of our brows in the Jakartan humidity. The air reeked of reptile excrement and rotten flesh. Some of these animals had liquefied into a necrotic soup, while others seemed to have mummified. But astonishingly, amid all the death, some of the snakes were still alive, if just barely. And so we kept at our task.

As we sorted the last of the snakes, a shriek pierced the stifling air. One of the ProFauna workers, a man who had worked by my side all day, screamed again as cobra venom made contact with his eyes. Either it had been on his hands and he had rubbed his eyes, or one of the snakes had spit at him. As we drove frantically to the hospital, turning the wrong way down one-way streets jammed with traffic, I bathed his eyes with water in an attempt to soothe his pain. Once we got him to the hospital, we spent hours on the phone with a venom expert in the United States as the worker came closer to losing his sight with every passing minute. Luckily, in the end, this man who devotes his life to saving animals didn't lose his vision. But the memory of that day will stay with me forever.

This is the reprehensible reality of the black market, an industry so pervasive that Interpol estimates its annual profits at more than $20 billion,[1] behind only the black markets for weapons and illegal narcotics. In fact, the crimes often become entangled, with smugglers branching out into animal trafficking in order to mask their *drug* trafficking, making enforcement even more complicated.

The trading of live endangered animals and animal products was outlawed by the Convention on International Trade in Endangered Species of Wild Fauna and Flora (CITES) in 1977, but the black market thrives just the same. Poaching and the illegal trade in wildlife are insidious activities whose business plays out in the back-alley markets of London, Paris, Miami, New York, Phnom Penh, Bangkok, and the DRC. In some countries, enforcement is strict and penalties steep. In others, black market activities receive only a legal slap on the wrist. In still others, the animal trade is openly celebrated. Regardless of the enforcement practices in a given country, the trade is a global epidemic in which an animal killed in the jungles of the DRC can end up as bushmeat for human consumption. Bushmeat can be found everywhere, from subsistence villages to urban centers in Africa, and even on the dinner tables of expatriates living around the world. In addition to being slaughtered for their meat, the animals are also harvested for their parts, which are used in Asian folk medicines and for ornamental purposes, such the use of rhino horn for dagger handles in Yemen and Oman and the use of furs and reptile skins for clothing and accessories. Sometimes they're kept alive to be sold as pets—especially parrots, reptiles, and small primates. In conjunction with habitat loss, the black market trade is responsible for the near extinction and critical endangerment of hundreds of animal species. When poachers slaughter an animal to harvest a specific part of its body, such as a rhino's horn, a tiger's bones, or an elephant's tusks, it can decimate the species' population and cause entire ecosystems to falter.

There's little in life that's more disturbing than the sight of a dead rhino flat on its side with a bloody hole in its head where its horn used to be. Or a gorilla that's been reduced to little more than a stump, its hands and feet having gone the way of its dignity. Or an elephant that's been stripped of its face and its once-mighty trunk—powerful enough to knock over a tree—to give poachers access to the bases of the tusks. How can we reconcile the moral chasm that lies between a 5,000-pound rhino carcass and a few pounds of harvested horn? It's difficult not to feel that all of humanity has let these animals down by failing to protect them from our species' worst impulses.

While you might think (or hope) that such impulses and acts are so rare that they couldn't endanger an entire animal species, the elephant, for one, knows differently. According to the IUCN, the Asian elephant (*Elephas maximus*) is endangered, and the African bush elephant (*Loxodonta africana*) is listed as near threatened. Richard G. Ruggiero, PhD, of the USFWS Division of International Conservation, has witnessed the elephants' decline in horrifying detail.

"A lot of the work I did [in Africa] was walking around with my head to the ground following elephants, trying to see how they behave, what they eat, etc. I'd see tracks of an elephant that had been dragging its leg and intuit that something was wrong," he says. "After following the tracks, I'd realize that the elephant was lagging behind the herd because it had five or six spear wounds in its upper thighs and back legs."

Ruggiero worked in the Republic of the Congo, where such spears are wielded by the Janjaweed, armed horsemen in the Darfur region of Sudan and Chad whom Ruggiero describes as "probably the best horsemen since the Middle Ages."

"Basically, they are a culture of roving warriors that ride on horseback and take everything of value, be it women, ivory, slaves, or bushmeat," he says. "They've been running around in the absence of law and order and government, taking whatever they want."

And when it's ivory they want, the results are shocking. "They ride up on a horse and then spear an elephant in its hindquarter. When the elephant runs forward, they catch up to it and they spear it again. They do it maybe 10 times until they hamstring it, cut its sciatic nerve, or it bleeds to death. Or they harass it until it becomes so weak and confused that it falls over, and then they give it a heart thrust if it isn't already dead from the loss of blood. And they leave it there until it gets rotten enough to be able to pull the tusks out, or if they're in a hurry because they think guys like me are around, they cut its trunk off and then take an axe and chop away at the upper jaw, the maxillary, to pull the tusks out.

"I've seen a cow elephant that's been killed, her trunk and her face cut off, lying in about 3 inches of liquid, which is a combination of body fluids and blood. And standing in that pool is her 2-year-old calf. Even though her mama is bloated and reeking of death, she doesn't want to leave. She'll stay and starve to death or the lions will get her."

For me, the heartbreak of poaching is encapsulated in that image: a distraught elephant calf who literally can't live without her mother. Tactile creatures, elephants are very dependent on a mother's touch, and they're also highly emotional animals—maybe nearly as emotional as humans—capable of both despondency and joy.

I once had the opportunity to visit the David Sheldrick Elephant Orphanage in Nairobi, Kenya, while filming an episode of my show. I was designated as the *mahout*—or keeper—for the night of a 3-month-old calf that had lost his family to poachers. As we bedded down in his cage, my main job was to make sure the 350-pound calf had the tactile contact with me that he needed to sleep peacefully. Things began well enough, with him nodding off easily, but in the middle of the night, I felt a knocking at my back. He was having a nightmare, and I instinctively cupped his eyes so he couldn't see the light from the oil lamp hanging from the ceiling. The trembling of his trunk slowed, and his breathing softened. Just as he was drifting off again, he started to twist a lock of my hair with the tip of his trunk. All 40,000 muscles in that miniature proboscis were working together to make sure that its tip—which is 10 times more sensitive than a human finger—brought him the soothing contact he needed. Suddenly, I grasped the trauma that a creature this sensitive must experience in the presence of a poacher's brutality.

———

I hadn't thought about that experience for a long time. Then, one night at home, my daughter Maya fell out of bed. As I held her, rocking her back to sleep, I felt her breathing calm and slow down, just as the calf's had. It was a moment that reminded me of why I'm a conservationist. Though I try to maintain some distance from the heartache and brutality I sometimes witness, I can't avoid having a strong emotional connection to my work.

"It becomes a very personal thing when you see the degree of an elephant's suffering," Ruggiero says. "A mentor of mine who was an ex–concentration camp internee and a brilliant conservationist once said the Sudanese poachers are committing genocide on elephants. He used that term. This is a guy who was in a concentration camp during World War II. He said that humanity is committing genocide on elephants and that the elephants know it but they don't know why. And when you think about it, when you know what normal elephant behavior is when they're not being hunted, and then you see how they act when they *are*—how they change their behavior in such a sophisticated way, in terms of socializing, in terms of diet, in terms of nocturnal versus diurnal—he's right. They know that people are trying to kill them. But they obviously don't know why. When they find a fresh carcass, they touch it; they realize that the tusks are gone. When they do come across tusks that are not intact, they pick them up and carry them around."

Poaching is devastating many other animals besides the elephant, including the rhinoceros. Blessed—and cursed—with a horn that's worth five times more than gold in Hong Kong, Singapore, and the Mideast, this animal bears the holy grail of the black market on its face as conspicuously as a hood ornament.

# THE RHINOCEROS: POACHING'S POSTER CHILD

When we look at rhinos, we see something vaguely prehistoric in their appearance. Their armor, their famous sickle-shaped horns, and their lumbering gait give them the look of having stepped out of the Ice Age, barely transfigured by evolution. Rhino species are among the few remaining megafauna species, which are characterized by their massive body size. The woolly rhino (*Coelodonta antiquitatis*) of the Ice Age, in fact, is a direct ancestor of the Indian rhino (*Rhinoceros unicornis*), which is native to Asian countries such as India and Nepal, as are the Sumatran rhino (*Dicerorhinus sumatrensis*) and the Javan rhino (*Rhinoceros sondaicus*). The black rhino (*Diceros bicornis*) and the white rhino (*Ceratotherium simum*), meanwhile, are native to Africa. Grouped in the family Rhinocerotidae, rhinos are also distantly related to the horse. In the rhino sections of some zoos, you'll find posters illustrating how rhinos and horses evolved from common prehistoric ancestors, and you can suddenly see the family resemblance. (You may never look at horses the same way again.)

All species of rhino can weigh more than a ton, and the white rhino can weigh more than 6,600 pounds—making it nearly the largest land mammal alive, second only to the African elephant (which weighs in at up to 11,000 pounds). All rhinos are herbivores, eating only plants, but some are browsers—eating a great variety of vegetation, including the leaves of bushes and trees—while others are grazers, consuming grass like giant lawn mowers. Rhinos can have one or two horns, and their hide is made thick by latticelike layers of collagen. The Indian rhino's appearance is the most dramatic; it looks as if it's wearing a suit of armor, with enormous plates of that durable skin and one large horn at the end of its snout. Despite their size and capacity for brute force, rhinos are remarkably agile and self-possessed. Ernest Hemingway, who famously hunted rhinos early in the 20th century, wrote in "Notes on Dangerous Game: The Third Tanganyika Letter":[2]

> The rhino is a joke. He may be a bad joke, too, but his atrociously poor eyesight gives the hunter an advantage over him that his bulk, his really remarkable speed

and agility, and his sometimes idiotic pugnacity cannot overcome unless aided by advantage of terrain. . . . He is, too, very fast. . . . But fundamentally, to me, he seems a dangerous practical joke let loose by nature and armed with a horn which the Chinese pay high prices for to grind up and use as an aphrodisiac.

Even staunch conservationist President Theodore Roosevelt hunted white rhino in Uganda in 1910, at a time when its numbers had dwindled to hundreds. "The expedition," the *New York Times* reported on January 9 of that year, "as made up in the presidential hunt includes Col. Roosevelt, Kermit Roosevelt with 30 porters and boys. They have 200 [boatloads] of supplies."[3]

Clearly, they were determined to bring home a rhino. Referred to as a "rare beast" even then, if it hadn't been for drastic conservation measures taken years later, the rhino mounted in the parlor of Roosevelt's summer home in Oyster Bay, New York, would have been a rare trophy indeed.

As Hemingway noted, the rhino horn is highly prized. Its value stems largely from a centuries-old belief drawn from Chinese folk medicine that it can reduce fever. Rhino horn is also sold as a cure for impotence and lack of desire (a belief probably inspired by the fact that rhinos mate for 2 hours at a time). In Taiwan, a pound of Asian rhino horn can command $10,000 to $30,000, and a pound of African rhino horn goes for $1,000 to $1,500. It's estimated that each year of the 1970s, an average of 17,600 pounds of rhino horn was traded illegally in global markets. Though this number decreased to about 6,600 pounds a year during the 1980s, it still translates into at least 1,300 annual rhino deaths, according to the WWF.

Three rhino species—the Sumatran, the Javan, and the black rhino—are now *critically* endangered, and the Indian rhino is listed as threatened. Only the white rhino is a comfortable distance from the brink, due largely to the conservation efforts at South African nature reserves. The Sumatran rhino, with 275 members remaining, faces the most immediate threat because of the rapid rate at which its numbers are declining, though the Javan rhino is even rarer, with only 50 surviving.

Though poaching had taken a serious toll in the 1980s and 1990s, some rhino populations (mostly white rhinos) mounted a comeback with the help of new conservation programs. But progress comes hard in the face of a resurgent demand for rhino horn in Asia and ongoing civil strife and political upheaval in parts of Africa such as Zimbabwe. In 2008, the incidence of poaching rose sharply in Zimbabwe as well as South Africa, where at least 40 white rhinos reportedly were killed. And for the northern white rhino—whose population is confined to the DRC's Garamba National Park—the situation is grave.

Though some white rhino populations are thriving on nature reserves in Botswana and South Africa, the northern white rhino has been decimated by poachers. By August 2006, only four remained.[4] In fact, according to the WWF, the northern white rhino may now be functionally extinct. Wildlife protection is a tall order in a region still plagued by violence that has left an estimated 5.4 million people dead, many as a result of hunger and disease. And besides simply serving as an obstacle, the war also feeds the problem, with rebels reportedly funding their armies with poaching proceeds.

The same problem is vanquishing the rhino population in Zimbabwe, even though penalties for poaching there are extremely harsh. But in a country like Zimbabwe, where the average annual income is $480, the allure of making half a year's salary by killing a rhino and selling its horns can make it a worthwhile risk. Sadly, however, it's not the starving people who are getting rich. It's the dealers, who can make more than $4,500 on the black market for a single Asian rhino horn weighing about 5 pounds. African rhino horns, which weigh about 3.5 pounds, sell for about $3,500.

# A Medicinal Myth

This lucrative market for rhinoceros horn endures despite proof that this animal part has no medicinal value. In 1983, in an effort to educate the public, the WWF sponsored a study to investigate the purported "health benefits" of rhino horn. As expected, the study proved conclusively that it has no effect on fever or libido. But 26 years later, belief in these mythical benefits persists.

Most animal horn consists of a bony center covered by a thin layer of keratin, the same protein that's the principle component of our fingernails, toenails, and hair. Rhino horns are unique because they're *just* keratin. In a recent Ohio University study,[5] computed tomography scans of the heads of rhinos that had died of natural causes revealed that the keratin contained dense deposits of calcium and melanin in the middle of the horns. The calcium makes the core strong, and the melanin—which we have in our own skin—protects the core from the sun's ultraviolet rays. Because the keratin in the outer portion of the horn doesn't contain melanin, the sun is able to weaken it. As it's worn down by horn-to-horn clashes with other rhinos and by being rubbed on the ground during grazing, a sharp point—bolstered by the calcium—takes shape.

"Ultimately, we think our findings will help dispel some of the folk wisdom attached to the horn. The more we can learn about the horn, the better we can understand and manage rhino populations in the wild and in captivity," says Lawrence Witmer, the study's director and a professor of anatomy at Ohio University in Athens.

## Beating the Black Market

While white rhinos in South Africa have been threatened by increased poaching in recent years, they're currently considered a conservation success story. Their numbers dwindled to a mere 100 at the height of the "great white hunter" era in 1895. Today, with more than 14,000 living members of the subspecies, the white rhino is the healthiest rhino population in the world.

Unfortunately, black rhinos haven't been as successful at evading poachers. Their population of 4,240 is down from close to 70,000 in the late 1960s—a 94 percent drop. There are four subspecies of black rhino, but the western black rhinoceros (*Diceros bicornis longipes*) has been declared possibly extinct. Between poaching and habitat loss, tremendous effort is still needed to secure the future of the black rhino, but thanks to unrelenting conservation efforts, its numbers are stabilizing and slowly rising. Today, the last black rhinos of other subspecies are living in several national parks, primarily in Namibia, South Africa, Zimbabwe, Zambia, Malawi, Tanzania, and Kenya.

In Zimbabwe, the black rhino's population has rebounded to more than 500 animals. Though that makes it the third-largest rhino population in Africa, it actually needs the most help, as poaching remains a serious threat. Due to the country's tumultuous political and social climates, Zimbabwe's national parks and private conservancies are plagued by severe staffing and equipment shortages. And large-scale park invasions have resulted in the death and displacement of many black rhinos in captivity.

Fortunately, the International Rhino Foundation (IRF) has made inroads, mainly in the protected areas in the Lowveld region of Zimbabwe, where it works closely with local communities to protect the animals via monitoring and antipoaching patrols. Crews remove snares, provide veterinary care, and move rhinos to safe areas.

The plight of the rhino in Africa is a clear example of what happens when political and social instability impact a government's ability to protect animals. In South Africa and Botswana, where the political climate is stable, the white rhino population is also secure. But in areas where the savanna was once liberally dotted with the black rhino, political chaos has created an array of issues for the species, putting their survival—and that of an entire ecosystem—in danger.

"Rhinos function as landscape engineers," says Eric Dinerstein, PhD, chief scientist for WWF. "One of the things people don't realize is that when you have a forest or any kind of habitat without its giant mammals, it looks much different than it would if the giant mammals were there."

When large animals such as rhinos and elephants are present in an *understory*—the part of a forest that grows in the shade of the canopy above—they control the spread of plants in an area by eating the species they find palatable. "The same principle is true in the eastern United States," Dinerstein says. "If we put mountain lions back in the forest and the white-tailed deer became scarce, we'd have a different forest."

Like the IRF, the WWF is aggressively defending rhino populations—and ecosystems—against further damage. "We're doing all that we can to combat, infiltrate, report on poachers, use local people to form antipoaching information networks, and, more important, provide incentives for locals to want to live next to rhinos and tigers," Dinerstein says. The goal is to tie their economic future to the well-being of endangered animals through ecotourism and revenue-generating systems at places like Chitwan National Park in Nepal, where 50 percent of everything from hotel concession fees to park entry fees goes to communities in the buffer zone around the park. "So basically, the more rhinos there are, the more tourists are attracted. The more tourists are attracted, the more money they pay. The more money they pay, the more revenue goes back to community development. Last year, an estimated $400,000 (from ecotourism) went back to community development around Chitwan, which is far, far greater than what government puts into the local development office."

All of these efforts add up. "The fact that there are any rhinos alive today is a miracle," Dinerstein says. "And when you think about how the white rhinos have gone from under a hundred individuals at the turn of the last century to well over 10,000 today, that's a double miracle. Black rhinos' recovery in certain populations in Africa, given all the poaching and the unrest and the instability of that continent, is remarkable."

If you've ever doubted that a small group of people can make a big difference in the face of a tide that seems inexorable, organizations like the WWF and the IRF are proof that such a change is possible.

## The Indian Rhino: Encounter with a Giant

Along with the Sumatran and black rhinos, the Indian rhino—also called the *greater one-horned rhino*—shares the unfortunate distinction of being one of the most actively endangered species of rhinoceros, and it's one I know well. As I traveled through Chitwan National Park, one of the species' last remaining safe havens, I had the opportunity to search for one of these elusive protected animals while riding an Asian elephant named Rajkali.

Located in the Terai—subtropical lowlands at the base of the Himalayas—Chitwan is 125 miles from Nepal's capital, Kathmandu. But even though it sounds as if it's at the end of the world—an isolated place as far from the "real world" as the mythical Shangri-la—the truth is that very few natural places are isolated from man and his assaults on the last remaining wilderness. In Chitwan, when you're beneath the tree canopy and surrounded by mountains, it's easy to believe that you're walking through pristine wilderness, but the illusion is soon shattered by the sound of rushing tires on a roadway nearby or the droning engine of a low-flying plane overhead. The dense, once-uncharted forests that inspired the poetic nickname *green mansions* are now more like small apartments clinging to existence on the outskirts of civilization.

While on elephant-back at Chitwan, my camera crew in tow, we sighted a lone rhino bull escaping the sultry afternoon heat in the river. We moved in and dismounted from our elephants, the cameramen getting into position with cautious elation. We were *all* elated—we hoped to film this rare, massive animal in an up-close and intimate way that would help us share the species' plight with the world.

My heart pounded as it always does when I get close to such an incredible creature. We were only 100 yards from the rhino, which was in the river up to his shoulders, enjoying the coolness of the muddy water on this brutally hot afternoon. We were so excited that we walked right to the river's edge. Though we took cover behind a thicket of trees, it was still a risk. These animals are very territorial, and they've been known to kill or injure people when they've felt threatened. They don't use their horns, incidentally, but rather bite—Indian rhinos have very sharp teeth, and one bite can take out a 5-pound chunk of flesh. Naturally, we were trying to avoid direct contact of *any* kind.

So there we were, sitting and filming in silence, awestruck by the size of this rhino standing in 4 feet of water, when suddenly he towered above us, water streaming down the folds of skin separating his formidable plates of armor. He hadn't been *standing* in 4 feet of water—he'd been kneeling in 5 *inches* of water—and now, as if shot from a cannon, all 3 tons of him were making their presence known to us.

We scattered in every direction. Rajkali, my faithful companion of 2 days, took off with the rest of the elephants, shrieking and crashing through the forest. The cameraman grabbed his equipment and sprinted through the underbrush as if his life depended on it—which it probably did. I don't think any of us had ever moved so fast in our lives, and my heart was in my throat until I knew everyone was safe.

The experience left me in awe of the brute power of that rhino and renewed my respect for this magnificent species. I felt fortunate to have witnessed one of the world's most formidable animals in a rare defensive encounter with humans—and one that didn't result in the rhino's death.

The Indian rhino is a success story in rhino conservation. Thanks to vigilant protection from the Indian and Nepalese wildlife authorities, its numbers have recovered from fewer than 200 at the turn of the 20th century to the current estimate of 2,600. However, poachers have kept the pressure on in both countries, even around such highly popular and safe parks as Chitwan. It's also a concern that more than 85 percent of these rhinos inhabit a single protected area—India's Kaziranga National Park—exposing the population to the risk that just one natural disaster, disease outbreak, or other catastrophe could undo all the progress this species has made.

Conservationists are well aware of these risks and are diligently working to overcome them. In 2005, the IRF began a project with the San Diego Zoo's Wild Animal Park to return Indian rhinos to safe reserves in their native India. The program also supports breeding exchanges between parks and zoos in India, which are vital to preserving the species' genetic diversity, something that will help the rhinos maintain healthy populations in places where they live in close quarters with one another, like Kaziranga. Fashion designer Marc Ecko, who is famous for his clothing brand Eckō Unltd. (which uses a depiction of a chunky rhino as its logo), helped to launch the project with a large donation. Ecko has said that he has a "true affinity" with the animals. "More than just a logo, the rhino took on a whole new meaning as we began to coexist with it," Ecko has said. "We always said that the rhino is a survivor, so when we overcame our early financial struggles, it was only natural that we gave back to the animal that provided the inspiration."

As a tribute to his dedication to the cause, a baby Indian rhino at the Wild Animal Park has been named "Ecko."

## The Sumatran Rhino:
## A Portrait of Passion

Geographically close to the Indian rhino but worlds away in terms of physiology and genetics, the Sumatran rhino clings to survival as its numbers decline faster than those of any other extant species. Half the size of the Indian rhino, the Sumatran rhino—featured along with me on the cover of this book—is the smallest of the living rhino species. It's also the only Asian rhino with two horns and with hair that covers its entire body, a remnant of the thick fur coat that allowed its ancestor, the woolly rhinoceros, to live in cold climates. Sumatran rhinos once lived throughout

Indonesia, Malaysia, and parts of Southeast Asia, but today their range consists only of the islands of Sumatra and Borneo and the Malay Peninsula, where 275 survivors remain. Over the past 15 years, poachers have killed more than half the world's population of Sumatran rhinos, making it the most endangered rhino on Earth.

At the Carl H. Lindner Jr. Family Center for Conservation and Research of Endangered Wildlife, based at the Cincinnati Zoo, Terri Roth, PhD, is working to stave off the powerful tide of extinction that's closing in on the Sumatran rhino.

A slim, ash-blonde woman with the visionary look of a zoological Virginia Woolf, Roth appears oddly at ease in a birthing pen with a large, hairy Sumatran rhino. Maybe it's because of her experience with horses in California—a background that would ultimately stand her in good stead when trying to breed the rare rhino.

Roth is the only scientist in the world to have successfully bred the Sumatran rhino in captivity, and she used her horse sense to do it. Working with a fertile female named Emi and her male partner, Ipuh, Roth suffered right along with Emi as she endured several heartbreaking miscarriages. "Each time, I just felt sick inside," Roth says.

Remembering that rhinos are distant relatives of horses, Roth took a chance. The next time Emi became pregnant, she was fed a dose of horse progesterone soaked into bread slices. To this day, Roth isn't sure whether the hormones created the lucky "perfect storm" of fertility, but Emi finally carried a calf to full term. He was named Andalas, an ancient name for Sumatra.

Today, Andalas lives at the Way Kambas National Park in Indonesia, one of the few protected parks where Sumatran rhinos can live without the constant threat of poaching. Andalas, fast becoming a viable partner for the park's fertile females, is the great hope for the survival of the species. If Sumatran rhinos can be bred at the park, they may be able to be moved to other viable protected areas.

The dynamics of Sumatran rhino mating are very tricky, Roth says. The species is physiologically unique and can't, for instance, be interbred with any other rhino species, even other Asian species. When working with Emi at the Cincinnati Zoo, Roth was the first scientist to discover that the Sumatran rhino is an induced ovulator, which means that a female's egg doesn't leave the ovary until the animal starts mating.

"A Sumatran rhino and an Indian rhino are more biologically distinct than a tiger and a lion," says Roth. "Their reproductive systems are very different, and the same is probably true for the Javan rhino, though it has yet to be studied."

The critical work is being done with the Sumatran rhino because the Javan rhino population lives in two very remote locations in national parks and isn't seeing the swift decline the Sumatrans are, she says. "The wild Javan rhino population has been relatively stable, even though there are very few individuals. But the species are similar enough that the Javan rhino can benefit from the research. They're both solitary, forest-dwelling rhinos in similar habitats facing similar threats."

In the meantime, Roth is crossing her fingers and counting on Andalas to help revive his species. "There's a lot riding on Andalas's shoulders," she says. "But he's mature now, and there seems to be no reason why he can't be mated with the three available females at the reserve."

For Roth and her colleagues in Indonesia and Cincinnati, rhinos have become an unshakable passion.

"There's something special about rhinos," she says. "They can be extremely personable and can act a little like large puppy dogs.

They like to be rubbed and scratched. They have a lot of character. Unlike some other animals, rhinos, especially Sumatrans, lose their fear of humans very quickly. This is a problem for them in the wild, but when you're working with them, it creates a special bond."

All of the animals of our planet are lucky that people like Roth are working hard to preserve the futures of even the most intimidating species. We're going to need as many of these dedicated souls as we can find if we're going to solve the bushmeat crisis that threatens Africa's endangered wildlife.

## CONTINENT IN CRISIS

While most people are aware that chimpanzees (*Pan troglodytes*) have a lot in common with humans, I have to admit that I didn't realize just how similar to us these complex animals are until I paid a visit to a chimp sanctuary on Ngamba Island in Lake Victoria, Uganda, in 2002. I was sitting with Debby Cox, then the director of the Chimpanzee Sanctuary and Wildlife Conservation Trust, in an area of forest where the chimps are set free each day to socialize, explore, and play. When she opened the gate, it was as if a party had erupted. Everywhere, young chimps wrestled and shrieked happily. Six of them rushed over and climbed on me as if I were a human jungle gym. Amid all the excitement, I felt a wet spot forming in my hair, and when I looked behind me, I saw the sly grin of a chimp who was casting a perfect arc of urine onto my head. I'm convinced he was in cahoots with the chimps that then began reaching into my pockets, hoping to distract me from the pickpockets' fingers. Actually, I have to admit it worked, as they ended up with my passport and everything else I'd been carrying.

But at least they entertained me in return. Two chimps used sticks to stage an elaborate sword fight complete with drama and lots of emoting. After taking a lunge to the face, the defeated chimp slumped to the ground, cupping his eye. When he turned his sad gaze on me, I couldn't resist picking him up. Of course, that's when he knew he had me. He reached up to my mouth, carefully pinched my lips into a kiss and pulled them to his face. There was nothing wrong with his eye—he just wanted a kiss, and he knew how to get one.

There was one chimp, though, that wasn't having such a good time. When others tried to include her in the fun, she sighed and stared at the ground like a lonely child on the playground. When I sat next to her, she breathed another long sigh and looked up into the trees. When I asked Debby what was wrong, she told me that though the chimp's name, Ikuru, means "the happiness" in the Lugbara language, she sometimes had low moments, particularly in large-group settings. All the chimps that are brought to Ngamba Island have been orphaned by the pet and bushmeat industries, and Ikuru's story is especially traumatic.

A Ugandan army officer found Ikuru during a raid on a rebel camp. He'd noticed a chimp roasting in a pot over a fire and thought he saw something move. When he looked closer, he realized that there were actually two chimps in the pot: 2-year-old Ikuru and her dead mother, to whom she was clinging despite the scalding heat. The soldier gently pried her off, careful to avoid the third-degree burns on her lower back, and asked a local villager to keep her until he could return. Unfortunately, he wasn't able to come back for another 6 months, and when did, it was clear that Ikuru was suffering from malnutrition and other maladies. When the officer tried to take her with him across the northwest border between the DRC and Uganda, he was told he couldn't keep her because of her protected species status, and she was sent to Ngamba Island.

When Ikuru sighed again and put her hand on my knee, I could feel a weight settle on *me*.

That officer, who probably made very little money, could have sold Ikuru to be eaten as bushmeat, but he opted to go back where he'd left her and save her life instead. Maybe he recognized her as a cousin, realizing like I did that day that we have more in common with chimps—genetically, biologically, behaviorally, socially, even cognitively—than we have differences. Maybe he realized that sacrificing the life of a chimp to the bushmeat trade would be akin to cannibalism.

Debby has told me that Ikuru has since overcome her social difficulties and is a great surrogate mother to young chimps, but the bushmeat trade that orphaned her has only grown worse. In fact, it's reached epidemic proportions, with 1 million to 5 million tons of meat from African forest animals being consumed every year in Central Africa. One million tons of bushmeat is equivalent to 4 million cattle—or roughly 9 *billion* quarter-pound burgers. Bushmeat is inexpensive in rural areas—a third of the price of farmed meat—and with the human population expanding rapidly, the demand for inexpensive protein will only intensify without successful intervention. It's estimated that at the current rate of consumption, almost all of the six countries in the Congo Basin will be unable to provide sufficient protein for the human population by 2050.[6]

Ruggiero first saw this problem close-up in the early '80s as a Peace Corps volunteer working at Manovo-Gounda-St. Floris National Park in the northern part of the Central African Republic. The park supports large populations of elephants, rhinos, buffaloes, giraffes, "and everything else you can think of," he says. In turn, it was also popular with the Janjaweed, who were on the hunt for rhino horn, ivory, and bushmeat. When he and fellow volunteer Michael Fay, PhD, who now works with the Wildlife Conservation Society and the National Geographic Society, followed elephant trails in the jungle, they would sometimes see horseshoe prints, as well. "And then we'd see a bunch of vultures—that was the give-away that a bushmeat camp was close," Ruggiero says. "We'd come to a clearing and find an enormous camp set up in a natural salt lick area. There would be dozens of wooden drying racks with tons of meat in various stages of preparation, from fresh carcasses to butchered pieces to dried product. It would be transported out on camel or donkey or bicycle, either directly back to Sudan or to the national highway, where trucks would pick it up. It was all indus-trial scale and extremely efficient.

"We'd walk into these camps, and everybody would run away, completely desert the camp, and we'd see the smoking remnants of dozens if not a hundred animals. All the trees are cut down to be used for smoking the meat, so there are piles of firewood, there are bones, there are animal heads they're not using. It's a surrealistic scene, like walking into one of Dante's circles of hell—100°F, smoking fires, vultures in the trees, stinking carcasses."

That was 30 years ago. When the slaughter expanded from the savannas to the forests, the great apes came under increasing fire, and suddenly it all hit home. "This was no longer an issue of bush pigs and duikers [forest antelopes]—now it was affecting our clos-est living relatives," Ruggiero says. "It's a different sort of emo-tional resonance when it's chimpanzees and gorillas."

The term *bushmeat* applies to any wildlife hunted in Africa's bush or forest—elephants, apes, lions, crocodiles, porcupines, cane rats, pangolins, monitor lizards, guinea fowl—but poachers prefer the larger animals because they bring the highest returns on their investment. This poaching has led to huge animal population declines in Central and East Africa and to outright local extinctions in West Africa. And as commercial logging operations clear the land, making it more accessible to hunters, and an expanding road infrastructure connects rural areas to city markets, the poaching threat has become even more severe.

"There are very few species or populations that can withstand commercial-level exploitation—period," Ruggiero says. "There's a huge difference between that and hunting something, bringing it home, and eating a third of it and selling or trading two-thirds to your neighbor in the same village. It's easy to satisfy that market and not create undue demand. But when you open the market to insatiable populations of people, you ensure a species' destruction."

"When you look at the data over the last 30 years, there has also been an absolute reduction of wildlife in many parts of East Africa, to the tune of 50 to 80 percent, including many large mammal species," says Heather Eves, PhD, who has worked in Africa since the mid-'80s and is director of the Bushmeat Crisis Task Force (BCTF), which she has led since it was established in 2000. She and Ruggiero are married, having met while working in Africa. "Now it's farmland everywhere, no wildlife. But where did all the animals go?" she continues. "Some people in the region question whether there's a bushmeat issue. A colleague from East Africa suggested that either animals will move on to other places, or we should be seeing carcasses—evidence of the loss of wildlife due to the loss of land. But we're not seeing that because the animals are being consumed as bushmeat."

While bushmeat is cheaper than farmed meat in rural areas, many Africans consider it superior to beef and chicken in both taste and nutrition, and it's considered an expensive delicacy in urban areas. Any bushmeat that makes it to cities in West Africa, where the black market isn't as open, fetches a higher price than filet mignon. Some people even believe it has medicinal properties. And then there are the cultural traditions that die hard, if at all.

"You definitely have a challenge," says Natalie Bailey, MS, assistant director of the BCTF. "You have a whole generation that's grown up consuming bushmeat as part of their day-to-day culture. In Central and West Africa, the demand for bushmeat is very high among the urban elite. When you're an important businessman or government official and you have a dinner party, it's important that you serve bushmeat."

And when members of this culture move to the United States, bushmeat finds its way here, too. Bailey estimates that several thousand pounds' worth makes it into the country every month, brought by travelers from African countries on airplanes, transported in shipping containers, and even sent by mail.

"We're always going to want a connection to where we came from, and food is such a powerful connector," Bailey says. "For African-born people living in the US, bushmeat very often is that connector. In a focus group, they said bushmeat isn't *necessary* for a special occasion, but having it is what really makes it *special*."

While it's forbidden to bring bushmeat into the United States, the logistical reality is that there isn't enough manpower to enforce the law. As of 2008, there were only about 120 USFWS agents to inspect wildlife-related shipments around the clock at 38 US ports of entry designated for wildlife imports. But with 327 official American ports, there are many more ports than available agents. Baltimore Washington International Airport is a designated port of entry for wildlife, but the inspectors there also must cover the Dulles International and Reagan National airports when US Customs and Border Protection officials alert them to wildlife issues at those airports. "And when bushmeat is detected and intercepted, it's typically incinerated to prevent the potential spread of disease," Bailey says, "so it never gets tested to identify the species."

Because bushmeat represents such an important cultural tradition for many people, it's understandably difficult to stop the illegal slaughter of rare animals.

Uganda Wildlife Authority lawyer Vincent Opyene says that besides inadequate wildlife laws and enforcement, judges, magistrates, state attorneys, and prosecutors aren't well versed in environmental law, the scope of which tends to focus more on pollution than on illegal hunting.

"From my experience as a prosecutor, if a poacher removes all the morphological features like the skin, horns, and hoofs from poached wildlife, it becomes very difficult for the prosecution to prove that the poached species is protected wildlife," says Opyene.

"This is because our law puts the burden of proof on the person alleging that a specific species was poached. The standard of proof in this region is proof beyond reasonable doubt. If the rangers fail to differentiate between bushmeat and domestic animal meat, the poacher can't be found guilty."

Opyene also blames the lack of coordination among enforcement agencies in the region for a rise in poaching. "In order to control this trend, there needs to be a coordinated law enforcement effort among all stakeholders and partners, and we need to attach value to all wildlife species, since it is impossible to award damages for unvalued resources," he says. To those ends, Opyene is now also a member of the Bushmeat-Free Eastern Africa Network. This interdisciplinary and multi-institutional network monitors bushmeat in and around protected areas and increases awareness of the problem.

But in order to truly stem the tide of bloodshed for bushmeat, people need alternatives. Specifically, alternative sources of both protein and income. Eves says the answer lies in educating local communities and creating options that include microfinancing for businesses and families. For example, the Wildlife Conservation Society, the government of the DRC, and a private logging company created a three-way partnership in Central Africa. "They found a few individuals in the town to be the project leaders, and they helped start butcheries," Eves says. "They bought freezers and set up shops with sanitary conditions, and they imported livestock and provided the market with alternative sources of meat. If you create opportunities for people to succeed individually, others will watch, and if they see their neighbors succeeding, they will repeat it. That is the success that has to spread across the continent. You have to create wealth and opportunities where there are none."

Practically speaking, impoverished hunters and consumers have no choice, and giving them choices is the only hope for ending the crisis. "Commercial poachers are coming in and hiring all of these local unemployed people who have no way to earn a living but need malaria medicine for their children," Eves says. "They're hiring these people to spend hours and hours with hundreds of wire snares, or handing them guns with all the ammunition they can carry."

As with any situation where two parties have different objectives, compromise is key. "The people living next to the wildlife have the real, absolute stewardship of that wildlife," Eves says. "And like everyone else in the world, they want three things: jobs, education for their children, and good medical care. Providing these is a very clear part of successful conservation outcomes, along with effective wildlife management. That's why partnerships with human development agencies and local communities are essential. It *is* possible if there's a global commitment to conserve biodiversity."

From the comfort of our own homes (equipped with our well-stocked refrigerators), it's easy to judge people who eat bushmeat as cruel. But it's not that simple. If you're unemployed and impoverished, you feed your family what you can and take any work that's offered to you. You need a really good reason to abandon a strategy that you believe has allowed you to survive thus far. Think of it this way: Such a sudden, radical change in ideology would be the equivalent of waking up one morning and deciding to quit your job because you've decided that capitalism is unfair.

"We as Americans want to know that, whether or not we can ever afford the ticket to Africa, there are free-ranging elephants and gorillas out there," Eves says. If you've been *surrounded* by magnificent wildlife for your whole life, though, it can be difficult to imagine that it can simply disappear, even if you've been told otherwise. But the sad truth is, if we don't stop bushmeat poaching, all of Africa's big animals—many of them endemic species—will disappear. Consider these numbers: Since the 1970s, the human population has grown 600 percent in Central Africa;[7] meanwhile, the African elephant population has dropped from 1.3 million to an estimated 470,000 to 690,000.[8] If human numbers continue to grow at that pace and the elephant population continues to respond in the same way, they'll be gone within another 3 decades. It doesn't help that elephants have the longest gestation period of any mammal—22 months—and that a female will bear a single calf only every 4 or 5 years.

It's a tragic, complicated issue, and it requires the efforts of everyone along the trade chain—"everybody from the leader of a nation to somebody who's just learning about this for the first time," says Bailey. Perhaps the most important component of any possible solution is having the *will* to find one. "We know what to do, we know how to do it. The problem is, we're not fast enough or spread widely enough to compensate for the rate at which nature is being destroyed," Ruggiero says. "You need political will, you need the will of the local people who make the sacrifice to live with conservation, you need the money to do it—you need human will at whatever level you define it."

In the DRC, about 250 rangers have been killed while defending wildlife in the past 10 years, and most of them were owed months or even years of back pay at the times of their deaths. "They're out there without proper gear, without pay, they're alone against very well armed militias, and still they're trying their best to protect wildlife," Ruggiero says. "And when I ask them, 'Why do you do this?' they look me right in the eye and say that it's the right thing to do, that a world without nature and wildlife is not a good place to be. There is hope in that."

And hope is a powerful thing. When the American alligator teetered on the edge of extinction, the actions of local residents, conservationists, and law enforcement officials proved that hope can move mountains . . . and save swamps.

# THE AMERICAN ALLIGATOR: A STORY OF SURVIVAL

There have been many moments in my career when I've been privileged to be in the presence of the magnificent, unnerving creature known as the alligator. What's it like to hold a baby gator that's just emerged from its shell, shiny and slippery from the clear white albumen that surrounded it in the egg? Well, it's a short and sweet experience—short because it wouldn't be wise to push your luck if its mother is nearby. In the same moment that you take that young life into your hands, you also take your *own* life into your hands, because when these babies call, Mama comes running. As the eggs begin to hatch, the babies emit what sounds like a cross between a croak and a chirp, alerting the mother to the fact that it's time to dig them out from under the mound of reeds and grasses she carefully, deliberately buried them in. As the vegetation decays, it produces heat—just like a compost pile does—and keeps the eggs at a temperature ranging from 82° to 93°F. Far from the cannibals they're made out to be in old science journals, alligators are award-winning mothers and fascinating creatures.

On one memorable morning while we were taping a show on the Louisiana bayou, I stood on the bank of a murky freshwater breeding pond in a postcard southern swamp where Spanish moss dripped from cypress trees. I watched as two huge adult alligators sized me up, their goggle eyes showing through the muck like knots on a decaying log. As I explained to the camera how young gators emerge from their nests, I heard the familiar *aaawwk awwk* sound emerge from a heap of leaves and twigs where a mother had laid her eggs. I reached in and pulled out an egg that had just broken open, the miniature dragonlike creature inside poking out its head for the first time. It was hard to believe it would one day weigh up to half a ton and be 13 or 14 feet long, like the adults who had their unblinking eyes on me. And there's a good chance it *wouldn't* have had the opportunity to grow into one of those enormous eating machines if we hadn't gone above and beyond in our efforts to bring the American alligator (*Alligator mississippiensis*) back from the brink of extinction.

When you see an alligator, it's astonishing to think that *anything* could threaten its existence. It has a head that looks as if it's armored with plates of solid rock, an arsenal of about 80 teeth in its long jaw, and a tail that can function very much like a mace and is capable of breaking a human leg. Even as babies, they're equipped with caruncles, or egg teeth, that they use to tear through the leathery membrane of their eggs and enter the world. Could there be a sturdier creature? These reptiles are so beautifully designed for survival that even their eyes are camouflaged to blend in with their swampy home.

Members of the crocodilian order, which also includes crocodiles, gharials, and caimans, have been patrolling swamps for 240 million years. Alligators' survival skills are so advanced that they can crack a turtle shell like a walnut and pull a white-tailed deer into a watery grave. They can also build their own feeder holes along waterways, using their claws and their mighty mouths to clear vegetation by the roots and their great, slashing tails to create a depression that fills with water and fish, crustaceans, and turtles. During the dry season, the holes hold rainwater that benefits not only alligators but also swamp mates such as snakes, birds, and insects. And gators sometimes add to their holes by digging as far as 20 feet into a bank, carving out a perpetually wet, sheltered den where it can survive during the dry season.

The perils of the dry season are nothing compared with the perils of sharing their environment with man, though, and the American alligator was hunted nearly to extinction for its skin. In Florida, hunting restrictions were put in place in the 1940s, but that didn't stop the hunters—who, with the laws in place, were now poachers—and by 1967, the American alligator was listed as an endangered species. (Before passage of the Endangered Species Act in 1973, laws passed in the 1960s provided limited protections for species that were considered endangered.) But in 1970, the interstate shipment of poached alligators was declared a federal offense, and when the Endangered Species Act took effect, it banned alligator hunting altogether. Since then, the species' recovery has been so successful that it's become a glowing example of what can happen when government agencies and the private sector put their heads and hearts together. Just as June 28, 2007, was a day to celebrate the American bald eagle's removal from the endangered species list, June 4, 1987, was another historic delisting day, this time for the American alligator. In its wake, fish, game, and wildlife commissions in southern states instituted alligator-hunting seasons as a way to promote conservation. People tend to want to preserve the things that have value to them, in this case economic value. The states also study and monitor alligator populations, and that knowledge and vigilant harvest control have combined to help them strike a perfect conservation balance. Meanwhile, the USFWS very attentively regulates the alligator skin trade. And on the private front, large-scale farms in Florida, Georgia, Louisiana, and Texas harvest eggs in the wild and raise alligators in captivity. They release a certain percentage back into the wild after they reach the juvenile stage, giving them a leg up on survival.

The story isn't quite over, though. While that chapter had a happy ending, the tension is already building in the next one as global warming takes hold. The sex of an alligator is determined by the temperature at which the egg is incubated. If the temperature is 82° to 86°F, it will be a female. If it's 90° to 93°F, it will be a male. If it's 87° to 89°F, it could be either. So global warming could result in fewer and fewer females, and that in turn could result in disaster. Furthermore, in Florida's Everglades, the hottest part of American alligators' range, they're growing to a shorter average length than they do in other parts of their range, and sexual maturity is setting in later, according to a 2000 study by Florida scientists and wildlife officials. Scientists suspect that global warming has raised temperatures enough to change their metabolism, which leads to bigger appetites and more competition for food.

In addition to the impact of global warming, alligators are facing the loss and degradation of their habitat. Drainage of swampland and diversion of water to neighboring towns supply the needs created by urban sprawl. Increased levels of dioxins—chemicals that can disrupt hormones and interfere with alligator reproduction—have also been found in the water. Different species respond differently to environmental toxins, and it's important to recognize that a species can be ravaged by chemicals that may not produce any visible symptoms in humans. *We're* not the canaries in the coal mine.

Water is as vital to alligators as oxygen is to humans. They spend as much of their lives in it as we spend outside of it. Imagine living a life that requires you to pack up and move whenever the air around you becomes more polluted, making it hard for you to breathe. We saved the alligator from poachers, but can we save it from the invisible, insidious assaults affecting all of Earth's creatures?

———

In the open waters of a private wildlife sanctuary near the Everglades, I had my most incredible alligator experience to date as I watched their mating ritual play out before my eyes. I was right in the water with them, squatting at the edge of the swamp as several bull alligators took turns inhaling deeply, submerging all but their heads and letting out their best bellows to impress nearby females. Most of an alligator's bellow is of such a low frequency that humans can't hear it, but it produces sound waves that females can feel up to 5 miles away with the highly sensitive skin along their jaw lines. Those sound waves also cause water to bubble off the bull's back like raindrops falling upside down, and I could feel the vibrations passing through the water, unnerving me to my hips. The result of all the bellowing? A female nuzzled up to the "winner."

This ancient reproductive behavior has remained unchanged over the geologic eras, and it's the product of a tiny primordial brain. That hardwired programming keeps the alligators single-mindedly focused on the task of mating rather than eating. Otherwise, I'd have quickly become part of the food chain.

For me, alligators are a constant reminder of *our* species' best qualities, and what we're capable of in terms of conservation. It's easy to care about our national bird or a cuddly, playful otter. It's harder to have the same concern and compassion for something big and powerful enough to eat you. At an aquarium, it's a thrill to see these ancient, intimidating reptiles face-to-face—foreign and familiar at the same time—with just two sheets of "plastic glass" between you. But what if you were to suddenly come face-to-face with one in your backyard swimming pool or while floating in an inner tube on an otherwise peaceful pond? You'd be terrified, and with good reason: This is a predator that has proved capable of taking down animals as strong as the Florida panther and the American black bear. But that fear didn't stop us from protecting alligators when they were in jeopardy. We were able to look past our prejudices to see the big picture: If a creature's lineage can be traced back 240 million years, there's good reason for it to continue. That creature has a powerful purpose. The planet needs it. In the case of American alligators, we need them to preserve our wetlands.

Wetlands are a microcosm of Earth's complex biodiversity. They're home to an astonishing array of life-forms, many of which cannot exist elsewhere. These habitats also serve vital ecological functions, storing water and acting as storm and flood barriers for terrestrial areas. The slow flow of water from these ponds acts as a filter, taking sediment—including toxins—out of circulation by allowing it to settle at the bottom. Alligators control populations of animals that could otherwise deplete marsh areas. They also contribute to the food chain with their hatchlings, which are an important source of food for snakes, raccoons, egrets, herons, and largemouth bass. Even their feces provide nutrients for fish and aquatic invertebrates.

If we had failed to protect the American alligator, the ramifications would have extended far beyond the swamps. In 2008, former senator Fred Thompson made a now-infamous remark at the 2008 Republican National Convention: "When [Sarah Palin] and John McCain get to Washington, they're not going to care how much the alligators get irritated—they're going to drain that swamp." The rousing applause drawn by that statement betrayed a distressing lack of ecological concern. Had that been the prevailing attitude when the American alligator was fighting for survival, the alligator almost surely would have lost. And now that we know what's at stake, we can never let it get so close to the brink again. Next time, our best efforts might not be enough.

# CHAPTER 7

# EXPLOITED TO EXTINCTION

A T THE HARVARD MUSEUM of Natural History in Cambridge, Massachusetts, there's a skeleton hanging from the ceiling that looks like an aquatic dinosaur, colossal and entirely alien. With massive ribs and a craggy formation of thick plates for a skull, it's the stuff of horror films—surely, I thought, it must have been a vicious predator that struck fear in the heart of any creature unlucky enough cross its path. Were I afloat in a kayak, watching this monster surface, I can't imagine I'd feel anything but sheer terror.

Then I read the placard hanging on the wall. This wasn't a monster at all, but rather a gentle animal called a Steller's sea cow (*Hydrodamalis gigas*), an extinct relative of the manatee. I was surprised to learn that these gigantic bones weren't from the body of a prehistoric creature that had become extinct 65 million years ago. In fact, this creature still meandered along the Alaskan and Russian coastlines as recently as 240 years ago. As a wildlife biologist, this realization provided a sobering moment.

Shaped a little like a fat torpedo, the Steller's sea cow had a massive body that tapered at one end to a small head. Its neck was short but flexible, possibly to allow it to graze over a large area without having to expend the energy it would take to move its colossal body. These enormous creatures measured about 25 feet long and weighed from 11,880 to 24,631 pounds, making them up to 12 times heavier than Florida manatees (*Trichechus manatus latirostris*).

Unlike other marine mammals, manatees (and their close relatives, the dugongs) are herbivores. Steller's sea cows were toothless, gentle giants that spent most of their time grazing. They ate mainly sea grasses and other aquatic vegetation, so throughout the Pliocene and Pleistocene periods—from 24 million years ago to 1.6 million years ago—they inhabited shallow coastline waters from Japan to Mexico. Classified in the order Sirenia, this marine mammal was as big as a whale and fully aquatic, meaning it lived only in water. Interestingly, though, marine biologists believe these creatures evolved from four-legged terrestrial mammals. Protein analysis has revealed that the sirenians' closest living relatives are elephants, aardvarks, and small mammals called hyraxes.

Despite thriving for millions of years, Steller's sea cows were commercially hunted to near extinction over just a 14-year period. They were last spotted in the 1760s and thought to be extinct by 1768. The species was survived by three other manatee species (in the family Trichechidae) and the dugong (in the family Dugongidae), all of which are currently endangered. The sea cow's fastest speed was slow, and my encounters with Florida manatees have convinced me that hunting these laid-back foragers wouldn't have required much skill. But sportsmanship wasn't the objective for commercial hunters—the goal was profit, and as they prospered, the sea cows steadily disappeared from the water.

Like many marine mammals, the Steller's sea cow originally occupied a vast range, but by historical times its known territory was confined to the Bering Sea. The German naturalist Georg Wilhelm Steller first spotted the creatures grazing on kelp in the frigid, shallow waters just off the coast of the Komandorski Islands in 1741, when he and the other members of a Russian expedition were shipwrecked. They had been exploring the far north Pacific with Vitus Bering, who was mapping the Arctic coast to find routes from Siberia to North America. During a punishing winter that claimed the lives of nearly half the crew, including Bering, Steller wrote *De Bestiis Marinis*, or *The Beasts of the Sea*, and described the fauna of the island, including the sea otter, the northern fur seal, and the spectacled cormorant (*Phalacrocorax perspicillatus*)—a species that would become extinct within 100 years of the sea cow's demise.

Steller, who often named newly discovered species after himself (including Steller's cider, a sea duck), wrote in *De Bestiis Marinis* that sea cows lost so much weight during the winter that their ribs and vertebrae could be seen beneath their hides. It's possible that the sea cows didn't have enough food to sustain them through the winter. Marine biologists theorize that the algae, sea grass, and kelp beds that were their main food sources may have been depleted by a sea urchin population that exploded after sea otters—the urchins' natural predators—were hunted to the edge of extinction in that area.

Steller described the sea cows as social creatures that gathered and grazed in herds. He wrote that when one sea cow was attacked, its fellow herd members often gathered to help defend it. But sadly, as the herd of sea cows plodded toward the victim in distress, it was that much easier for a hunter to kill several members of the herd at once.

The fact that these giant creatures grazed close enough to the shoreline for hunters to wade out and spear them also made the sea cows easy prey. In fact, Steller reported that the animals behaved as if they were tame; when men waded or rowed boats among them, the sea cows showed no signs of alarm. I can only imagine that for a hungry, shipwrecked crew, these friendly, slow-moving marine mammals must have seemed like a godsend. One sea cow provided 7,000 pounds of meat and fat. Steller described the meat as tasting like beef, and Russian sailors even likened it to prime rib.

The sea cow was hunted mainly for food—including its milk, which was drunk or churned into butter. Its blubber was also used for cooking and lamp oil. And its thick, rugged hide was used to make durable shoes, belts, and even boats. But probably because sea cows were so plentiful and easy to kill, hunters didn't exercise foresight. It wasn't unusual for a hunter to wade into the water, spear a sea cow, and wait for it to die and wash ashore, sparing him the trouble of hauling in the heavy creature himself. Obviously, when the tide didn't push a dead sea cow's body back to shore, this hunting practice was a deplorable waste of both a resource and a life. But there were no hunting regulations in place to sustain the population, so until 1755, when hunting sea cows was finally prohibited, it was a virtual bloodbath. For these marine mammals with a low reproductive rate (Sirenia species bear one or occasionally two young every 2½ to 7 years), their suboptimal environment ensured their demise.

# LYING DOWN WITH LIONS

It's hard not to feel haunted by the ghosts of bygone species like the Steller's sea cow when you visit Gir Forest National Park in Gujarat, India—the last wild refuge of the Asiatic lion.

When my crew and I went to India to film this lion, I was pretty accustomed to encountering big cats in the wild. I'd been mere yards away from jaguars, African lions, cheetahs, leopards, and many other wild felines, from the tiny margay to tigers as long as Cadillacs. But as my camera crew and I rode into the park, I felt an unexpected thrill at the prospect of seeing the Asiatic lion (*Panthera leo persica*), also called the Indian lion, in its habitat.

Our driver deposited us and our gear by the side of the road and told us to wait. This was the appointed meeting place for our segment with Ravi Chellam, PhD, the foremost expert on Asiatic lions in the world. After 5 or 10 minutes had ticked by, I suddenly felt vulnerable, sitting in the dust in the baking sun—a toasted lunch for whatever predator might happen to walk by. As anyone who has watched my shows is aware, snakes don't faze me a bit, but hungry carnivores certainly inspire in me an acute awareness of my place in the food chain. I know what to do when faced with a venomous king cobra, but it's a lot more difficult to defend yourself against a lion.

After what felt like a very long time, Ravi arrived in an open-top truck, smiling at my nervousness. "Where were you?" I asked, climbing up beside him, relieved to be less of a target in the open bush.

"It takes a while to get through the forest, you know," Ravi said. "There was a sighting of a female and some cubs. Let's go."

The day was getting long, and lions typically come out to hunt as the heat of the noonday sun diminishes. The female sighted was probably looking for easy prey.

As we drove through a parched landscape of withered vegetation, the fine, choking dust of the road collected in the corners of our eyes and in our noses. After 10 minutes that seemed like an hour, we pulled over and headed into the bush on foot. This was a rare occasion when armed animal trackers accompanied us, but we still knew we had to be just as cautious. After walking only a few hundred yards, we saw her: Less than 50 feet away, the lioness was watching her cubs play in the grass, her amber eyes sleepy, as if she'd just fed. I felt my heart leap into my throat. "Can we get in closer?" I asked, almost hoping the answer would be no. "We can try," said Ravi. Squatting and crab-walking, we made our way into a tangle of brush, and that's when we heard the heavy *chuff, chuff* sound behind us, like a train engine coming to life—the sound of a male lion in the mood for love. I don't know how the lioness felt about it, but it sent shivers up *my* spine.

Asiatic lion males aren't as social as their African brethren, and they associate with their pride, or social group, only to mate or take part in a large kill. We were able to catch a glimpse of this shaggy-maned male only as he disappeared into the trees at our backs, leaving us alone again with the lioness and her cubs. As it turned out, the male hadn't made much of an impression on her— her white, whiskery chin was sinking toward the ground, her eyes heavy with the need for a nap. Played out, the cubs followed suit, settling in beside her and gazing at her for a moment before letting their heads settle onto their paws.

As we watched this magnificent lion that was tolerating our presence, I was deeply grateful for the opportunity to share that wild space with her. But at the same time, her precarious position in relation to my species became sharply obvious. Even here in Gir, surrounded by protective measures, these lions aren't safe from the presence of humans.

Though it has been banned since the 1950s, hunting took a large toll on the lion population—forcing it into a range much closer to the human population. This proximity to people has created an impossible situation. For centuries, humans and these large, powerful carnivores had been able to keep a respectful distance from one another. Historically, lions and tigers weren't known to purposely seek human prey, according to big-cat expert

Mahendra Shrestha, director of the Save the Tiger Fund. But in recent years, circumstance has brought humans and the lions of Gir closer together. Drought has plagued the region, drying up watering holes that had been frequented by the lions' prey—mainly the chital, sambar, and chinkara. As their natural prey has become more elusive, the lions have turned to livestock, which has inevitably drawn them closer to herders and ranchers and led to a rise in attacks on humans. Before the drought began in 1987, an average of 7½ human attacks occurred every year; since the drought, the number has risen to 40 annual attacks.[1]

When most people think of lions, they tend to think of Africa. But the lion that humans first encountered—in the Middle East, the Mediterranean, and India—was the Asiatic lion. The smallest of the subspecies, at 240 to 400 pounds, the Asiatic lion is most likely the species referred to in the biblical story of Daniel and the lion's den. It is also likely to be one of the species pitted against gladiators and Christians in Roman arenas. The Asiatic lion makes an appearance in ancient Greek literature, as well. Hercules fought an Asiatic lion and wore its hide for strength. At one time, these tawny beauties ranged freely throughout the Middle East, India, and Afghanistan, roaring their way into our history and culture for several thousand years. The Asiatic lion is regarded as sacred in Hinduism, representing the animal half of the half-man Narasimha, an incarnation of the god Vishnu, "the preserver." Now, sadly, it's the lions that are in need of preservation.

Although these lions were once widespread throughout Asia, trophy hunting was such a popular pastime among British colonialists and Indian royalty in the 19th and early 20th centuries that, by 1910, the Asiatic lion had become a member of the Hundred Heartbeat Club.[2] India's royal families were fond of decorating their palaces with the stuffed "trophies," and their appetite for the *shikar*—the hunt—was matched by that of the British colonialists who arrived after Great Britain assumed control of India in the 1850s. One British officer alone was reported to have shot as many as 80 lions over the course of just 3 years.[3] At the end of the 19th century, with the Asiatic lion population believed to be at just 20 (though census information from the time indicates that the number may have been closer to 100), lion hunting was banned except for occasional royal *shikars*. In the 1950s, it was finally banned completely. Since then, it's been a slow recovery for this critically endangered subspecies. Today, there are about 350 individuals left in the wild, all in Gir Forest National Park. Some Asiatic lions are scattered around the world in captivity, but the lions in the park are the only hope the subspecies has for surviving in the wild.

Complicating matters even further, the Maldharis, a group of poor, nomadic herdsmen, graze about 14,000 head of cattle within the protected parklands, damaging the fragile ecosystem. Small villages that existed long before the land was designated as a sanctuary are also located in the protected area. Such close proximity to humans and cattle has led lions to attack both species when their natural prey is scarce. Sadly, these attacks often lead to retaliation by angry villagers, who poison the lions.

It can be difficult to convince the Maldharis that saving the lions is worthwhile. After all, you can't expect a local villager to be eager to protect lions when he has lost livestock or even a friend or family member to an attack. Unfortunately, there's just no easy way for man and this particular beast to coexist side by side.

One of the best possible solutions, suggested by Chellam and Shrestha, is to breed lions in captivity and move a number of them to other protected areas. In addition to shielding humans from lion attacks, this would create separate lion populations—a safeguard in the event of a disease or natural disaster that could devastate an entire population inhabiting the same small area. Placing the lions in additional regions would also help to diversify and strengthen the gene pool, giving them another competitive edge.

## INSPIRATION OUT OF AFRICA

In addition to the last remaining Asiatic lions in the Gir park, five endangered subspecies of lion still roam the savannas of Africa. In Kenya, where tourism generates more than half of the country's foreign income, trophy hunting is illegal and lions are vigilantly protected from poachers, but that doesn't save them from deadly encounters with indigenous people.

The most significant human threat to lions in Kenya is Maasai warriors, or *murrans*. The Maasai generally kill lions for two reasons: either as part of an initiation ritual in which male tribe members are inducted into manhood or as retaliation when their livestock are attacked, which is happening more and more frequently. A hundred years ago, when lions and land were more plentiful, the Maasai respected the lion as a part of their culture. But now that lions are going after livestock, they're increasingly viewed as pests.

While there's no way for the Maasai and the lions to sit down at the same table and negotiate land boundaries, the Kilimanjaro Lion Conservation Project, part of an organization called Living with Lions, has been attempting to mitigate these conflicts. As part of an agreement with the Maasailand Preservation Trust, the Maasai owners of the Mbirikani Group Ranch are now being compensated for livestock losses due to lion attacks. Specifically, they receive payments of $200 per cow, $100 per goat, and $80 per donkey, all doled out from the proceeds of ecotourism and donations. In a country where most people live on about $1 a day, that's impressive compensation.

A new program on the Mibrikani ranch educates the Maasai tribe members about becoming stewards of the lions, or Lion Guardians. The Maasai guardians monitor both collared and uncollared lions with the help of staff research scientists.[4] They work and live in the community and are respected *murrans*, so they're able to persuade other Maasai not to seek vengeance for lost livestock. Since the program began in 2006, only 4 lions have been killed on the ranch—a huge decline from the 22 killed in the 18 months before the program started.[5] This project, built on principles of mutual respect and interest, works *with* the Maasai and has been such a success that plans are now under way to expand it to a neighboring ranch.

In a display of adaptability as significant as the Mauritius kestrels moving their nests from a tree to a cliff side, the Maasai warriors have become lion caretakers. Long-held traditions of hunting lions for ritual and revenge have been replaced with a plan of action that takes into account the health of the planet as a whole. It is a story that both illustrates the powerful connection between humans and animals and shows that positive outcomes are possible when we increase awareness and find solutions that incorporate the needs of all the species sharing the same lands. It was a historic day in 2007 when a Maasai leader involved with the project declared, "From this day forward, on Mbirikani, the warrior and the lion are brothers."[6]

# FALL OF THE PASSENGER PIGEON

Sometimes, extinction comes from out of nowhere. Well, out of nowhere in the sense that we didn't see it coming. That was the case with the passenger pigeon (*Ectopistes migratorius*), which went from being the most abundant bird in North America to extinction in the span of a century.

Though we're used to seeing flocks of pigeons—originally known as European rock doves and introduced by colonists from Europe—their numbers are nothing compared with the multitudes of passenger pigeons that once filled the skies. Most estimates of the passenger pigeon population number them at 3 billion to 5 billion at the time of Europeans' arrival in America— 25 to 40 percent of the total US bird population. Highly social birds, passenger pigeons lived in enormous colonies that spanned hundreds of square miles of forest. Sometimes, hundreds of nests could be found in a single tree. In fact, courtship and reproduction were initiated only within large groups. The pigeons summered in forests east of the Rockies across North America and migrated to the South during colder months. Many early explorers and settlers wrote about the vast migrating flocks of birds. Cotton Mather, a 17th-century Puritan minister probably best known for his affiliation with the Salem witch trials, was also a prolific writer who noted that he'd observed one flock about a mile wide and "taking several hours to pass overhead." In fact, that's how the passenger pigeon got its name: *passenger* comes from the French *passager,* "to pass by."

The passenger pigeon was so densely populous that only the desert locust traveled in larger flocks. But by 1900, not a single passenger pigeon could be found in the wild.

In the early 1800s, hunters began killing the birds in staggering numbers—a feat made easy by the fact that they lived in large groups. Pigeons were mainly killed to feed slaves and the indigent, but they were also captured and sold to trapshooters for use as live targets and to farmers, who ground up the birds and used them as fertilizer. Pigeons were shipped by the thousands in tightly packed boxcars to various East Coast destinations. For many slaves in the 18th and 19th centuries, pigeons were the only meat they were served. Later, as happened with the heath hen in the 1700s, indentured servants often requested in their contracts that they be served pigeon no more than two or three times a week. (These people would no doubt be shocked to see squab— the humble pigeon—listed on menus at high-end restaurants for up to $30 a plate.)

In 1805, you could buy a pair of passenger pigeons in New York City for just two cents. When a resource is so abundant, it's easy to believe that it's inexhaustible. But by the 1850s, people finally began to realize that these birds were no longer coloring the landscape with their gray, brown, and red plumage or turning the sky black as their flocks passed overhead. Unfortunately, this realization coincided with the American Industrial Revolution; and a cheap source of protein was needed to feed the more than 30,000 men who were building the first transcontinental railroad. And so, despite awareness of the passenger pigeon's diminishing population, hunting accelerated.

Though there were some early attempts at captive-breeding programs, all of them failed, perhaps because these birds typically required the presence of large colonies to reproduce. In 1857, the Ohio legislature rejected a bill that would have protected the passenger pigeon. A committee report said: "The passenger pigeon needs no protection. Wonderfully prolific, having the vast forests of the North as its breeding grounds, traveling hundreds of miles in search of food, it is here today and elsewhere tomorrow, and no ordinary destruction can lessen them, or be missed from the myriads that are yearly produced."[7]

In April of the same year, the pigeons arrived in especially great numbers in Petoskey, Michigan, and hunters from throughout the Great Lakes region quickly descended on the nesting grounds. Estimates of the number of pigeons killed in Petoskey that year range from 1.5 million to 7 million—up to 50,000 a day for almost 5 months. In response to pleas from conservationists, the Michigan legislature banned the practice of netting the pigeons (in which large nets were placed on the ground to capture hundred of birds at a time) in the vicinity of nesting areas, but enforcement was lax. In the early 1890s, with the pigeons' population nearly wiped out, Michigan passed a 10-year hunting suspension, but it was far too little and far too late.

The last confirmed sighting of a wild passenger pigeon occurred on March 22, 1900, and the last captive pigeon died September 1, 1914, at the Cincinnati Zoo. Martha (named for Martha Washington) was mounted and is now on display with other extinct creatures at the Smithsonian Institution's Museum of Natural History.

The fate of the passenger pigeon is a textbook example of the consequences of unsustainable exploitation. The math should have been obvious: When you hunt an animal at a rate that exceeds its ability to reproduce, the species cannot endure. Many ecologists also believe that passenger pigeons relied on their strength in numbers for protection against their predators— another obstacle to reviving their population. When they were able to live in large, communal groups, predators took a proportionately small toll. But as America became increasingly colonized and land was used for housing, agriculture, and industry, the pigeons' patches of habitat became smaller. As they dispersed into diminished, fragmented groups, predators—including man—took a proportionately larger toll.

In conjunction with the plight of the heath hen (see Chapter 1), the extinction of the passenger pigeon stirred the fires of conservationism in America. It raised people's awareness of the consequences of their actions, in this case unsustainable exploitation. And it fed the national dialogue about our *accountability* for those actions.

We learned something from this tragic mistake. And while we still have a lot more to learn—judging by the number of species on the brink of disappearing—there's hope as long as we're committed to not repeating our oversights. The survival of magnificent species like the harpy eagle depends on it.

# THE HARPY—A HUNTER IS HUNTED

When I scan the area around the base of a kapok tree deep in the Amazon rainforest, I notice ribbons of sloth fur strewn on the ground. When I stoop to look closer, I also notice specks of flesh, and it's easy for me to imagine the violence that led to this carnage.

In all likelihood, a harpy eagle had perched at the top of a towering kapok tree in the dark night, still as stone, supporting her 3-foot body on legs as thick as the small end of a baseball bat. As dawn broke, she cast her piercing glare down through the cover of leaves, hoping to glimpse one of the tree dwellers she prefers, such as a monkey, an opossum, a macaw, or a sloth. After patiently watching and waiting, she spotted a patch of fur slowly inching its way up the slender, bamboolike trunk of the cecropia. She spread her wings to their full 6-foot span (relatively small for an eagle, but perfect for negotiating tight turns in the forest) and swooped in for an easy kill, her talons ripping out the sloth's spine like a wishbone from a chicken carcass. Neither the sloth's powerful grip on the tree trunk nor its perfect camouflage created by the algae growing in its fur could protect it from this predator. Wings loudly beating the air, the harpy carried off her 10-pound catch with no loss of momentum.

Sadly, as a species, the harpy eagle (*Harpia harpyja*) *is* losing its momentum. Time is running out for Panama's national bird and the largest and most powerful raptor in the Americas. Once populous from southern Mexico to northern Argentina, harpies are now rarely sighted. In Brazil, where harpies used to live throughout the Atlantic rainforest, the birds are now confined to the most remote pockets of the Amazon basin—one of the few places where there's still enough pristine rainforest brimming with prey to support these hungry raptors. Though they're fully protected in both Panama and Brazil, humans have forced harpies to retreat to habitats so remote and difficult to access that protecting them is much easier said than done. As apex predators, harpies are hunted mainly by ranchers who fear that these skillful birds of prey will attack livestock. Harpies are also hunted for their tail and flight feathers, which Amazonian tribes use in ceremonial headdresses. Deforestation compounds the problem by creating open areas that are accessible to hunters who kill not only the harpy but also its prey, cutting into the birds' food sources.

In Greek mythology, a harpy is a winged monster with the head and trunk of a woman and the tail, legs, and talons of a bird. While a harpy eagle can't whisk humans off to the underworld like its namesake, it *is* a powerful and intimidating creature. If you've never seen one, imagine a 15-pound bird with 5-inch talons and feathers sprouting from the back of its head like the disheveled locks of mad scientist. It's safe to say that if you ran into one in the wild, the ornately designed harpy—complete with black "cape"— would give you pause. As big as the claws of a grizzly, their talons can exert 530 pounds of pressure per square inch as they shred flesh, crunch bones, and pierce spines. When it comes to flight, they're quite an anomaly: The vast majority of birds are designed to be light and ethereal and to achieve lift easily, but harpy females range from 14 to 20 pounds and can carry prey up to three-quarters of their weight. At 8 to 12 pounds, the males are quicker and go after smaller prey, such as birds and reptiles.

Built to get their way, these "jaguars of the canopy" were historically situated very comfortably at the top of the food chain. Now, however, the IUCN classifies the harpy eagle as near threatened. The Peregrine Fund considers harpies to be "conservation-dependent," meaning that intensive captive breeding and release as well as habitat protection are required to prevent the eagles from becoming endangered.

In conjunction with Panama City's Neotropical Raptor Center (NRC), the Peregrine Fund began a captive-breeding program in 1998 that has released more than 40 harpies throughout Panama and Belize. Normally, a couple produces two eggs a year and ignores one of them, allowing it to go unhatched. But conservationists at the Peregrine Fund have successfully employed the double-clutching method—and even *triple*-clutching—when an eagle lays her eggs, so instead of raising a single hatchling, a harpy couple may find itself raising a brood of as many as six. And once those chicks become independent, they're monitored via GPS to allow scientists to learn more about their hunting, breeding, and movement patterns. The Peregrine Fund also leads an antipoaching education campaign aimed at raising awareness of harpies' vital role in the ecosystem.

In 2004, four eagles that had been shot in Panama were sent to the NRC. Of the two eagles that survived, one had been shot in the wing and suffered trauma to her eye—two body parts vitally important to a harpy's survival in the wild. The bird with the eye injury ended up losing that eye, and wildlife biologist Marta Curti says that no one expected the bird to be able to leave the safety of captivity. But after 2 years of encouraging recovery, the staff decided to release her and keep very close tabs on her. If things didn't go well, they would have recaptured her. But in a humbling display of tenacity and fortitude, she began to hunt almost immediately. Three years later, this one-eyed eagle flies free in the skies over Panama.

"This is why we do what we do," Curti says.

# THE GRAY WOLF
# RECOVERY MISSION

There's nothing like the thrill of seeing a wolf in the wild, especially with Yellowstone National Park as your backdrop. Imagine a snow-covered early spring day in Yellowstone's Lamar Valley, with the Druid Peak gray wolf pack hovering about 150 yards from a herd of elk. When the wolves decide the time is right, they begin the chase, separating the herd into smaller groups. The snow is deep, and in some spots, it reaches as high as the wolves' chests. But they appear to be unfazed by the extra exertion as they execute arc after perfect arc, like swimmers doing the butterfly stroke. Three wolves succeed in isolating a cow that's grown tired, and they bite at her legs until she collapses into the snow. Having run off the rest of the elk herd, the other wolves in the pack settle in around the carcass. It's not long before the snow around them has turned red with the blood of their feast.

"Wolves kill big things for a living, and it's bloody and nasty," says Yellowstone Wolf Project leader Doug Smith, PhD. "They've been demonized for thousands of years because of it. Old beliefs die hard, and some people still think we'd be better off without wolves."

But the truth is that, just like every species, the gray wolf (*Canis lupus*), which is an apex predator, plays a vital role in the ecosystem it inhabits.

"Yellowstone was overpopulated with elk before wolves were reintroduced to the park in 1995," Smith says. "We had 18,000 to 20,000 elk then, and now we have 8,000 to 10,000." What's an ecologically sound number of elk? "It's probably less than 10,000," he says. "Ecosystems are shaped by dominant carnivores like wolves, and when you lop off that level of the food chain, the ecology of an area becomes, in a sense, artificial."

As incredible as it sounds, the presence of wolves has an effect on almost every living creature that inhabits Yellowstone. The most obviously affected animals, of course, are the wolves' prey, which includes bison, moose, deer, and pronghorn. And then there are the other animals that prey on these same species, such as bears, mountain lions, and coyotes. The effect even trickles down to reptiles, amphibians, birds, insects, and trees.

Before the wolf was reintroduced to Yellowstone to help control the elk population, the elk ate so many shoots and so much bark from willow shrubs and aspen that, besides hindering the park's recovery from the 1988 fire that burned nearly a million acres, they robbed songbirds of homes and almost squeezed out beavers from the park altogether. By 1996, there was only one colony of beavers in northern Yellowstone, Smith says, but in 2009—14 years after wolves were reintroduced to the park—12 colonies were identified.

This wide-ranging environmental response is known as a *trophic cascade*, a series of effects caused by a trigger—in this case, the reintroduction of wolves—that impacts the entire food chain. These cascades gain momentum more easily in aquatic environments, Smith says, but a carnivore as dominant as the wolf can bring the same kind of dramatic change to terrestrial landscapes. Keep in mind, though, that if they hadn't disappeared in the first place, their role would be just the opposite of bringing about change— they would simply maintain the long-established natural order.

That isn't to say these top predators can shape the ecosystem at will. Though a wolf pack is capable of taking down an elk, sometimes it's the elk that wins, using antlers and hooves—front and rear—to chase the wolves off, most likely injuring some of them in the process. Far from invincible, half of adult wolves in the wild bear battle scars from wounds inflicted by prey. "Wolves can't kill any animal they want," Smith says. And on the heels of a hard winter, like the one Yellowstone experienced in 2007–2008, the wolves can face additional challenges. The park received heavy snowfall that winter, and as a result, the elk that survived the brutal season came through with hardier constitutions—making them even more difficult for the wolves to catch. This effect has, in turn, created an increase in *intraspecific strife*, a phenomenon that occurs when members of the same species attack one another. In this case, wolves battled other wolves in violent clashes over elusive prey. That's one of the reasons why, in 2008, the wolves' population dropped by a significant 27 percent for the first time since returning to Yellowstone. Another cause attributed to the population decline is a deadly disease that took a huge toll on the pup survival rate that year. Typically, 70 to 80 percent of wolf pups survive; in

2008, only 29 percent survived. Smith suspects that a disease known as distemper was responsible for this dramatic shift.

Despite this evidence of wolves' physical limitations and vulnerability, they've been regarded with fear and hatred and viewed as invincible predators for centuries. Wolves were hunted to extinction in England around 1500, and in 1603, within 50 years of British colonization, America's first wolf bounty was established in the Massachusetts Bay Colony. As Americans headed west to establish ranches in the following centuries, so did the bounties, because wolves were seen as threats to the livestock the ranchers depended upon.

In 1850, American Fur Trading Company records indicate that 20 wolf pelts were shipped down the Mississippi to be sold; just 3 years later, in 1853, that number increased to 3,000.[8] By the 1870s, it's estimated that 100,000 wolves were being killed annually.[9] In 1915, federal authorities established a wolf-poisoning program, and between the poisoning and the hunting, Yellowstone wolves were driven to extinction in 1926. By the 1960s, they were absent from all of the lower 48 states except for Minnesota.

Today, the wolf population stands at about 1,400 in the recovery areas of northwestern Montana, central Idaho, and the greater Yellowstone ecosystem (which includes millions of national forest acres bordering the park). In May 2009, the wolves in Montana and Idaho as well as Michigan, Minnesota, Wisconsin, Oregon, Washington, and Utah were removed from the endangered species list. "The recovery of the gray wolf throughout significant portions of its historic range is one of the great success stories of the Endangered Species Act," secretary of the interior Ken Salazar said at the time. Wyoming's wolves weren't part of the delisting because the USFWS recognizes that the state's regulatory mechanisms may put the wolf population in danger. Specifically, Wyoming has designated most of the state as a "predator zone," where wolves could be shot at will if they were delisted.

In 2008, we saw what could happen when wolves don't have sufficient protection. After the gray wolf population in the northern Rockies was classified as fully recovered in March, 110 wolves were hunted and killed in 110 days.[10] As Jamie Rappaport Clark, executive vice president of the nonprofit Defenders of Wildlife, explained, "The wolf population in [a] region needs to be treated as a total distinct population segment, not managed on a state-by-state basis. This is a recipe for small, isolated pockets of wolves that cannot move and breed across the region."

As in the past, much of the animosity toward wolves comes from ranchers, whose livelihoods can be seriously affected by wolf attacks on their animals. Though Defenders of Wildlife compensates livestock owners for losses caused by wolves, many ranchers say they're compensated for only a fraction of their actual losses. They also say the wolves' presence stresses their cattle, which keeps their weight—and the ranchers' profits—down.

When a wolf continues to prey on livestock after repeated attempts to deter it, management does become necessary. "It's better for all parties, including wolves, if chronic killers are taken out," Smith says. "A big part of wolf recovery is engendering local support."

Incidentally, while wolves are protected in Yellowstone, that doesn't mean wolves in the park are immune to what goes on outside its boundaries. Wolves are drawn from areas of high population density to areas of low density—so if hunting has markedly reduced the wolves' population just outside of the park, they may venture out of the protected area. In other words, as nonprotected wolves disappear outside the park, Yellowstone wolves will move into their old habitats for the "solitude" they offer.

Clearly, wolves need positive leadership on our part—something the wolves themselves exemplify. "Wolves never feel sorry for themselves," Smith says. "I've seen an alpha female with a broken leg get right in there while her pack was attacking a bison. She was doing her part like there was nothing wrong with her. I've necropsied wolves and found that they had broken legs that had healed over, in essence giving them a solid new leg. These animals just never quit."

Outside of the protection of national parks, 80 percent of wolf deaths come at the hands of man, and it all comes down to perceptions—and misperceptions—of wolves' place in the ecosystem. As Smith says, "Wolves' future depends on human attitudes." And historically, their only defense against humans, besides governmental protection, has been living far away from them. But as the human population continues its relentless expansion, that becomes harder and harder to do.

And it's not just gray wolves that have paid the price for our misplaced fear and hatred. The Mexican wolf (*Canis lupus baileyi*), a subspecies of the gray wolf, is on a much longer path to recovery. Since the first 11 captive-raised Mexican wolves were released in 1998 in the Blue Range Wolf Recovery Area in eastern Arizona, the population has grown to only 52 wolves; 23 have been illegally shot and killed along the way. With 7,000 square miles to call home, lack of habitat clearly isn't the problem. What the Mexican wolf most needs is an increased public awareness of the severity of its plight. Sometimes wolves are shot because they're mistaken for coyotes; other times, they're shot simply because they're viewed as nuisances. It's important that the humans who inhabit the same land as these wolves understand the long-term ecological consequences of having a quick trigger finger.

The conservation of the Mexican wolf is managed by a collaboration of the Arizona Game and Fish Department, the New Mexico Department of Game and Fish, the White Mountain Apache tribe, the USDA and the USFWS. The only way for the Mexican wolf to survive is if these authorities are called in to resolve conflicts between ranchers and wolves. Wildlife management can be successful and beneficial to all parties when it's placed in the knowledgeable hands of professionals.

Wolf conservation efforts *can* succeed. The red wolf is living, thriving proof of that.

# A BEAUTIFUL SHADE OF RED

The moment I came eye-to-eye with a red wolf (*Canis rufus*) was the beginning of one of the most moving experiences of my life. This particular red wolf had just been transported from a facility on Florida's Gulf Coast to North Carolina's Alligator River National Wildlife Refuge. As USFWS biologists Art Beyer and Chris Lucash opened the door of her kennel, she stared at us with hazel eyes. At 18 months old and weighing just 70 to 80 pounds, she was about half the size of a gray wolf but more robust than a coyote. Covered in coarse, ocher fur, the red wolf's sleek build allows it to pursue small game and deer through the merciless mazes of brambles and nettles that make up portions of its habitat.

Art carefully reached in through the top of the cage and, grasping the wolf by the scruff of her neck, secured and muzzled her. Without the risk of being bitten, we were free to loop a radio/GPS collar around her neck that would track her every move and even report her heart rate.

But before we released her and two younger wolves, Art and Chris wanted to show me one more thing.

"Give me your hand," Art said. When I offered it, he guided it to the wolf's belly. "Do you feel how full it is?"

She was plump and thus likely pregnant, and in the world of red wolves, that's an especially rare and happy occasion.

"For us, this is what it's about," Chris said, "seeing these animals get to that point where they feel comfortable enough in a habitat to reproduce."

The unsustainable hunting and aggressive predator-control programs of the past are ultimately to blame for the red wolf's precarious position. The species once ranged as far north as southern New England, throughout most of the Southeast, and as far west as Oklahoma. For centuries, it was hunted for its beautiful pelt and because it was considered a threat to livestock. The population decline reached grave proportions in the 1970s, and the USFWS responded by capturing the remaining wolves for captive breeding. With the red wolf declared extinct in the wild in 1980, the species was down to just the 400 survivors in captivity, and morphological testing revealed that only 14 were purebred red wolves. The others? Wolf-coyote hybrids.

During my visit to the Alligator River refuge, I had the opportunity to participate in the capture of a coyote, an animal whose species has become the greatest threat to the recovery of the wolf population. The cross-breeding between wily coyotes and red wolves is a major concern because it jeopardizes the wolves' genetic lineage. Standing in a large enclosure in which a female coyote had just been trapped, Art handed me a 6-foot-wide net and delivered an unnerving order: "Whatever you do, don't miss."

Our "adventure" was being filmed for the companion documentary to this book, so I steeled myself for the cameras as the coyote bared her teeth, seeming to grin at me. "Coyotes aren't big predators," I told myself. "But they *do* have big *teeth* . . . Why does Art think I know what I'm doing?"

Before I could talk myself out of it, I took a breath and went in for the capture. To my surprise, I didn't come up empty-handed. When the coyote tried to shoot past me at 20 mph, I held out the net, and somehow, that's exactly where she ended up. I proudly handed over my "catch" to the staff on hand, who secured her and whisked her away to the vet.

As I stood there, the flurry of excitement having blown over, a thought dawned on me: *How am I going to explain the euthanasia of this creature to a TV audience?*

When I arrived at the vet's office, I reluctantly asked him what would happen to the coyote, half-afraid to hear the answer.

"We're going to sterilize her and take her back," he said.

The coyote couldn't have known it, but this "problem animal" had just become part of the solution.

Try as we might to classify and organize nature into neat, orderly categories, nature doesn't follow anyone else's rules. The truth is, a canine is a canine. In the case of red wolf-coyote hybrids, females of both species will mate with members of the other species when they're in heat and can't find mates of their own species. The USFWS has responded to this problem by controlling the coyote population. Initially, the invasive coyotes were euthanized, but other coyotes simply moved into previously occupied territory and took their place, so the program had little effect. USFWS field biologists decided to switch gears and began capturing coyotes that had established territories and mated with red wolves—for life—and sterilized them via tubal ligations and vasectomies. Because their hormone-producing organs aren't removed, the coyotes can continue to form pair bonds and maintain their instinctive territorial behavior. This allows them to be returned to their habitat, where they maintain positions within their wolf families and, most important, defend red wolf turf against coyotes that *haven't* been sterilized. As the wolf population continues to grow and young wolves continue to be reintroduced, the adult wolves will chase off more and more coyotes and tip the balance in the favor of the wolves.

The projection is that after 50 more years of this adaptive management, the red wolf population's genes will be 99 percent pure, with coyote genes accounting for only a biologically acceptable 1 percent.

A month after filming the red wolves, I was having dinner in New York City when I got a call from the producer of my documentary urging me to get the film crew back to North Carolina as soon as possible. He wouldn't tell me what was happening, saying he didn't want to get my hopes up. But I would soon find out myself. A few days later, we were back in red wolf country, following a radio collar's signal through the most vicious, unforgiving network of vegetation I've ever confronted: poison ivy, poison oak, thistles, nettles and every type of thorn you can imagine. Incredulous at the fact that an animal the size of a red wolf was somewhere in this snarl, we crept on hands and knees until we came upon a depression in the earth not far from the origin of the radio signal. In it were three week-old wolf pups.

Ryan Nordsven, one of the biologists with us, and I put on surgical gloves so that we wouldn't pass on pathogens—or our scent—to the pups during handling. Then Ryan carefully reached a fist through the treacherous tangle. Seconds later, he held a newborn wolf, as soft as a puppy and its eyes still closed. Somehow, from this absolutely forbidding, fortresslike setting, surrounded by nature's version of barbed wire, had come this beautiful creature. But then, such a cruel landscape is exactly the kind of protection that this precious next generation of red wolves needs to survive.

When it was my turn to reach in and hold the pup, my gloved hands shook as I thought about this tiny creature's amazing contribution to its species. As overwhelmed as I was, though, there was business to tend to. I applied gentle pressure to the pup's front leg so Chris could use a syringe to extract a mere half-droplet of blood that would yield a veritable reservoir of information— information that will be used to create and structure family lines and reclaim the red wolf's natural heritage. Next I pinched the nape of the pup's neck to allow Chris to inject a transponder chip. This part of the process prompted a tiny yelp, but the knowledge to be gained from it is well worth the moment of pain. That chip gives biologists a front-row seat for this wolf's entire life. When it comes to understanding a species—and learning how to aid in its recovery—you can't get any more of an edge than that.

After we'd done the same with the other two pups, we put them back in their den and made our way back through the bramble. This time, I found I didn't mind the discomfort quite so much.

Since 1987, red wolves raised in captivity have been reintroduced to 1.7 million wild acres in North Carolina's Alligator River and Pocosin Lakes National Wildlife Refuges. The result: an estimated 100 freely roaming wolves 29 years after the species had bottomed out at just 14 members. And that's in addition to the 178 in captivity. Let's just hope that if global warming brings about the rise in sea level that scientists expect to occur in the next century, the wolves will be moved to a safe habitat before any of this coastal refuge is affected.

Also working on the wolves' behalf is the Red Wolf Coalition, which solicits private support for the recovery program and educates the public on wolves' ecological importance as apex predators. Luckily for the red wolves, cattle ranching isn't a major industry in the recovery area—the reintroduced wolves haven't met with the opposition that gray wolves have in the West. In the absence of hunting as a primary threat, the USFWS can focus its resources on managing the coyote population.

And judging by the program's success so far, the red wolf is on a different kind of brink now—it's on the cusp of graduation from the Hundred Heartbeat Club.

# How a Tiger Lost Its Stripes

If we had the ability to restock the Pacific Ocean with Steller's sea cows, should we? Would it be ecologically sound to return massive flocks of passenger pigeons to the skies above North America if we could? To what degree are we responsible for reversing the damage we've done—and where do we draw the ethical line in the sand?

These are the kinds of questions that scientists must consider when exploring the possibility of cloning the extinct thylacine, or Tasmanian tiger (*Thylacinus cynocephalus*), from preserved DNA. Reintroducing an extinct species to the wild could drastically alter an entire ecosystem, as evidenced by the effects of the gray wolves brought back to Yellowstone.

The Tasmanian tiger wasn't actually a tiger at all, but rather a carnivorous marsupial much like the Tasmanian devil. Despite this similarity, the two creatures looked nothing alike—a fact that I learned firsthand one day at the Harvard Museum of Comparative Zoology. A curator placed what I thought was the skull of a wolf (a classic placental carnivore) in my hands. When she said that it was a Tasmanian tiger skull, I was stunned. My initial assessment had been based entirely on looks rather than on what I knew about biology and evolution. With teeth clearly designed for killing prey and shredding flesh, I'd assumed it must be the skull of a coyote or a small wolf.

The Tasmanian tiger and the Tasmanian devil also shared a common habitat—both were native to Australia and New Guinea and became extinct on the Australian mainland (as well as New Guinea) before European settlers arrived, probably as a result of hunting by humans and dingoes alike. Its range thus confined to Tasmania, the tiger came under threat nearly as soon as humans arrived on the once-isolated island off Australia's southeastern coast. Ranchers blamed the tiger for attacks on their sheep, and a bounty was eventually placed on its head. Far from offering protection, the Australian government actually endorsed unsustainable hunting by offering a payment of £1 per dead tiger.

With a large, long body; short, sandy fur; and a tail that reached to the ground, the Tasmanian tiger looked more canine than feline. But it was the eye-catching stripes that ran from its shoulder area down its long body that gave the "tiger" its nickname. Like Tasmanian devils, females had pouches that opened to the rear and concealed four teats. Unique among Australia's marsupials, males had scrotal pouches that protected their reproductive organs from injury in the thick brush of their habitat. But maybe the most unusual characteristic of this one-of-a kind animal was its ability to open its jaws to a 120-degree angle. When you see a photo of a yawning Tasmanian tiger, your first thought is likely to be that you're looking at either a doctored photo or a genetically aberrant dog that's been trained as part of a carnival sideshow. Now picture this unique creature hopping on its hind legs like a kangaroo and you'll have an idea of what an extraordinary creature the Tasmanian tiger was.

Sightings of the tiger in the wild had become increasingly rare by the late 1920s, and in 1930 the last one was shot by a farmer who'd spotted it lurking around his henhouses. Captivity proved no safe haven for the species, either. The last captive tiger died at the Hobart Zoo in Tasmania in 1936—locked out of its shelter and at the mercy of Hobart's winter weather. In the years since, sightings of Tasmanian tigers have been reported regularly, including a report by a Tasmania Parks and Wildlife Service officer as recently as 1995, but subsequent searches failed to turn up any tigers.

Although a conservation movement had been afoot since 1901, the tiger ultimately fell victim to a reluctance to fight the status quo. Saving the thylacine was a politically unpopular position in the face of the commonly held belief that it posed a threat to livestock and, therefore, livelihoods. By the time the Tasmanian government finally extended protection to the tiger in 1936, there were none left in the wild—and the last one in captivity died 59 days later.

# LAND OF THE LOST

Imagine an Australia where Macquarie Island red-crowned parakeets, black emus, paradise parrots, and gray-headed blackbirds once again splash their colors across nature's canvas. An Australia where Norfolk Island pigeons still coo and Lord Howe warblers still warble and the Lord Howe boobook owl still hoots. Where gastric-brooding frogs still protect their eggs by swallowing them, desert rat-kangaroos still sprint across the plains, pig-footed bandicoots still groom themselves with the two fused toes on their rear feet, eastern hare-wallabies still leap 6 feet into the air, big-eared hopping mice still do their best kangaroo imitation, crescent nail-tail wallabies still escape predators by climbing the insides of hollow trees, and Tasmanian tigers still shy away from humans as if they know the danger they pose. So many unique species we've never seen have been lost that if they were to magically reappear, Australia would look like the set of a science-fiction movie.

And things aren't getting any better. Australia is home to more threatened amphibians (38) and reptiles (35) on the IUCN's Red List than any other country. And with 1,324 species on that list, it's second only to the United States in terms of overall number of threatened animals. In fact, according to the WWF-Australia, more than 20 percent of Australia's mammals are threatened with extinction.

"Land clearing and its consequences, such as salinization of rivers and landscapes, are the foremost threat to the majority of species on this list," says WWF-Australia conservation director Ray Nias, PhD. "For many species, the additional impact of climate change is now providing the final straw."[11]

And it's not just animals that are affected, but plants as well—and the decline of plants, of course, affects animals and the rest of the ecosystem. "The impact is on the entire landscape," Nias says. "The fact that a large number of plants are now reaching threatened status means that animals relying on these for food and shelter are also directly affected."

Species at immediate risk include the regent honeyeater, the northern hairy-nosed wombat, the western swamp tortoise, Gilbert's potoroo, the grassland earless dragon, the Mary River cod, the southern corroboree frog, the Gouldian finch, and the gray-headed flying fox.

"There is no question that land clearing throughout Australia must be stopped," Nias says. "This is the minimum measure for halting this alarming rate of species decline."

In the face of such widespread loss, why don't we simply bring the Tasmanian tiger—and any other species for which we have preserved DNA—back into the wild? After all, we don't appear to be far from having that capability. In 2008, Andrew Pask, PhD, and Marilyn Renfree, PhD, of the University of Melbourne injected DNA sequences from 100-year-old Tasmanian tiger samples into very early stage mouse embryos and, after 14 days, discovered that the tigers' genetic material was functioning. The researchers reported that this technique could provide us with a more accurate picture of what dinosaurs looked like and reveal why the Tasmanian tiger more closely resembled a dog than its fellow marsupial, the kangaroo.

Pask says this line of investigation isn't a precursor to cloning the Tasmanian tiger, because the existing DNA samples have deteriorated beyond the point of being replicable. But University of New South Wales science dean Mike Archer, PhD, who began a thylacine-cloning project as director of the Australian Museum in 1999, says he hopes technological advances will lead to the cloning of some recently extinct species. His project was halted in 2005 because of the DNA's deterioration.

After all that we've done to engender the decline of so many species, is it our responsibility to restore the natural order of things? If we lived in a world where species' populations and habitats were stable (and one in which time and money were less precious resources), this might be a viable option. But unfortunately, our world is far from perfect, and while the loss of the Tasmanian tiger is tragic, it also provides a valuable lesson. When we extinguish an entire animal species, we don't have the ability to travel back in time and reverse the situation, but we do have an obligation to act now to prevent future tragedies. Endangered species depend not on our hindsight but on our foresight.

———

"We do not inherit the earth from our ancestors; we borrow it from our children," a Native American proverb instructs. Given our planet's current condition, we must do everything in our power to pay back future generations—with interest. We owe it to them to hand down a wealth of natural resources—animals, plants, habitats, minerals, fuel, timber, productive soil. We need to literally make up for lost ground.

What does the future hold for the members of the Hundred Heartbeat Club? That depends largely on us, our priorities, and our allocation of resources. Consider this: Every month, it takes $12 billion to fund America's involvement in the Iraq War. For only $450,000, we could buy almost all the habitat needed to protect Ecuador's remaining frogs. The price tag of an endangered Asian or African elephant's care and protection for a year is $125,000. And it takes a mere $250 to sponsor a tracker with the Dian Fossey Gorilla Fund's antipoaching patrols.

We really do hold hope in our hands, just as I held that priceless red wolf pup in mine. What will happen when climate change raises sea levels and the refuge that the wolf pups call home is submerged? Will we have moved the red wolf population to safer ground? While we're hardwired to protect species for aesthetic, commercial, and economic motives, the impetus to preserve biodiversity should be our greatest—and most urgent—call to arms.

Chances are that in any given community, there's a river that needs to be cleaned up. Or an animal that could use the aid of human intervention, such as the Florida panther, which has benefited from the culverts built to help it safely cross highways. Saving the world's animals—and, in turn, the health of our planet—

begins in your own backyard, when you allow a garter snake bathing in the afternoon sun to slither back into your garden unharmed. It begins with showing your children the miracles that take place every day in the neighborhood pond. That's where the seeds of conservation are planted.

Most things start small. Consider all the steps it took to create our massive carbon footprint. Now we just need to step in a different direction. We can—and we must.

# GLOSSARY

**Amphibian:** a cold-blooded vertebrate able to live both on land and in water and to metamorphose from a water-breathing juvenile into an air-breathing adult

**Amplexus:** the mating clasp in which a male frog clings to a female, stimulating her to release her eggs, which the male then fertilizes

**Apex predator:** a species positioned at the top of the food chain in its range by virtue of having few or no predators

**Biodiversity:** the variety of life-forms present in a particular ecosystem

**Browser:** an herbivore that feeds on high-growing plants

**Bushmeat:** the meat of wildlife that's hunted throughout sub-Saharan Africa, often through illegal poaching, and offered for sale on the black market

**Canopy:** the uppermost layer of foliage in a forest

**Captive-breeding program:** a program in which a species is bred in captivity and individuals are later released into the wild

**Carnivore:** a meat-eating animal

**Carrion:** the rotting flesh of a dead animal, especially when regarded as a food source for scavenger species

**Charismatic-species syndrome:** the attachment of human-inspired values to other life-forms, especially animal species having popular appeal

**Chytrid (*Batrachochytrium dendrobatidis*):** a fungus that burrows into the skin of amphibians and causes chytridiomycosis, a fatal condition that prevents the animal from regulating the movement of oxygen, water, and carbon dioxide through its skin

**Cloud forest:** a tropical or subtropical mountain forest usually enshrouded in low-level cloud cover

**Conservation-dependent species:** a species that requires intensive captive breeding and release as well as habitat protection in order to avoid becoming extinct

**Corridor:** a linear tract of land that links patches of the preferred habitat for an animal species

**Critically endangered species:** a species that has experienced or is expected to experience a population decline of at least 80 percent in three generations or 10 years, whichever is longer. It is the highest risk category assigned by the International Union for the Conservation of Nature (ICUN).

**Deforestation:** the destruction of forest to allow for uses such as agriculture and urban development

**Double-clutching:** the technique of removing one set of an animal's eggs to stimulate production of another set while the first set is artificially incubated

**Ecology:** the study of the relationships between organisms and their environments

**Ecosystem:** an environment and all the organisms living in it

**Ecotourism:** a form of tourism that promotes ecological awareness and often donates a portion of the proceeds to conservation efforts

**Edge lands:** areas in which the natural habitat of wildlife borders land inhabited by humans

**Endangered species:** a species that has experienced a population loss of at least 50 percent in three generations or 10 years, whichever is longer. It is the second-highest risk category assigned by the ICUN. In the United States, a species is considered endangered under the Endangered Species Act if it is at risk of extinction throughout all or a significant portion of its range.

**Endemic species:** a species found only in a particular region or type of habitat

**Extirpate:** to destroy completely, as in the elimination of a species from a particular region

**Family:** a taxonomic category of several related genera

**Fauna:** the animals of a particular region

**Feral species:** a species that has escaped domestication and returned to the wild

**Flora:** the plants of a particular region

**Generalist species:** a species that can thrive in a wide range of environmental conditions and capitalize on a wide range of resources, such as food sources

**Genus (*pl* genera):** a group of species with common attributes

**Grazer:** an herbivore that feeds on low-growing vegetation

**Habitat degradation:** the deterioration of an environment to the point where it can no longer support the species living there

**Habitat fragmentation:** division of a species' habitat into smaller, disconnected parts

**Herbivore:** an animal that eats mainly grass or other plants

**Indicator species:** a species, often one of the most sensitive in its environment, that embodies the effects of an environmental condition such as a disease outbreak, pollution, or climate change

**International Union for the Conservation of Nature (IUCN):** the largest global environmental network, having more than 1,000 governmental and nongovernmental member organizations and almost 11,000 volunteer scientists in more than 160 countries. Headquartered in Switzerland, it supports scientific research; manages field projects; and convenes governments, institutions, companies, and local communities to develop and implement policies, laws, and best practices.

**Introduced species:** a nonnative plant or animal species that is transported to and released into a new habitat, often by humans

**Invasive species:** a nonnative animal species that outcompetes native species for food and other limited resources, preys on native animals, or degrades the landscape

**Invertebrate:** an animal lacking a spinal column

**"Island" habitat:** an isolated patch of a particular animal population's habitat

**Keystone species:** a species that has a greater stabilizing effect on its ecosystem than the size of its population would suggest

**Mammal:** a warm-blooded vertebrate species that nurses its young with milk from mammary glands and is at least partially covered with hair or fur

**Marsupial:** a species of mammal whose females have a pouch in which they carry their young

**Metapopulation management:** the relocation of members of an animal species from habitat to habitat for the purpose of creating greater genetic diversity

**Necropsy:** an autopsy performed on an animal

**Neotropical:** pertaining to the geographic region of South and Central America, the Mexican lowlands, the Caribbean islands, and southern Florida, where particular plants and animals are found

**Obligate carnivore:** a mammal that eats only meat

**Omnivore:** an animal that eats both plants and meat

**Palm oil:** oil derived from the fruit of the *Arecaceae elaeis* oil palm that's used as cooking oil and in processed food products, low-fat dairy products, and toiletries such as soap and cosmetics. Indonesia and Malaysia produce 80 percent of the world's palm oil.

**Passive integrated transponder (PIT) tag:** a device used by biologists to study an animal in the wild over time. The tag, which is implanted in the animal, contains a microchip that captures and transmits information.

**Pinniped:** a semiaquatic, fin-footed marine mammal, such as a walrus or seal, that derives from the Odobenidae, Otariidae, or Phocidae family

**Poaching:** the act of illegally hunting or fishing protected wildlife

**Radiotelemetry:** the use of radio signals to convey information. In its wildlife application, a transmitter in a tag or collar conveys information about an animal's movements and behavior.

**Rainforest:** a forest that receives enough rainfall to sustain foliage year-round

**Range:** a plant or animal's native region

**Scavenger:** an animal that eats trash and decaying organic matter

**Sirenian:** a member of the Sirenia order of fully aquatic, herbivorous mammals that possess armlike forelimbs used for steering and paddle-like tails

**Slash-and-burn agriculture:** the cutting and burning of vegetation to clear land for planting crops

**Specialist species:** a species that can tolerate only a narrow range of environmental conditions or has a very limited diet

**Species:** the basic unit of classification of organisms, consisting of a population or a group of populations of closely related organisms that reproduce with one another but not with other species

**Subspecies:** a subdivision of a species that's usually geographically isolated from other populations of the same species and exhibits one or more morphological differences

**Taxonomy:** the science of naming and classifying organisms

**Threatened species:** critically endangered, endangered, and vulnerable species as a single group, as defined by the ICUN

**Trophic cascade:** the series of effects that occurs across the food chain when a predator suppresses the abundance of its prey or the prey is hunted to extinction. The organism at the next-lower position on the food chain is then freed from predation and can prey on another organism in greater numbers.

**Umbrella species:** a species whose protected status benefits other species that share its habitat

**Ungulate:** a hoofed mammal, such as a rhinoceros

**Unsustainable hunting:** the hunting of a species at a rate that puts its survival at risk

**Vertebrate:** an animal that possesses a spinal column

**Vulnerable species:** a species that has experienced a population loss of at least 30 percent in three generations or 10 years, whichever is longer, as defined by the ICUN

# END NOTES

## Chapter 1

1. Ian Stirling and Andrew E. Derocher, "Melting Under Pressure: The Real Scoop on Climate Warming and Polar Bears," *Wildlife Professional* 1, no. 3 (Fall 2007): 24–27.
2. WWF–India, "Sundarbans Programme," n.d., http://www.wwfindia.org/about_wwf/what_we_do/cc_e/ccai/ccw.
3. National Aeronautics and Space Administration, "Arctic Sea Ice Reaches Lowest Coverage for 2008," September 16, 2008, Release 08-234, http://www.nasa.gov/home/hqnews/2008/sep/HQ_08234_Artic_Sea_Ice.html.
4. Worldwatch Institute, *State of the World 2009: Into a Warming World* (New York: W. W. Norton, 2009), p. 194.
5. S. Robert Lichter, "Climate Scientists Agree on Warming, Disagree on Dangers, and Don't Trust the Media's Coverage of Climate Change," April 24, 2008, http://stats.org/stories/2008/global_warming_survey_apr23_08.html.
6. National Wildlife Federation, "Global Warming," n.d., http://www.nwf.org/globalwarming.
7. Natural Resources Defense Council, "Issues: Global Warming: Global Warming Puts the Arctic on Thin Ice," November 22, 2005, www.nrdc.org/globalwarming/qthinice.asp.
8. Ibid.
9. S. Schliebe and others, "*Ursus maritimus*," in *The 2008 IUCN Red List of Threatened Species*, n.d., http://www.iucnredlist.org/details/22823. Accessed April 5, 2009.
10. Edward O. Wilson, "Vanishing Before Our Eyes," *Time* 155, no. 16A (April/May 2000): 17–19, http://www.time.com/time/magazine/article/0,9171,996747,00.html.
11. Eric W. Sanderson and others, "The Human Footprint and the Last of the Wild," *BioScience* 52, no. 10 (2002): 891–904.
12. Stuart L. Pimm and Peter Raven, "Biodiversity: Extinction by Numbers," *Nature* 403 (2000): 843–845.
13. Bruce A. Stein, Lynn S. Kutner, and Jonathan S. Adams, editors, *Precious Heritage: The Status of Biodiversity in the United States* (New York: Oxford University Press, 2000), Chapter 7.
14. Stuart Chape and others, compilers, *2003 United Nations List of Protected Areas* (Gland, Switzerland: IUCN, and Cambridge, England: UNEP-WCMC, 2003), p. 21.
15. Food and Agriculture Organization of the United Nations, "Results of the Global Forest Resources Assessment 2000," March 2001, http://www.fao.org/DOCREP/MEETING/003/X9591E.HTM.
16. Stein, *Precious Heritage*.
17. Charles Darwin Foundation for the Galapagos Islands, "Pinta Giant Tortoise," "Charles Darwin Research Center Fact Sheet," 2006, http://www.darwinfoundation.org/files/species/pdf/pinta-en.pdf.
18. Josep del Hoyo and others, editors, *Handbook of the Birds of the World* (Barcelona: Lynx Edicions, 1994).
19. US Fish and Wildlife Service, "Bald Eagle: Fact Sheet: Natural History, Ecology, and History of Recovery," June 2007, http://www.fws.gov/midwest/eagle/recovery/biologue.html.

20. US Fish and Wildlife Service, "Bald Eagle Soars Off Endangered Species List: Secretary Kempthorne: The Eagle Has Returned," June 28, 2007, http://www.fws.gov/news/NewsReleases/showNews.cfm?newsId=72A15E1E-F69D-06E2-5C7B052DB01FD002.

# Chapter 2

1. Richard Grant, "Siberian Tigers—the Hunted Ones," *Daily Telegraph* November 30, 2007, http://www.telegraph.co.uk/earth/3316744/Siberian-tigers-the-hunted-ones.html.
2. Fiona Govan, "Iberian Lynx Population Is Growing," *Daily Telegraph* November 7, 2007, http://www.telegraph.co.uk/earth/earthnews/3313369/Iberian-lynx-population-is-growing.html.
3. Chen Hong, "Scientists Map Panda Genome," *China Daily* October 13, 2008, http://www.chinadaily.com.cn/cndy/2008-10/13/content_7097966.htm.
4. Global Footprint Network and WWF Hong Kong, *Hong Kong Ecological Footprint Report 2008,* November 2008, www.wwf.org.hk/eng/pdf/conservation/living-planet/2008/Ecological%20Footprint_English.pdf.
5. Denis D. Gray, "Panda Porn Helps Spark Birthing Boom in Captive Breed," Associated Press November 22, 2006.
6. Malaysian Palm Oil Association, "Malaysian Palm Oil Association (MPOA) and Sustainable Palm Oil," January 6, 2005, http://www.rspo.org/PDF/Communications/Public%20Forum%20KL/MPOA%20&%20Sustainable%20Palm%20Oil%20(Ven geta%20Rao%20MPOA).pdf.
7. Charles Victor Barber and others, *The State of the Forest: Indonesia: Key Findings,* February 2002, http://www.wri.org/publication/content/8508.
8. Christopher Barr, *Banking on Sustainability: Structural Adjustment and Forestry Reform in Post-Suharto Indonesia,* 2001, p. 131, www.cifor.cgiar.org/publications/pdf_files/books/profits.pdf.
9. Ibid, p. 169.
10. Friends of the Earth, *Import of Illegal Tropical Timber to the UK,* June 2001, p. 3, http://www.foe.co.uk/resource/briefings/import_illegal_timber.pdf.
11. Conservation International, "Madagascar to Triple Areas Under Protection," September 16, 2003, http://www.conservation.org/newsroom/pressreleases/Pages/091603_mad.aspx.
12. Alex Kirby, "Hopes Rise for Mountain Gorillas," BBC News October 17, 2002, http://news.bbc.co.uk/2/hi/science/nature/2332527.stm.

# Chapter 3

1. National Audubon Society, "2007 Audubon Watchlist," n.d., http://web1.audubon.org/science/species/watchlist.
2. The Nature Conservancy, "Protecting Native Plants and Animals," n.d., http://www.nature.org/initiatives/invasivespecies.

# Chapter 4

1. Environmental Protection Agency Office of Pesticide Programs, "Promoting Safety for America's Future," April 2003, http://www.epa.gov/oppfead1/annual/2002/2002annualreport.pdf.

2. David Patterson, *"Homo sapiens Linnaeus,* 1758: General Description," Encyclopedia of Life, August 3, 2008, http://www.eol.org/pages/327955.

## Chapter 5

1. S. Schliebe and others, "IUCN Red List Status," in *The 2008 IUCN Red List of Threatened Species,* http://www.IUCNredlist.org/amphibians/redlist_status. Accessed April 19, 2009.
2. Darrel R. Frost, *Amphibian Species of the World: An Online Reference,* Version 5.3, February 12, 2009, http://research.amnh.org/herpetology/amphibia/index.php. Accessed May 11, 2009.
3. Agency for Toxic Substances and Disease Registry, "Public Health Statement for Atrazine," October 1, 2007, http://www.atsdr.cdc.gov/toxprofiles/phs153.html.
4. Benjamin Lester, "Amphibian Annihilation," *Cosmos* no. 16 (August 2007), http://www.cosmosmagazine.com/features/print/2393/amphibian-annihilation.

## Chapter 6

1. Thomson Reuters, "New UN Database to Help Combat Wildlife Crime," Reuters. com June 4, 2007, http://www.reuters.com/article/environmentNews/idUSL0476594320070604.
2. Ernest Hemingway, "Notes on Dangerous Game: The Third Tanganyika Letter," *Esquire* 2, no. 2 (July 1934): 19, 94.
3. *New York Times* January 9, 1910.
4. International Union for the Conservation of Nature, "Rhinos on the Rise in Africa but Northern White Nears Extinction," June 16, 2008, http://cms.iucn.org/what/species/mammals/?uNewsID=1146.
5. Lisa Forster, "Scientists Crack Rhino Horn Riddle," Research Communications, Ohio University, November 6, 2006, http://news.research.ohiou.edu/news/index.php?item=338.
6. John E. Fa, Dominic Currie, and Jessica Meeuwig, "Bushmeat and Food Security in the Congo Basin: Linkages between Wildlife and People's Future," Environmental Conservation 30, no. 1 (2003): 71–78.
7. World Bank, World Development Indicators, 2009, Africa. http://web.worldbank.org/WBSITE/EXTERNAL/COUNTRIES/AFRICAEXT/0,,menuPK:258649~pagePK:158889~piPK:146815~theSitePK:258644,00.html
8. WWF, "African Elephant: A Powerful Symbol of Nature," n.d., http://www.worldwildlife.org/species/finder/africanelephants/africanelephant.html.

## Chapter 7

1. Vasant K. Saberwal and others, "Lion-Human Conflict in the Gir Forest, India," *Conservation Biology* 8, no. 2 (June 1994): 501–507.
2. Asiatic Lion Information Centre, "The Lion of India," n.d., http://www.asiatic-lion.org/intro.html.
3. Ram Bir Singh Kushwah and Vijay Kumar, *Economics of Protected Areas and Its Effect on Biodiversity* (New Delhi: APH Publishing, 2001), p. 21.
4. Rhett A. Butler, "Africa's Lion Population Is Falling," Mongabay.com, March 25, 2008, http://news.mongabay.com/2008/0325-interview_hazzah.html.

5. Conservation International, "Ol Donyo Wuas Trust: Community Protection for Predators," n.d., http://www.conservation.org/Documents/pcf_lionfactsheet.pdf.
6. Tony Perry, "Maasai Tribesmen Become Brothers with a Former Foe," *Los Angeles Times* July 5, 2007, p. B-2, http://articles.latimes.com/2007/jul/05/local/me-lions5.
7. George Shiras 3rd, "The Wild Life of Lake Superior, Past and Present," *National Geographic* 40, no. 2 (August 1921): 113–204.
8. Barry Holstun Lopez, *Of Wolves and Men* (New York: Scribner, 1978).
9. Peggy Struhsacker, *Wolves in the Northeast: Principles, Problems and Prospects* (Reston, Virginia: National Wildlife Federation, 2003), p. 6.
10. Natural Resources Defense Council, *Nature's Voice* January/February 2009.
11. WWF-Australia, "Wave of Extinction Hits Australia," November 19, 2003, http://www.wwf.org.au/news/n48.

# BIBLIOGRAPHY
# AND SOURCES

## Ecology, Environment, and Extinction

Forsyth, Adrian, and Miyata, Ken (1984). *Tropical Nature: Life and Death in the Rain Forests of Central and South America*. New York: Macmillan.

Friedman, Thomas L. (2008). *Hot, Flat, and Crowded: Why We Need a Green Revolution—and How It Can Renew America*. New York: Farrar, Straus, and Giroux.

Gore, Al (2006). *An Inconvenient Truth: The Planetary Emergence of Global Warming and What We Can Do About It*. New York: Rodale.

Groom, M. J.; Meffe, G. K.; Carroll, C. R. (2006). *Principles of Conservation Biology* (3rd ed.). Sunderland, MA: Sinauer Associates.

Groves, C.; Wilson, D. E.; Reeder, D. M. (eds.) (2005). *Mammal Species of the World* (3rd ed.). Baltimore: Johns Hopkins University Press.

Grzimek, B. (1990). *Grzimek's Encyclopedia of Mammals*, Volume 1. New York: McGraw-Hill.

Krichner, John (1997). *A Neotropical Companion: An Introduction to the Animals, Plants, and Ecosystems of the New World Tropics*. Princeton, NJ: Princeton University Press.

Quammen, David (1996). *The Song of the Dodo: Island Biography in an Age of Extinctions*. New York: Touchstone.

Wilson, Edward O. (2000). "Vanishing before our eyes." *Time Europe*, Special Edition, 155 (16A): 17–19.

Wilson, Edward O. (2002). *The Future of Life*. New York: Alfred A. Knopf.

## Amphibians

Alford, R. A., and Richards, S. J. (1999). "Global amphibian declines: A problem in applied ecology." *Annual Review of Ecology and Systematics*: 133–165.

Andre, S. E.; Parker, J.; Briggs, C. J. (2008). "Effect of temperature on host response to *Batrachochytrium dendrobatidis* infection in the mountain yellow-legged frog (*Rana muscosa*)." *Journal of Wildlife Diseases* 44: 716–720.

Beebee, T. J. C., and Griffiths, R. A. (2005). "The amphibian decline crisis: A watershed for conservation biology?" *Biological Conservation* 125: 271–285.

Beltz, Ellin (2005). *Frogs: Inside Their Remarkable World*. Buffalo: Firefly Books.

Blaustein, A. R., and Kiesecker, J. M. (2002). "Complexity in conservation: Lessons from the global decline of amphibian populations." *Ecology Letters* 5: 597–608.

Blaustein, A. R.; Romansic, J. M.; Kiesecker, J. M.; Hatch, A. C. (2003). "Ultraviolet radiation, toxic chemicals and amphibian population declines." *Diversity and Distributions* 9: 123–140.

Blaustein, A. R., and Wake, D. B. (1990). "Declining amphibian populations—a global phenomenon." *Trends in Ecology and Evolution* 5: 203–204.

Bovero, S.; Sotgiu, G.; Angelini, C.; Doglio, S.; Gazzaniga, E.; Cunningham, A. A.; Garner, T. W. J. (2008). "Detection of chytridiomycosis caused by *Batrachochytrium dendrobatidis* in the endangered Sardinian newt (*Euproctus platycephalus*) in southern Sardinia, Italy." *Journal of Wildlife Diseases* 44: 712–715.

Brito, D. (2008). "Amphibian conservation: Are we on the right track?" *Biological Conservation* 141: 2912–2917.

Burrowes, P. A.; Longo, A. V.; Joglar, R. L.; Cunningham, A. A. (2008). "Geographic distribution of *Batrachochytrium dendrobatidis* in Puerto Rico." *Herpetological Review* 39: 321–324.

Campbell Grant, E. H.; Bailey, L. L.; Ware, J. L.; Duncan, K. L. (2008). "Prevalence of the amphibian pathogen *Batrachochytrium dendrobatidis* in stream and wetland amphibians in Maryland, USA." *Applied Herpetology* 5: 233–241.

Carey, C., and Alexander, M. A. (2003). "Climate change and amphibian declines: Is there a link?" *Diversity and Distributions* 9: 111–121.

Collins, J. P., and Storfer, A. (2003). "Global amphibian declines: Sorting the hypotheses." *Diversity and Distributions* 9: 89–98.

Crump, M. L.; Hensley, F. R.; Clark, K. L. (1992). "Apparent decline of the golden toad: Underground or extinct?" *Copeia* 2: 413–420.

Daszak, P.; Cunningham, A. A.; Hyat, A. D.; et al. (2003). "Infectious disease and amphibian population declines." *Diversity and Distributions* 9: 141–150.

Fisher, R. N., and Shaffer, H.B. (1996). "The decline of amphibians in California's Great Central Valley." *Conservation Biology* 10: 1387–1397.

Gascon, C.; Collins, J. P.; Moore, R. D.; Church, D. R.; McKay, J. E.; Mendelson III, J. R. (eds.) (2007). "Amphibian Conservation Action Plan." International Union for the Conservation of Nature, Species Survival Commission, Amphibian Specialist Group. Gland, Switzerland: The World Conservation Union.

Grismer, L. L., and Aun, P. K. (2008). "Diversity, endemism, and conservation of the amphibians and reptiles of southern peninsular Malaysia and its offshore islands." *Herpetological Review* 39: 270–281.

Gupta, B. K. (2006). "Amphibian biodiversity conservation (ABC) course." *Solitaire* 17: 11.

Hayes, T. B.; Collins, A.; Lee, M.; Mendoza, M.; Noriega, N.; Stuart, A. A.; Vonk, A. (2002). "Hermaphroditic, demasculinized frogs after exposure to the herbicide atrazine at low ecologically relevant doses." *Proceedings of the National Academy of Sciences of the United States of America* 99: 5476–5480.

Hedges, B.; Joglar, R.; Thomas, R. (2004). "*Bufo lemur.*" IUCN Red List of Threatened Species.

Hero, J. M., and Kriger, K. M. (2008). "Threats to amphibians in tropical regions." *Encyclopedia of Life Support Services (EOLSS): Tropical Zoology.* Oxford, UK: EOLSS.

Hofrichter, R. (ed.) (2000). *Amphibians: The World of Frogs, Toads, Salamanders and Newts.* Buffalo: Firefly Books.

Holdridge, L. R. (1967). *Life Zone Ecology.* San Jose, Costa Rica: Tropical Science Center.

Houlahan, J. E.; Findlay, C. S.; Schmidt, B. R.; Meyer, A. H.; Kuzmin, S. L. (2000). "Quantitative evidence for global amphibian population declines." *Nature* 404: 752–755.

Hutchins, M.; Duellman, W. E.; Schlager, N. (eds.) (2003). *Grzimeck's Animal Life Encyclopedia*, Volume 6 (2nd ed.). Farmington Hills, MI: Gale Group.

International Union for the Conservation of Nature (2005). *Amphibian Conservation Summit Declaration*. http://intranet.iucn.org/webfiles/doc/SSC/SSCwebsite/GAA/ ACAP_Summit_Declaration.pdf

Jacobson, S. K., and Vandenberg, J. J. (1991). "Reproductive ecology of the endangered golden toad (*Bufo periglenes*)." *Journal of Herpetology* 25 (3): 321–327.

Kats, L. B., and Ferrer, R. P. (2003). "Alien predators and amphibian declines: Review of two decades of science and the transition to conservation." *Diversity and Distributions* 9: 99–110.

Kiesecker, J. M.; Blaustein, A. R.; Belden, L. K. (2001). "Complex causes of amphibian declines." *Nature* 410: 681–684.

Lannoo, M. J.; Lang, K.; Waltz, T.; Phillips, G. S. (1994). "An altered amphibian assemblage: Dickinson County, Iowa, 70 years after Frank Blanchard's survey." *American Midland Naturalist* 131: 311–319.

Lehtinen, R. M.; Kam, Y. C.; Richards, C. L. (2008). "Preliminary surveys for *Batrachochytrium dendrobatidis* in Taiwan." *Herpetological Review* 39: 317–318.

Lester, Benjamin (2007). "Amphibian annihilation." *Cosmos* 16, August.

Lips, K. R. (2000). "Decline of a tropical amphibian fauna." *166th National Meeting of the American Association for the Advancement of Science and Science Innovation Exposition*, Washington, DC, February 17–22, 2000.

Lovich, R.; Ryan, M. J.; Pessier, A. P.; Claypool, B. (2008). "Infection with the fungus *Batrachochytrium dendrobatidis* in a non-native *Lithobates berlandieri* below sea level in the Coachella Valley, California, USA." *Herpetological Review* 39: 315–317.

Marsh, D. M., and Trenham, P. C. (2001). "Metapopulation dynamics and amphibian conservation." *Conservation Biology* 15: 40–49.

McCallum, M. (2007). "Amphibian decline or extinction? Current declines dwarf background extinction rate." *Journal of Herpetology* 41: 483–491.

McCranie, J. R.; Wilson, L. D.; Adler, K.; Perry, T. D. (eds.) (2002). "The amphibians of Honduras." *Contributions to Herpetology*, Volume 19. Ithaca, NY: Society for the Study of Amphibians and Reptiles. pp. 1–625.

Mendelson III, J. R., et al. (2006). "Confronting amphibian declines and extinctions." *Science* 313: 48.

Myers, C. W. (1992). "Frog secretions and hunting magic in the Upper Amazon: Identification of a peptide that interacts with an adenosine receptor." *Proceedings of the National Academy of Sciences of the United States of America* 89: 10960–10963.

Myers, C. W.; Daly, J.; Malkin, B. (1978). "A dangerously toxic new frog (*Phyllobates*) used by Emberá Indians of western Colombia, with discussion of blowgun fabrication and dart poisoning." *Bulletin of the American Museum of Natural History* 161: 307–366.

Pounds, J. A., and Crump, M. L. (1994). "Amphibian declines and climate disturbance: The case of the golden toad and the harlequin frog." *Conservation Biology* 8: 72–85.

Pounds, J. A.; Fogden, M. P. L.; Savage, J. M.; Gorman, G. C. (1997). "Tests of null models for amphibian declines on a tropical mountain." *Conservation Biology* 11 (6): 1307–1322.

Pounds, J. A.; Fogden, M. P. L.; Campbell, J. H. (1999). "Biological response to climate change on a tropical mountain." *Nature* 398 (6728): 611–615.

Relyea, R. A., and Diecks, N. (2008). "An unforeseen chain of events: Lethal effects of pesticides on frogs at sublethal concentrations." *Ecological Applications* 18: 1728–1742.

Rohr, J. R.; Raffel, T. R.; Sessions, S. K.; Hudson, P. J. (2008). "Understanding the net effects of pesticides on amphibian trematode infections." *Ecological Applications* 18: 1743–1753.

Rohr, J. R., et al. (2008). "Agrochemicals increase trematode infections in a declining amphibian species." *Nature* 455: 1235–1239.

Rothermel, B. B., et al. (2008). "Widespread occurrence of the amphibian chytrid fungus *Batrachochytrium dendrobatidis* in the southeastern USA." *Diseases of Aquatic Organisms* 82: 3–18.

Sánchez, D.; Chacón-Ortiz, A.; León, F.; Han, B. A.; Lampo, M. (2008). "Widespread occurrence of an emerging pathogen in amphibian communities of the Venezuelan Andes." *Biological Conservation* 141: 2898–2905.

Savage, J. M. (1966). "An extraordinary new toad (*Bufo*) from Costa Rica." *Revista de Biologica Tropical* 14 (2): 153–167.

Savage, J. M. (2002). *The Amphibians and Reptiles of Costa Rica.* Chicago: University of Chicago Press.

Scherer, R. D.; Muths, E.; Lambert, B. A. (2008). "Effects of weather on survival in populations of boreal toads in Colorado." *Journal of Herpetology* 42: 508–517.

Snider, A., and Zippel, K. (2000). "Amphibian conservation at the Detroit Zoological Institute." *FROGLOG* (40), August 2000. http://www.open.ac.uk/daptf/froglog/FROGLOG-40-4.html.

Stebbins, R. C. (2003). *A Field Guide to Western Reptiles and Amphibians* (3rd ed.). Boston: Houghton Mifflin. p. 217.

Stuart, S.; Chanson, J. S.; Cox, N. A.; Young, B. E.; Rodrigues, A. S. L.; Fishman, D. L.; Waller, R. W. (2004). "Status and trends of amphibian declines and extinctions worldwide." *Science* 306: 1783–1786.

Sumanadasa, D. M.; Wijesinghe, M. R.; Ratnasooriya, W. D. (2008). "Effects of diazinon on larvae of the Asian common toad (*Bufo melanostictus*, Schneider 1799)." *Environmental Toxicology and Chemistry* 27: 2320–2325.

Venesky, M. D., and Brem, F. M. (2008). "Occurrence of *Batrachochytrium dendrobatidis* in southwestern Tennessee, USA." *Herpetological Review* 39: 319–320.

Vredenburg, V. T. (2004). "Reversing introduced species effects: Experimental removal of introduced fish leads to rapid recovery of declining frog." *Proceedings of the National Academy of Sciences of the United States of America* 101 (20): 7646–7650.

Wake, D. B. (1991). "Declining amphibian populations." *Science* 253: 860.

Wiese, R. J., and Hutchins, M. (1994). "The role of zoos and aquariums in amphibian and reptile conservation." In J. B. Murphy, K. Adler, J. T. Collins (eds.), *Captive*

*Management and Conservation of Amphibians and Reptiles.* Contributions to Herpetology, Volume 11. Ithaca, NY: Society for the Study of Amphibians and Reptiles. p. 37–45.

Young, B. E.; Lips, K. R.; Reaser, J. K.; Ibanez, R.; Salas, A. W.; Cedeno, J. R.; Coloma, L. A.; Ron, S.; La Marca, E.; Meyer, J. R.; Munoz, A.; Bolanos, F.; Chaves, G.; Romo, D. (2001). "Population declines and priorities for amphibian conservation in Latin America." *Conservation Biology* 15: 1213–1223.

Zippel, K.; Lacy, R.; Byers, O. (eds.) (2006). *CBSG/WAZA Amphibian Ex Situ Conservation Planning Workshop Final Report.* Apple Valley, MN: International Union for the Conservation of Nature, Species Survival Commission, Conservation Breeding Specialist Group.

Zippel, K. C. (2004). "Zoos play a vital role in amphibian conservation." AmphibiaWeb. http://www.amphibiaweb.org/aw/declines/zoo/index.html.

Zippel, K. C. (2002). "Conserving the Panamanian golden frog: *Proyecto Rana Dorada.*" *Herpetological Review* 33: 11–12.

Zippel, K. C. (2007). "Prepare your staff to aid in the amphibian extinction crisis." *Connect* (Association of Zoos and Aquariums) February: p. 67.

## Sources

Amphibian Ark, http://www.amphibianark.org.

AmphibiaWeb, http://amphibiawcb.org.

Blanco L., Dr. Juan Felipe (n.d.). "Puerto Rican crested toad (*Bufo lemur*)." http://jfblanco.tripod.com/crestedtoad.html.

Encyclopedia Britannica Online (n.d.). "*Anotheca spinosa.*" http://www.britannica.com/EBchecked/topic/26669/Anotheca-spinosa.

Houston Zoo (2008). "2008: Year of the Frog." http://www.houstonzoofrogs.org.

International Union for the Conservation of Nature, 2008 IUCN Red List of Threatened Species, http://www.iucnredlist.org.

University of California at Berkeley, Department of Integrative Biology, http://ib.berkeley.edu/people.

University of Manchester, Manchester Museum, http://www.museum.manchester.ac.uk/aboutus/ourresearch.

ZipcodeZoo.com (2009). "*Bufo lemur* (Puerto Rican crested toad)." May 12. http://www.zipcodezoo.com/Animals/B/Bufo_lemur.

## Bears

### Giant Panda

Bailey, Deborah Smith. (2004). "Understanding the giant panda." *Monitor on Psychology* 35 (1): 22.

Baskin, John A. (1998). "Procyonidae." In C. M. Janis, K. M. Scott, L. L. Jacobs (eds.), *Evolution of Tertiary Mammals of North America*, Volume 1. Cambridge, UK: Cambridge University Press. pp. 144–151.

Benford, G. (1992). "Saving the 'Library of Life.'" *Proceedings of the National Academy of Sciences of the United States of America* 89 (22): 11098–11101.

Bininda-Emonds, O. R.; Gittleman, J. L.; Purvis, A. (1999). "Building large trees by combining phylogenetic information: A complete phylogeny of the extant Carnivora (Mammalia)." *Biological Reviews of the Cambridge Philosophical Society* 74: 143–175. PMID: 10396181.

Brown, Gary (1996). *Great Bear Almanac.* New York: Lyons Press.

Chorn, J., and Hoffmann, R. S. (1978). *Ailuropoda melanoleuca. Mammalian Species* 110: 1–6.

Ciochon, Russell L., and Eaves-Johnson, K. Lindsay (2007). "Bamboozled! The curious natural history of the giant panda family." Scitizen.com, July 20. http://www.scitizen.com.

Davis, D. D. (1964). "The giant panda: A morphological study of evolutionary mechanisms." *Fieldiana Zoology* 3: 1–339.

de Beaumont, G. (1982). "Qu'est-ce que le *Plesictis leobensis* Redlich (mammifere carnivore)?" *Archives of Science Geneva* 35: 143–152.

Endo, H.; Hayashi, Y.; Yamagiwa, D.; Kurohmaru, M.; Koie, H.; Yamaya, Y.; Kimura, J. (1999). "CT examination of the manipulation system in the giant panda (*Ailuropoda melanoleuca*)." *Journal of Anatomy* 195: 295–300. PMID: 10529064.

Endo, H.; Yamagiwa, D.; Hayashi, Y.; Koie, H.; Yamaya, Y.; Kimura, J. (1999). "Role of the giant panda's 'pseudo-thumb.'" *Nature* 397: 309–310. PMID: 9950422.

Flynn, J. J.; Finarelli, J. A.; Zehr, S.; Hsu, J.; Nedbal, M. A. (2005). "Molecular phylogeny of the Carnivora (Mammalia): Assessing the impact of increased sampling on resolving enigmatic relationships." *Systematic Biology* 54: 317–337. PMID: 16012099.

Flynn, J. J.; Nedbal, M. A.; Dragoo, J. W.; Honeycutt, R. L. (2000). "Whence the red panda?" *Molecular Phylogenetics and Evolution* 17: 190–199. PMID: 11083933.

Flynn, J. J., and Nedbal, M. A. (1998). "Phylogeny of the Carnivora (Mammalia): Congruence vs incompatibility among multiple data sets." *Molecular Phylogenetics and Evolution* 9: 414–426. PMID: 9667990.

Gambaryan. P. P. (1974). *How Mammals Run: Anatomical Adaptations.* New York: Wiley.

Goldman, D.; Rathna Giri, P.; O'Brien, S. J. (1989). "Molecular genetic-distance estimates among the Ursidae as indicated by one- and two-dimensional protein electrophoresis." *Evolution* 43: 282–295.

Goodman, Brenda (2006). "Pandas eat up much of zoos' budgets." *New York Times,* February 12.

Gould, S. J. (1980). *The Panda's Thumb.* New York: Norton.

Hawes, A., and Huy, M. (2001). "What's in a name? Giant panda." Smithsonian National Zoological Park. http://nationalzoo.si.edu/Animals/GiantPandas/WhatsInAName/default.cfm.

Ledje, C., and Arnason, U. (1996). "Phylogenetic analyses of complete cytochrome b genes of the order Carnivora with particular emphasis on the Caniformia." *Journal of Molecular Evolution* 42: 135–144. PMID: 8919865.

Li, De-Zhu; Guo, Zhenhua; Stapleton, Chris (2007). *"Fargesia dracocephala."* In Z. Y. Wu; P. H. Raven; D. Y. Hong (eds.), *Flora of China*, Volume 22. Beijing: Science Press. pp. 81, 93.

Lindburg, Donald G., and Baragona, Karen (2004). *Giant Pandas: Biology and Conservation.* Berkeley, CA: University of California Press.

Liu, M., and Wehrfritz, G. "China's panda politics." *Newsweek*, October 15, 2007.

Lumpkin, Susan, and Seidensticker, John (2007). *Giant Pandas.* London: Collins.

O'Brien, S. J.; Nash, W. G.; Wildt, D. E.; Bush, M. E.; Benveniste, R. E. (1985). "A molecular solution to the riddle of the giant panda's phylogeny." *Nature* 317: 140–144. PMID: 4033795.

Oleksyn, Veronika (2007). "Panda gives surprise birth in Austria." Associated Press, August 23.

Prapanya, Narunart (2006). "'Panda porn' to encourage mating." CNN.com, January 25.

Putatunda, Rita (2008). "Facts on pandas." Buzzle.com, February 15.

Roberts, M. S., and Gittleman, J. L. (1984). *"Ailurus fulgens."* *Mammalian Species* 222: 1–8.

Ryder, Joanne (2001). *Little Panda: The World Welcomes Hua Mei at the San Diego Zoo.* New York: Simon and Schuster.

Schaller, George B. (1993). *The Last Panda.* Chicago: University of Chicago Press.

Taylor, M. E., and Gittleman, J. L. (eds.) (1989). *Carnivore Behavior, Ecology, and Evolution*, Volume 1. Ithaca, NY: Cornell University Press. pp. 382–409.

Warren, Lynne (2006). "Panda, Inc." *National Geographic*, July.

# Sources

American Bear Association, http://www.americanbear.org/otherbears.htm.

Animal Diversity Web, http://animaldiversity.ummz.umich.edu/site.

Anonymous (2007). "Concern grows for smallest bear." BBC News, November 12. http://news.bbc.co.uk/1/hi/sci/tech/7087345.stm.

Anonymous (2002). "Pandas unexcited by Viagra." BBC News, September 9. http://news.bbc.co.uk/1/hi/world/asia-pacific/2246588.stm.

Anonymous (2008). "2008 pregnancy watch ends without cub." Smithsonian National Zoological Park, August 13. http://nationalzoo.si.edu/Animals/GiantPandas/PandaConservation/2008PregnancyWatch.Australian Broadcasting Corporation (2007). "Panda granny." June 12. http://www.abc.net.au/tv/btn/stories/s1947589.htm.

Briggs, Helen (2006). "Hope for future of giant panda." BBC News, June 20. http://news.bbc.co.uk/1/hi/sci/tech/5085006.stm.

International Union for the Conservation of Nature, http://www.iucn.org.

International Union for the Conservation of Nature, Bear Specialist Group. *"Ailuropoda melanoleuca."* 2006 IUCN Red List of Threatened Species.

Memphis Zoo, http://www.memphiszoo.org.

National Geographic Traveler (2008). "Panda rescue efforts in China." July 1. http://blogs.nationalgeographic.com/blogs/intelligenttravel/2008/07/panda-rescue-efforts-in-china.html.

Natural History Notebooks, http://www.nature.ca/notebooks/english/gpanda.htm.

Panda Channel, Ocean Park Hong Kong, http://pctv.netvigator.com/pctv/players/panda/loadPlayer.jsp?channel=panda2.

San Diego Zoo, http://www.sandiegozoo.org.

Smithsonian National Zoological Park, http://www.nationalzoo.si.edu.

Smithsonian National Zoological Park (n.d.). "Giant panda reproduction." http://newdesk.si.edu/kits/pandas/nzp_panda_reproduction.pdf.

Utah Education Network, http://www.uen.org/themepark/habitat/animal.shtml.

Wolong Nature Reserve, China Conservation and Research Center for Giant Pandas, http://www.chinagiantpanda.com/site/wolong.htm.

World Wildlife Fund (2009). "Giant panda." May 19. http://www.panda.org/what_we_do/endangered_species/endangered_species_list/giant_panda.

World Wildlife Fund China (n.d.). "Panda facts at a glance." http://www.wwfchina.org/english/pandacentral/htm/learn_about_giant_panda/panda_q_a/panda_behavior_habitat.htm.

Xinhua News Agency (2007). "China: 217 pandas bred in captivity." January 4. http://www.china.org.cn/english/news/194895.htm.

## Birds

Allston, W. P. (1991). "Why did the passenger pigeon become extinct?" *Boston Globe,* August 16. p. 22.

Bleyer Jennifer (2006). "The Don Quixote of the plumed set." *New York Times,* August 20. p. 7.

Boroughs, Don, (2001). "Not dead as a dodo." *International Wildlife* 31 (6): 44–51.

Bull, J., and Farrand Jr., J. (1977). *The Audubon Society Field Guide to North American Birds.* New York: Alfred A. Knopf. pp. 468–469.

Cade, T., and Jones, C. (1993). "Progress in the restoration of the Mauritius kestrel." *Conservation Biology* 7 (1): 169–175.

Carroll, J. R. (1988). "Bald eagle, *Haliaeetus leucocephalus.*" In R. F. Andrle and J. R. Carroll (eds.), *The Atlas of Breeding Birds in New York State.* Ithaca, NY: Cornell University Press. pp. 100–101.

Carter, J., and Jones, M. (1999). "Habitat composition of Mauritius kestrel home ranges." *Journal of Field Ornithology* 70 (2): 230–235.

Chung, J. (2002). "*Falco punctatus.*" Animal Diversity Web. http://animaldiversity.ummz.umich.edu/site/accounts/information/Falco_punctatus.html.

Cokinos, Christopher (2000). *Hope Is the Thing with Feathers: A Personal Chronicle of Vanished Birds.* New York: Putnam.

Cracraft, J.; Barker, F. K.; Donoghue, M. J.; Braun, J.; et al. (2004). *Phylogenetic Relationships Among Modern Birds (Neornithes): Toward an Avian Tree of Life.* New York: Oxford University Press.

Diamond, Anthony W., and the Roger Tory Peterson Institute (1989). *Save the Birds*. Boston: Houghton Mifflin.

Erritzoe, Johannes, and Erritzoe, Helga (1993). *The Birds of CITES and How to Identify Them*. London: Lutterworth Press.

Ferguson-Lees, James, and Christie, David A. (2001). *Raptors of the World*. Boston: Houghton Mifflin.

Gerrard, J. M., and Bortolotti, G. (1988). *The Bald Eagle: Haunts and Habits of a Wilderness Monarch*. Washington, DC: Smithsonian Institution Press.

Goodwin, Derek (1976). *Crows of the World*. Ithaca, NY: Cornell University Press.

Hartston, William (2004). "Ten things you never knew about...pigeons." *The Express*, May 4. p. 24.

Howard, Hildegarde (1947). "A preliminary survey of trends in avian evolution from Pleistocene to recent time." *Condor* 49 (1): 10–13.

Jones, C.; Heck, W.; Lewis, R.; Mungroo, Y.; Slade, G. (1995). "The restoration of the Mauritius kestrel (*Falco punctatus*) population." *Ibis* 137 (Suppl. 1): S173–S180.

Kiff, L. F.; Peakall, D. B.; Wilbur, S. R. (1979). "Recent changes in California condor eggshells." *Condor* 81 (2): 166 –172.

Liddell Henry George, and Scott, Robert (1980). *A Greek-English Lexicon* (abridged edition). Oxford, UK: Oxford University Press.

Marling, Karal Ann (1999). "The way of the dodo." *New York Times*, June 6. p. 44.

Nielsen, John (2006). *Condor: To the Brink and Back: The Life and Times of One Giant Bird*. New York: Harper Perennial.

Nye, P. (1990). "A second chance for our national symbol." *Conservationist*, July/August.

Pratt, H. D.; Bruner, P. L.; Berrett, D. G. (1987). *The Birds of Hawaii and the Tropical Pacific*. Princeton, NJ: Princeton University Press.

Remsen Jr., J. V.; Cadena, C. D.; Jaramillo, A.; Nores, M.; Pacheco, J. F.; Robbins, M. B.; Schulenberg, T. S.; Stiles, F. G.; Stotz, D. F.; Zimmer, K. J. (2007). *A Classification of the Bird Species of South America*. American Ornithologists' Union. http://www.museum.lsu.edu/~Remsen/SACCBaseline.html.

Safford, R., and Jones, C. (1997). "Did organochlorine pesticide use cause declines in Mauritian forest birds?" *Biodiversity and Conservation* 6 (10): 1445–1451.

Sibley, Charles G., and Monroe, Burt L. (1990). *Distribution and Taxonomy of the Birds of the World*. New Haven: Yale University Press.

Simpson, J., and Weiner, E. (eds.) (1989). "Raven." *Oxford English Dictionary* (2nd ed.). Oxford, UK: Clarendon Press.

Sorenson, M. D.; Cooper, A.; Paxinos, E. E.; Quinn, T. W.; James, H. F.; Olson, S. L.; Fleischer, R. C. (1999). "Relationships of the extinct moa-nalos, flightless Hawaiian waterfowl, based on ancient DNA." *Proceedings: Biological Sciences* 266 (1434): 2187–2193.

Staub, France (1976). *Birds of the Mascarenes and Saint Brandon*. Port Louis, Mauritius: Labama House.

Temple, S. (1987). "Foraging ecology of the Mauritius kestrel (*Falco punctatus*)." *Biotropica* 19 (1): 2–6.

Thacker, Paul D. (2006). "Condors are shot full of lead." *Environmental Science and Technology* 40 (19): 5826.

Watkins, Thomas (2007). "California condor lays egg in Mexico." *USA Today*, April 3.

Wetmore, Alexander, and Friedmann, Herbert (1938). "The California condor in Texas." *Condor* 35 (1): 37–38.

# Sources

American Bald Eagle Information, http://www.baldeagleinfo.com.

AnimalAqua.com, http://www.animalaqua.com/mauritius-kestrel.

Animal Diversity Web, http://animaldiversity.ummz.umich.edu.

Anonymous (2006). "Condors set up first nest in 100 years." SkyNews.com, March 30. http://news.sky.com/skynews/Home/Condors-Set-Up-First-Nest-In-100-Years/Article/200603413516474?chooseNews=Health.

BirdLife International, http://www.birdlife.org.

BirdLife International (2007). "California condor: *Gymnogyps californianus*." http://www.birdlife.org/datazone/species/index.html?action=SpcHTMDetails.asp&sid=3821. Accessed May 23, 2009.

BirdLife International (2009). "Hawaiian Crow: *Corvus hawaiiensi*." http://www.birdlife.org/datazone/species/index.html?action=SpcHTMDetails.asp&sid=5793&m=0. Accessed May 23, 2009.

California Condor Conservation, http://cacondorconservation.org.

California Condor Conservation Blog, Michael Wallace, PhD, http://cacondorconservation.org/content/blog/blogs/meet-the-bloggers/2008/michael-wallace-phd-wildlife-scientist.

Canadian Museum of Nature, http://nature.ca/notebooks/english/grtchick.htm.

Collar, N.; Crosby, M.; Stattersfield, A. (1994). *Birds to Watch 2*. Cambridge, UK: BirdLife International.

Conservation Commission of Missouri (2007). "Prairie chicken (*Tympanuchus cupido*)." http://www.mdc.mo.gov/landown/wild/pchicken/reference.

Convention on International Trade in Endangered Species of Wild Fauna and Flora, http://www.cites.org.

Cornell Lab of Ornithology. (n.d.) "California condor." All About Birds. http://www.birds.cornell.edu/AllAboutBirds/conservation/success/california_condor.

International Union for the Conservation of Nature (2006). "*Gymnogyps californianus*." IUCN Red List of Threatened Species.

Mauritian Wildlife Foundation, http://www.maurinet.com/wildlife.html.

Mongabay.com (n.d.). "News articles on extinction." http://www.mongabay.com/news-index/extinction1.html.

National Audubon Society (2007). "Audubon's WatchList 2007 in taxonomic order by geographic region: Red List species—continental U.S. and Alaska." http://www.audubon.org/bird/pdf/WatchList2007_Printable_List_Populations.pdf.

Peregrine Fund, http://www.peregrinefund.org.

Raymo, Chet (2008). "The thing with feathers." Science Musings Blog, June 7. http://www.sciencemusings.com/blog/2008/06/thing-with-feathers.html.

San Diego Zoo (n.d.). "Birds: California condor." http://www.sandiegozoo.org/animalbytes/t-condor.html.

Snyder, Noel F., and Schmitt, N. John (2002). "California condor (*Gymnogyps californianus*)." The Birds of North America Online. http://bna.birds.cornell.edu/bna/species/610/articles/introduction.

Stattersfield, Alison J., and Capper, David R. (eds.) (2000). *Threatened Birds of the World*. Cambridge, UK: BirdLife International.

Texas Parks and Wildlife Department (2008). "Attwater's prairie chicken (*Tympanuchus cupido attwateri*)." http://www.tpwd.state.tx.us/huntwild/wild/species/apc/.

US Fish and Wildlife Service (n.d.). "American bald eagle." USFlag.com. http://www.usflag.org/baldeagle.html.

US Fish and Wildlife Service (n.d.). "Birds, birds, birds." http://www.fws.gov/birds.

US Fish and Wildlife Service (n.d.). "California condor (*Gymnogyps californianus*)." http://ecos.fws.gov/speciesProfile/profile/speciesProfile.action?spcode=B002 .

US Fish and Wildlife Service, Hopper Mountain National Wildlife Refuge Complex (n.d.). "Biology of the California condor." http://www.fws.gov/hoppermountain/CACORecoveryProgram/CACO%20Biology.html.US Fish and Wildlife Service, Hopper Mountain National Wildlife Refuge Complex (n.d.). "California Condor Recovery Program." http://www.fws.gov/hoppermountain/CACORecoveryProgram/CACondorRecoveryProgram.html.

US Fish and Wildlife Service, Pacific Islands Fish and Wildlife Office (2009). "Endangered species in the Pacific Islands: Hawaiian crow." April 27. http://www.fws.gov/pacificislands/fauna/alala.html

US North American Bird Conservation Initiative, http://www.nabci-us.org/main2.html.

Ventana Wildlife Society (n.d.). "California condor reintroduction." http://www.ventanaws.org/species_condors.

Ventana Wildlife Society (n.d.). "California condors: Cool facts." http://www.ventanaws.org/species_condors_coolfacts.

Ventana Wildlife Society (n.d.). "California condor life history." http://www.ventanaws.org/species_condors_history.

Wildlife Trust (2000). "Mauritius kestrel." The Wild Ones Animal Index. http://www.thewildones.org/Animals/mKestrel.html.

## Canines

Allen, Glover M. (1942). *Extinct and Vanishing Mammals of the Western Hemisphere*. Cambridge, MA: American Committee for International Wild Life Protection. p. 400.

Asa, C., and Valdespino, C. (1998). "Canid reproductive biology: An integration of proximate mechanisms and ultimate causes." *American Zoologist* 38 (1): 251–259.

Brown, Wendy (1998). "El lobo returns." *International Wolf* 8 (4): 3–7.

Burrows, R. (1994). "Demographic changes and social consequences in wild dogs 1964–92." In A. R. E. Sinclair and P. Arcese (eds.), *Serengeti II: Research, Management and Conservation of an Ecosystem.* Chicago: University of Chicago Press.

Burt, W. H., and Grossenheider, R. P. (1980). *A Field Guide to the Mammals of North America North of Mexico.* New York: Houghton Mifflin.

Busch, Robert H. (1995). *The Wolf Almanac.* New York: Lyons and Burford.

Carbyn, Ludwig N.; Fritts, Steven H.; Seip, Dale R. (1995). *Ecology and Conservation of Wolves in a Changing World.* Edmonton, AB: Canadian Circumpolar Institute.

Chrisler, Lois (1956). *Arctic Wild.* New York: Ballantine Books.

Coppinger, Ray, and Coppinger, Lorna (2001). *Dogs: A Startling New Understanding of Canine Origin, Behavior and Evolution.* New York: Scribner.

Courchampa, Franck; Rasmussen, Gregory S. A.; Macdonald, David W. (2002). "Small pack size imposes a trade-off between hunting and pup-guarding in the painted hunting dog *Lycaon pictus.*" *Behavioral Ecology* 13 (1): 20–27. http://beheco.oxfordjournals.org/cgi/content/full/13/1/20.

Creel, Scott; Creel, Nancy; Krebs, J.; Clutton-Brock, T. (eds.) (2002). *The African Wild Dog: Behavior, Ecology, and Conservation.* Princeton, NJ: Princeton University Press. p. 59.

Darwin, Charles (1859). *On the Origin of Species by Means of Natural Selection, or the Preservation of Favoured Races in the Struggle for Life* (1st ed.). London: John Murray. p. 1.

Day, D. (1981). *The Doomsday Book of Animals.* London: Ebury Press.

Dixon, Robyn (2004). "Sad howl of wolves recalls apartheid in South Africa." *Los Angeles Times,* October 17.

Dutcher, Jim, and Dutcher, Jamie (2002). *Wolves at Our Door.* New York: Touchstone.

Ferguson, Gary (1996). *The Yellowstone Wolves: The First Year.* Helena, MT: Falcon Press.

Fischer, Hank (1995). *Wolf Wars: The Remarkable Inside Story of the Restoration of Wolves to Yellowstone.* Helena, MT: Falcon Press.

Fox, Michael W. (1984). *The Whistling Hunters: Field Studies of the Asiatic Wild Dog* (Cuon alpinus). Albany, NY: State University of New York Press. p. 150.

Frame, L.; Malcolm, J. R.; Frame, G. W.; van Lawick, H. (1979). "Social organization of African wild dogs (*Lycaon pictus*) on the Serengeti Plains, Tanzania, 1967–1978." *Zeitschrift für Tierpsychologie* 50: 225–249.

Frantzen, M. A.; Ferguson, J. W. H.; de Villiers, M. S. (2001). "The conservation role of captive African wild dogs (*Lycaon pictus*)." *Biological Conservation* 100: 253–260.

Fullbright, T. E., and Hewitt, D. G. (2007). *Wildlife Science: Linking Ecological Theory and Management Applications.* London: Taylor and London/CRC Press.

Garcia-Moreno, J.; Matocq, M. D.; Roy, M. S.; Geffen, E.; Wayne, R. K. (1996). "Relationships and genetic purity of the endangered Mexican wolf based on analysis of microsatellite loci." *Conservation Biology* 10: 376–389.

Geist, V. (2008). "When do wolves become dangerous to humans?" http://westinstenv.org/wp-content/Geist_when-do-wolves-become-dangerous-to-humans.pdf.

Ginsberg, J. R.; Alexander, K. A.; Creel, S.; Kat, P. W.; McNutt, J. W.; Mills, M. G. L. (1995). "Handling and survivorship in the African wild dog (*Lycaon pictus*) in five ecosystems." *Conservation Biology* 9: 665–674.

Grooms, Steve (1993). *The Return of the Wolf.* Minocqua, WI: NorthWord Press.

Hampton, Bruce (1997). *The Great American Wolf.* New York: Owl Books.

Harrington, Fred H., and Paquet, Paul C. (eds.) (1982). *Wolves of the World: Perspectives of Behavior, Ecology and Conservation.* Park Ridge, NJ: Noyes Publications.

Holaday, Bobbie (2003). *The Return of the Mexican Gray Wolf: Back to the Blue.* Tucson: University of Arizona Press.

Koler-Matznick, Janice (2002). "The origin of the dog revisited." *Anthrozoös* 15 (2): 98–118.

Lopez, Barry H. (1978). *Of Wolves and Men.* New York: Charles Scribner's Sons.

Lumpkin, S. (2003). "Hiding in plain sight." Smithsonian National Zoological Park, October 8. http://nationalzoo.si.edu/ConservationAndScience/SpotlightOnScience/fleischer2003108.cfm

Macdonald, D. W., and Sillero-Zubiri, C. (2004). "Wild canids—an introduction and dramatis personae." In D. W. Macdonald and C. Sillero-Zubiri (eds.), *The Biology and Conservation of Wild Canids.* Oxford, UK: Oxford University Press. pp. 3–36.

Matthiessen, Peter (2005). "Large carnivores and the conservation of biodiversity: Biodiversity." In Justina C. Ray, Kent H. Redford, Robert Steneck, Joel Berger (eds.), *Large Carnivores and the Conservation of Biodiversity.* Washington, DC: Island Press. p. 526.

McIntyre, Rick (1995). *War Against the Wolf: America's Campaign to Exterminate the Wolf.* Stillwater, MN: Voyageur Press.

Mech, David (1994). "Wolf-pack buffer zones as prey reservoirs." *Science* 198 (4314): 320–321.

Mech, L. D. (1999). "Alpha status, dominance, and division of labor in wolf packs." *Canadian Journal of Zoology* 77: 1196–1203.

Mech, L. David (1970). *The Wolf: The Ecology and Behavior of an Endangered Species.* Minneapolis: University of Minnesota Press.

*National Geographic* (2007). "A Man Among Wolves." DVD.

Naughton, Lisa; Treves, Adrian; Grossberg, Rebecca; Wilcove, David. "Summary report: 2004/2005 public opinion survey: Wolf management in Wisconsin." www.geography.wisc.edu/livingwithwolves/reports/2004_Survey_Results_Executive_Summary.pdf.

Nowak, R. (1992). "Wolves: The great travelers of evolution." *International Wolf* 2 (4): 3–7.

Phillips, Michael K., and Smith, Douglas W. (1996). *The Wolves of Yellowstone.* Stillwater, MN: Voyageur Press.

Robbins, J. (1998). "Weaving a new web: Wolves change an ecosystem." *Zoogoer* 27 (3). http://nationalzoo.si.edu/publications/zoogoer/1998/3/weavingwolfweb.cfm.

Saunders, Stephen C. (2000). "Endangered and threatened wildlife and plants; Proposal to reclassify and remove the gray wolf from the list of endangered and threatened wildlife in portions of the conterminous United States; Proposal to establish three special regulations for threatened gray wolves." *Federal Register* 65 (135): 43449–43496.

Scott, J. (1991). *Painted Wolves: Wild Dogs of the Serengeti-Mara*. London: Harnish Hamilton.

Sillero-Zubiri, C., and Laurenson, M. K. (2001). "Interactions between carnivores and local communities: Conflict or co-existence?" In J. L. Gittleman, S. M. Funk, D. W. Macdonald, R. K. Wayne (eds.), *Carnivore Conservation*. London: Zoological Society of London. pp. 282–312.

Steinhart, Peter (1996). *The Company of Wolves*. New York: Random House.

Stenlund, Milton H. (1991). *Wolves in Minnesota*. Cambridge, MN: Adventure Publications.

Stephens, P. A.; Sillero-Zubiri, C.; Leader-Williams, N. (2001). "Impact of livestock and settlement on the large mammalian wildlife of Bale Mountains National Park, southern Ethiopia." *Biological Conservation* 100: 307–322.

Vanderpool, Tim (2002). "Politics of the wolf." *Tucson Weekly*, June 20–26. http://www.tucsonweekly.com/tucson/politics-of-the-wolf/Content?oid=1070416.

Wilkinson, Todd (2007). "A brewing backlash against lobos." *Wildlife Conservation*, March/April.

Wozencraft, W. C.; Wilson, D. E.; Reeder, D. M. (eds.) (2005). *Mammal Species of the World* (3rd ed.). Baltimore: Johns Hopkins University Press.

Zarnke, R. L.; Evermann, J.; VerHoef, J. M.; et al. (2001). "Serologic survey for canine coronavirus in wolves from Alaska." *Journal of Wildlife Diseases* 37(4): 740–745.

Ziswiler, V. (1967). *Extinct and Vanishing Animals*. New York: Springer-Verlag. p. 113.

# Sources

African Wild Dog Conservancy, http://www.awdconservancy.org.

African Wildlife Foundation, http://www.awf.org.

Alaskawolves.org, http://www.alaskawolves.org.

Animal Planet (n.d.). "Gray wolf." Corwin's Carnival of Creatures. http://web.archive.org/web/20060524181949/http://animal.discovery.com/fansites/jeffcorwin/carnival/lilmammal/wolf.html.

Animal Welfare Institute (1983). "Persecution and hunting." Endangered Species Handbook. http://www.endangeredspecieshandbook.org/persecution.php.

Anonymous (n.d.). "Falkland Island fox." http://www.thewebsiteofeverything.com/weblog/pivot/entry.php?id=494.

Anonymous (2004). "Indian wolves are world's oldest." BBC News, July 17. http://news.bbc.co.uk/1/hi/world/south_asia/3804817.stm.

Anonymous (2005). "Wolves in national park becoming isolated, say biologists." CBC News, January 10. http://www.cbc.ca/health/story/2005/01/10/wolves-inbreeding050110.html.

Anonymous (2007). "Wolves find happy hunting grounds in Yellowstone National Park." ScienceDaily.com, August 31. http://www.sciencedaily.com/releases/2007/08/070830114825.htm.

Arizona Game and Fish Department (n.d). "Mexican Wolf Blue Range Reintroduction Project: Frequently asked questions." http://www.azgfd.gov/w_c/wolf/faq.shtml.

Binder, David (2000). "Wolves: From brink of extinction to the edge of the city." *New York Times,* March 14. http://www.nytimes.com/2000/03/14/science/wolves-from-brink-of-extinction-to-the-edge-of-the-city.html.

California Wolf Center, Mexican Wolf Project, http://www.californiawolfcenter.org/project.htm.

Conservation Science Institute (n.d.). "The gray wolf (*Canis lupus*)." http://conservationinstitute.org/pcn/pcn_gray_wolf.htm.

Defenders of Wildlife (n.d.). "Wolf predation plays small role in livestock losses in 2005." http://www.defenders.org/programs_and_policy/wildlife_conservation/solutions/wolf_compensation_trust/wolf_predation_and_livestock_losses.php.

Frankfurt Zoological Society, http://www.zgf.de/?id=14&language=en.

Grooms, Steve (2000). "Legends of the 'outlaw' wolves." *International Wolf* 10 (4). http://www.wolf.org/wolves/news/iwmag/2000/winter/winter2000.asp.

Heywood, N. C. "Antarctic fox (*Dusicyon australis*)." http://www.uwsp.edu/gEo/faculty/heywood/Geog358/extinctm/AntarFox.htm.

International Union for the Conservation of Nature, Hyaena Specialist Group. "Striped hyaena: Association with other species." http://www.hyaenidae.org/the-hyaenidae/spotted-hyena-crocuta-crocuta/crocuta-association-with-other-species.html.

International Wolf Center, http://www.wolf.org/wolves.

International Wolf Center (1996). Canis lupus: *Meet the Gray Wolf.* Ely, MN: International Wolf Center.

International Wolf Center (n.d.). "Frequently asked questions about wolves." http://www.wolf.org/wolves/learn/basic/faqs/faq.asp.

International Wolf Center (2004). "Wolf pup development." http://www.wolf.org/wolves/learn/basic/biology/pupdevelopment.asp.

International Wolf Center (2005). "Wolf depredation." http://www.wolf.org/wolves/learn/intermed/inter_mgmt/depstat.asp.

Line, Les (1996). "In long-running wolf-moose drama, wolves recover from disaster." *New York Times,* March 19. http://www.nytimes.com/1996/03/19/science/in-long-running-wolf-moose-drama-wolves-recover-from-disaster.html.

Maas, Peter (2005). "*Dusicyon australis.*" The Extinction Website. http://www.petermaas.nl/extinct/speciesinfo/falklandwolf.htm.

Mowry, Tim (2008). "Game board says yes to aerial shooting of wolves." *Fairbanks Daily News-Miner,* March 8. http://newsminer.com/news/2008/mar/08/game-board-says-yes-aerial-shooting-wolves.

NationalGeographic.com (n.d.). "African wild dog." http://animals.nationalgeographic.com/animals/mammals/african-hunting-dog.html.

NationalGeographic.com (n.d.). "Arctic fox." http://animals.nationalgeographic.com/animals/mammals/arctic-fox.html.

National Parks. "Red wolf (*Canis rufus*)." http://www.eparks.org/wildlife_protection/wildlife_facts/redwolf.asp.

National Wolfdog Alliance, www.wolfdogalliance.org.

Nordsven, Ryan (n.d.). "Red wolves of Alligator River: You win some, you lose some." Field Trip Earth. http://www.fieldtripearth.org/article.xml?id=1334.

Red Wolf Coalition (n.d.). "Historic timeline for the endangered red wolf." http://www.redwolves.com/about_recovery/timeline.html.

Rincon, Paul (2004). "Claws reveal wolf survival threat." BBC News, April 8. http://news.bbc.co.uk/1/hi/sci/tech/3602741.stm.

Route, Bill, and Aylsworth, Linda. "1999 world wolf status report." http://www.de5store.com/PDFArkiverade/wolves99.pdf.

Schmidt, Paul L., and Mech, L. David (1997). "Wolf pack size and food acquisition." *American Naturalist* 150 (4): 513–517. http://www.npwrc.usgs.gov/resource/mammals/wpsize/index.htm.

Sillero-Zubiri, Claudio; Hoffmann, Michael; Macdonald, David W. (eds.) (2004). *Canids: Foxes, Wolves, Jackals and Dogs.* International Union for the Conservation of Nature, Species Survival Commission, Canid Specialist Group. Gland, Switzerland: International Union for the Conservation of Species. http://www.canids.org/PRELIMS.pdf.

United States Department of Agriculture (1999). "Livestock guarding dogs: Protecting sheep from predators." Agriculture Information Bulletin #588. http://www.nal.usda.gov/awic/companimals/guarddogs/guarddogs.htm.

US Fish and Wildlife Service, Mexican Gray Wolf Recovery Program, http://www.fws.gov/southwest/es/mexicanwolf.

US Fish and Wildlife Service (1997). "Endangered red wolves." http://library.fws.gov/Pubs4/endangered_red_wolves.pdf.

US Fish and Wildlife Service (2009). "Gray wolf (*Canis lupus*): Biologue." March. http://www.fws.gov/Midwest/wolf/aboutwolves/biologue.htm.

US Fish and Wildlife Service, Mexican Wolf Recovery Program (2006). "Natural history." Mar 2. http://www.fws.gov/southwest/es/mexicanwolf/natural_history.shtml.

US Fish and Wildlife Service, Mexican Wolf Recovery Program (2006). "Mexican Wolf Recovery Program chronology." February 8. http://www.fws.gov/southwest/es/mexicanwolf/chronology.shtml.

US Fish and Wildlife Service, Alligator River/Pea Island National Wildlife Refuge (2008). "Red wolf update." http://www.fws.gov/alligatorriver/news/2008%20News/news-RedWolfUpdate.html.

Wildlife Committee of the Rio Grande Chapter of the Sierra Club and the Mexican Wolf Coalition (1993). *The Mexican Wolf.* Albuquerque, NM: Sierra Club.

Willems, Robert A. (1994/1995). "The wolf-dog hybrid: An overview of a controversial animal." *Animal Welfare Information Center Newsletter* 5 (4). http://www.nal.usda.gov/awic/newsletters/v5n4/5n4wille.htm.

Wisconsin Department of Natural Resources, Wisconsin Wolf Science Committee (2007). "Effects of wolves and other predators on farms in Wisconsin: Beyond verified losses." May. Pub-ER-658 2007. http://www.dnr.state.wi.us/org/land/er/publications/pdfs/wolf_impact.pdf.

Wolf Conservation Center, http://www.nywolf.org.

## Felines

Aldama, J. J.; Beltrán, J. F.; Delibes, M. (1991). "Energy expenditure and prey requirements of free-ranging Iberian lynx in south-western Spain." *Journal of Wildlife Management* 55 (4): 635–641.

Asadi, H. (1997). "The environmental limitations and future of the Asiatic cheetah in Iran." International Union for the Conservation of Nature, Species Survival Commission, Cat Specialist Group. www.catsg.org/cheetah/05_library/5_3.../A/ Asadi_1997_Environmental_limitations_and_future_of_Asiatic_cheetah_in_Iran. pdf.

Barnett, R.; Yamaguchi, N.; Barnes, I.; Cooper, A. (2006). "Lost populations and preserving genetic diversity in the lion *Panthera leo*: Implications for its *ex situ* conservation." *Conservation Genetics* 7 (4): 507–514. http://www.springerlink. com/content/t55636224161vn37.

Beltrán, J. F.; Aldama, J.; Delibes, M. (1992). "Ecology of the Iberian lynx in Doñana, SW Spain." In B. Bobek (ed.), *Global Trends in Wildlife Management*, Volume 2. Krakow, Poland: Swiat Press.

Bunsha, D. (2005). "Left high and dry." *Frontline* 22 (11), May 21. http://www.hindu. com/fline/fl2211/stories/20050603002308300.htm.

Bunsha, D. (2005). "A kingdom too small." *Frontline* 22 (10), May 7. http://www. hinduonnet.com/fline/fl2210/stories/20050520000106500.htm.

Burger, J., and Hemmer, H. (2006). "Urgent call for further breeding of the relic zoo population of the critically endangered Barbary lion (*Panthera leo leo* Linnaeus 1758)." *European Journal of Wildlife Research* 52 (1): 54–58.

Chellam, R., and Johnsingh, A. J. T (1999). "Translocating Asiatic lions." *India Re-Introduction News* (18): 11.

Cracraft, J.; Feinstein, J.; Vaughn, J.; Helm-Bychowski, K. (1998). "Sorting out tigers (*Panthera tigris*): Mitochondrial sequences, nuclear inserts, systematics, and conservation genetics." *Animal Conservation* 1: 139–150.

Delibes, M. (1989). "Factors regulating a natural population of lynxes." *Proceedings of the Conference on Reintroduction of Predators in Protected Areas*, Torino, Italy. pp. 96–99.

Ferreras, P.; Aldama, J. J.; Beltrán, J. F.; Delibes, M. (1992). "Rates and causes of mortality in a fragmented population of Iberian lynx, *Felis pardina*, Temminck, 1824." *Biological Conservation* 61: 197–202.

Fulbright, Timothy E., and Hewitt, David G. (eds.) (2007). *Wildlife Science: Linking Ecological Theory and Management Applications*. Boca Raton, FL: CRC Press.

Gibb, J. A. (1990). "The European rabbit." In J. A. Chapman and J. E. C. Flux (eds.), *Rabbits, Hares and Pikas: Status Survey and Conservation Action Plan*. Gland, Switzerland: International Union for the Conservation of Nature. pp. 116–120.

Johnsingh, A. J. T.; Goyal, S. P.; Qureshi, Qamar (2007). "Preparations for the reintroduction of Asiatic lion *Panthera leo persica* into Kuno Wildlife Sanctuary, Madhya Pradesh, India." *Oryx* 41: 93–96. doi:10.1017/S0030605307001512.

Johnsingh, A. J. T. (2004). "Is Kuno Wildlife Sanctuary ready to play second home to Asiatic lions?" *Newsletter of Wildlife Institute of India* 11 (4). http://www.wii. gov.in/publications/newsletter/winter04/wii%20in%20field.htm.

Luo, S. J., et al. (2004). "Phylogeography and genetic ancestry of tigers (*Panthera tigris*)." *PLoS Biology* 2 (12): e442. doi:10.1371/journal.pbio.0020442.

Matthiessen, Peter (2005). "Large carnivores and the conservation of biodiversity: Biodiversity." In Justina C. Ray, Kent H. Redford, Robert Steneck, Joel Berger (eds.), *Large Carnivores and the Conservation of Biodiversity*. Washington, DC: Island Press. p. 526.

Matthiessen, Peter, and Hornocker, Maurice (2001). *Tigers in the Snow*. Giroux, NY: North Point Press.

Miquelle, D. G.; Smirnov, E. N.; Goodrich, J. M. (2005). *Tigers of Sikhote-Alin Zapovednik: Ecology and Conservation*. Vladivostok, Russia: PSP. pp. 25–35.

Mitchell-Jones, A. J., et al. (1999). *The Atlas of European Mammals*. London: Academic Press.

Nowak, R. M. (1999). *Walker's Mammals of the World*. Baltimore: Johns Hopkins University Press.

Nowell, K., and Jackson, P. (eds.) (1996). "African lion, *Panthera leo* (Linnaeus, 1758)." In *Wild Cats: Status Survey and Conservation Action Plan*. International Union for the Conservation of Nature, Species Survival Commission, Cat Specialist Group. Gland, Switzerland: International Union for the Conservation of Nature. pp. 17–21. http://carnivoractionplans1.free.fr/wildcats.pdf.

O'Brien, S. J., et al. (1987). "Evidence for African origins of the founders of the Asiatic lion ssp." *Zoo Biology* 6 (2): 99–116.

Palomares, F.; Rodríguez, A.; Laffitte, R.; Delibes, M. (1991). "The status and distribution of the Iberian lynx, *Felis pardina* (Temminck), in the Coto Doñana area, SW Spain." *Biological Conservation* 57: 159–169.

Prynn, David (2002). *Amur tiger*. Edinburgh, Scotland: Russian Nature Press.

Rodríguez, A., and Delibes, M. (1992). "Current range and status of the Iberian lynx *Felis pardina* Temminck 1824 in Spain." *Biological Conservation* 61: 189–196.

Russello, M. A., et al. (2005). "Potential genetic consequences of a recent bottleneck in the Siberian tiger of the Russian Far East." *Conservation Genetics* 5 (5): 707–713. doi:10.1007/s10592-004-1860-2.

Seidensticker, John (1999). *Riding the Tiger: Tiger Conservation in Human-Dominated Landscapes*. Cambridge, UK: Cambridge University Press.

Sunquist, Mel, and Sunquist, Fiona (2002). *Wild Cats of the World*. Chicago: University of Chicago Press.

Thapar, Valmik (2004). *Tiger: The Ultimate Guide*. CDS Books.

Villafuerte, R., and Moreno, S. (1991). "Rabbit haemmorragic disease (RHD) in Doñana National Park (DNP)." *20th Congress of the International Union of Game Biologists*. pp. 107–108.

Werdelin, L. (1981). "The evolution of lynxes." *Annales Zoologici Fennici* 18: 37–71.

West, P. M., and Packer, C. (2002). "Sexual selection, temperature, and the lion's mane." *Science* 297: 1339–1343.

Wozencraft, W. C. (2005). "*Galidictis grandidieri*." In D. E. Wilson and D. M. Reeder (eds.), *Mammal Species of the World* (3rd ed.). Baltimore: Johns Hopkins University Press. p. 533. http://www.bucknell.edu/msw3.

Yamaguchi, N., and Haddane, B. (2002). "The North African Barbary lion and the Atlas Lion Project." *International Zoo News* 49: 465–481.

## Sources

Anonymous (2007). "EU 'put Portugal wildlife under threat.'" BBC News, April 8. http://news.bbc.co.uk/2/hi/science/nature/6530743.stm.

Anonymous (2005). "Iberian lynx in 'gravest danger.'" BBC News, March 10. http://news.bbc.co.uk/2/hi/science/nature/4336071.stm.

Anonymous (2005). "Hopes raised by Spain lynx births." BBC News, March 30. http://news.bbc.co.uk/1/hi/sci/tech/4394005.stm.

Anonymous (2003). "India seeks Iran's help with cheetahs." BBC News, January 31. http://news.bbc.co.uk/1/hi/world/south_asia/2714553.stm.

Asha for Education (n.d.). "Kuno Education Project, Sheopur District, Madhya Pradesh." http://www.ashanet.org/projects/project-view.php?p=421.

Asiatic Lion Information Centre (n.d.). "The Asiatic lion captive breeding programme." http://www.asiatic-lion.org/captive.html.

Asiatic Lion Information Centre (2007). "The Asiatic lion news archive–2007." September 11. http://www.asiatic-lion.org/news/news-0758.html.

Asiatic Lion Information Centre (n.d.). "Past and present distribution of the lion in North Africa and Southwest Asia." http://www.asiatic-lion.org/distrib.html.

Asiatic Lion Information Centre (n.d.). "The lion of India." http://www.asiatic-lion.org/intro.html.

Black and White Galleries, http://www.theblackandwhitegalleries.com.

Cat Action Treasury, http://felidae.org.

CatChannel.com, http://www.catchannel.com.

Central Zoo Authority of India, Government of India, http://www.cza.nic.in.

Chadwick, Alex (2007). "Biologist keeps track of Iran's rare cheetahs." NPR.org, March 12. http://www.npr.org/templates/story/story.php?storyId=7754357.

Clayton, Jonathan (2008). "Meet the other Tiger Woods—this one might save his species from extinction." Times Online, April 7. http://www.timesonline.co.uk/tol/news/world/africa/article3694774.ece.

International Union for the Conservation of Nature, Cat Specialist Group (n.d.). "Iberian lynx, *Lynx pardinus* (Temminck, 1827)." http://lynx.uio.no/jon/lynx/lynxib02.htm.

International Union for the Conservation of Nature (2006). "*Panthera tigris ssp. sumatrae.*" 2006 IUCN Red List of Threatened Species.

International Union for the Conservation of Nature (2007). "*Panthera leo persica.*" 2007 IUCN Red List of Threatened Species.

International Union for the Conservation of Nature (2006). "*Acinonyx jubatus venaticus.*" 2006 IUCN Red List of Threatened Species.

International Union for the Conservation of Nature (1987). "Position statement on the translocation of living organism." September 4. Gland, Switzerland: International Union for the Conservation of Nature.

Kamat, K. L. (2009). "The Indian cheetah." http://www.kamat.com/kalranga/prani/predators/cheetah.htm.

Large Carnivore Initiative for Europe, http://www.lcie.org.

Mielke, Mark (2008). "Animal bio: Barbary lion." Associated Content, August 13. http://www.associatedcontent.com/article/929613/animal_bio_barbary_lion.html?cat=58.

Miquelle, Dale G.; Stephens, Philip A.; Smirnov, Evgeny N.; Goodrich, John M.; Zaumyslova, Olga J.; Myslenkov, Alexander E. (2005). "Tigers and wolves in the Russian Far East: Competitive exclusion, functional redundancy, and conservation implications." In Justina C. Ray, Kent H. Redford, Robert Steneck, Joel Berger (eds.), *Large Carnivores and the Conservation of Biodiversity*. Washington, DC: Island Press. pp. 179–207.

Mongabay.com, http://www.mongabay.com.

National Geographic, Animals, http://animals.nationalgeographic.com.

Olney, H. (2009). "*Lynx pardinus*." Animal Diversity Web. http://animaldiversity.ummz.umich.edu/site/accounts/information/Lynx_pardinus.html.

Owen, James (2008). "'Tower lions' may help resurrect extinct African breed?" NationalGeographic.com, April 4. http://news.nationalgeographic.com/news/2008/04/080404-tower-lions.html.

Save China's Tigers, http://english.savechinastigers.org.

Save the Tiger Fund, http://www.savethetigerfund.org.

Sumatran Tiger Trust, http://www.tigertrust.info.

Tigers in Crisis, http://www.tigersincrisis.com/siberian_tiger.htm.

Toronto Zoo, animal fact sheets, http://www.torontozoo.com/Animals.

United Nations Development Programme (n.d.). "Conservation of the Asiatic cheetah in the Islamic Republic of Iran." http://www.undp.org.ir/project.aspx?projectID=26.

United Nations Environment Programme, World Conservation Monitoring Centre (n. d.). "Iberian lynx—*Lynx pardinus* (Temminck, 1827)." http://www.unep-wcmc.org/species/data/species_sheets/iberlynx.htm.

Ward, Dan (2004). "The Iberian lynx emergency." www.lcie.org/Docs/Iberian%20lynx/Ward%20REP%20The%20Iberian%20lynx%20emergency.pdf.

Wild About Cats (n.d.). "Asiatic cheetah." http://www.wildaboutcats.org/asiatic.htm.

Wildlife Conservation Society (n.d.). "Siberian Tiger Project." http://www.wcs.org/globalconservation/Asia/russia/siberiantigerproject.

Wildlife Conservation Society (n.d.). "Studies of the Asiatic cheetah in Iran." http://www.savingwildplaces.com/swp-home/swp-explorationandsurvey/239531.

Wildlife Conservation Society (n.d.). "Iran Cheetah Project." http://www.wcs.org/globalconservation/Asia/irancheetahproject.

Wildlife Conservation Trust of India, http://www.asiaticlion.org.

WildlifeExtra.com (n.d.). "Cheetahs in Iran; the last stronghold of the Asiatic cheetah." http://www.wildlifeextra.com/go/news/cheetah-iran.html.

World Wildlife Foundation (n.d.). "Sumatran tiger." http://www.panda.org/about_wwf/ what_we_do/species/about_species/species_factsheets/tigers/sumatran_tiger/index. cfm.

## Marine Mammals

Amstrup, S. C. (2003). "Polar bear (*Ursus maritimus*)." In G. A. Feldhamer, B. C. Thompson, J. A. Chapman (eds.), *Wild Mammals of North America: Biology, Management, and Conservation*. Baltimore: John Hopkins University Press. pp. 587–610.

Amstrup, S. C.; Durner, G. M.; McDonald, T. L.; Mulcahy, D. M.; Garner, G. W. (2001). "Comparing movement patterns of satellite-tagged male and female polar bears." *Canadian Journal of Zoology* 79: 2147–2158.

Amstrup, S. C.; McDonald, T. L.; Stirling, I. (2001). "Polar bears in the Beaufort Sea: A 30 year mark-recapture case history." *Journal of Agricultural, Biological, and Environmental Statistics* 6: 221–234.

Amstrup, S. C. (2000). "Polar bear." In J. J. Truett and S. R. Johnson (eds.), *The Natural History of an Arctic Oil Field: Development and Biota*. New York: Academic Press. pp. 133–157.

Amstrup, S. C., and Durner, G. M. (1995). "Survival rates of radio-collared female polar bears and their dependent young." *Canadian Journal of Zoology* 73: 1312–1322.

Amstrup, S. C., and Gardner, C. (1994). "Polar bear maternity denning in the Beaufort Sea." *Journal of Wildlife Management* 58 (1): 1–10.

Amstrup, S. C. (1993). "Human disturbances of denning polar bears in Alaska." *Arctic* 46 (3): 246–250.

Chen, P., and Hua, Y. (1989). "Distribution, population size and protection of *Lipotes vexillifer*." In W. F. Perrin, R. L. Brownell Jr., K. Zhou, J. Liu (eds.), *Biology and Conservation of the River Dolphins*. Occasional Papers of the International Union for the Conservation of Nature Species Survival Commission, Number 3. pp. 78–81.

Chen, P.; Liu, P.; Liu, R.; Lin, K.; Pilleri, G. (1980). "Distribution, ecology, behaviour and protection of the dolphins in the middle reaches of the Changjiang River (Wuhan-Yueyang)." *Oceanologica Limnologia Sinica* 11: 73–84.

Chen, P.; Zhang, X.; Wei, Z.; Zhao, Q.; Wang, X.; Zhang, G.; Yang, J. (1993). "Appraisal of the influence upon baiji, *Lipotes vexillifer* by the Three-Gorge Project and conservation strategy." *Acta Hydrobiologica Sinica* 17: 101–111.

Durner, G. M.; Amstrup, S. C.; Ambrosius, K. J. (2001). "Remote identification of polar bear maternal den habitat in northern Alaska." *Arctic* 54: 115–121.

Durner, G. M.; Amstrup, S. C.; McDonald, T. L. (2000). "Estimating the impacts of oil spills on polar bears." *Arctic Research of the United States* 14: 33–37.

Garner, G. W.; Amstrup, S. C.; Laake, J. L.; Manly, B. F. J.; McDonald, L. L.; Robertson, D. G. (eds.) (1999). *Marine Mammal Survey and Assessment Methods*. Rotterdam, The Netherlands: A. A. Balkema.

Kenyon, Karl W. (1970). *The Sea Otter in the Eastern Pacific Ocean.* Washington, DC: US Bureau of Sport Fisheries and Wildlife.

Lin, K.; Chen, P.; Hua, Y. (1985). "Population size and conservation of *Lipotes vexillifer.*" *Acta Zoologica Sinica* 5: 77–85.

Love, John A. (1992). *Sea Otters.* Golden, CO: Fulcrum.

Miller Jr., G. S. (1918). "A new river dolphin from China." *Smithsonian Miscellaneous Collections* 68 (9): 1–12.

Nickerson, Roy (1989). *Sea Otters: A Natural History and Guide.* San Francisco: Chronicle Books.

Paetkau, D.; Amstrup, S. C.; Born, E. W.; Calvert, W.; Derocher, A. E.; Garner, G. W.; Messier, F.; Stirling, I.; Taylor, M.; Wiig, O.; Strobeck, C. (1999). "Genetic structure of the world's polar bear populations." *Molecular Ecology* 8: 1571–1584.

Reeves, R. R.; Smith, B. D.; Wang, D.; Zhou, K. (2006). "*Lipotes vexillifer.*" 2006 IUCN Red List of Threatened Species.

Reeves, R. R.; Smith, B. D.; Crespo, E. A.; Notarbartolo di Sciara, G. (eds.) (2003). *Dolphins, whales and porpoises: 2002–2010 conservation action plan for the world's cetaceans.* International Union for the Conservation of Nature, Species Survival Commission, Cetacean Specialist Group. Gland, Switzerland: International Union for the Conservation of Nature.

Silverstein, Alvin; Silverstein, Virginia; Silverstein, Robert (1995). *The Sea Otter.* Brookfield, CT: Millbrook Press.

Simac, K.; Amstrup, S. C.; Weston York, G.; McDonald, T.; Durner, G. M.; Fischbach, A. (2001). "Forward looking infrared (FLIR): A new method for detecting maternal polar bear dens." *Abstracts, Society for Marine Mammalogy 14th Biennial Conference on the Biology of Marine Mammals,* November 28– December 3, 2001, Vancouver, BC.

Smith, B. D.; Zhou, K.; Wang, D.; Reeves, R. R.; Barlow, J.; Taylor, B. L.; Pitman, R. (2008). "*Lipotes vexillifer.*" 2008 IUCN Red List of Threatened Species.

Toy, Mary-Anne (2007). "Three Gorges Dam 'could be huge disaster.'" TheAge.com.au, September 27. http://www.theage.com.au/articles/2007/09/26/1190486394786.html.

Turvey, S. T.; Pitman, R. L.; Taylor, B. L., et al. (2007). "First human-caused extinction of a cetacean species?" *Biology Letters* 3 (5): 537–540. doi:10.1098/rsbl.2007.0292.

VanBlaricom, Glenn R. (2001). *Sea Otters.* Stillwater, MN: Voyageur Press.

Wang, D.; Zhang, X.; Liu, R. (1998). "Conservation status and the future of baiji and finless porpoise in the Yangtze River of China." *Report on the 8th International Symposium on River and Lake Environments,* Wuhan, China.

Zhou, K., and Li, Y. (1989). "Status and aspects of the ecology and behaviour of the baiji (*Lipotes vexillifer*) in the lower Yangtze River." In W. F. Perrin, R. L. Brownell Jr., K. Zhou, and J. Liu (eds.), *Biology and Conservation of the River Dolphins.* International Union for the Conservation of Nature Species Survival Commission Occasional Paper 3. pp. 86–91

Zhou, K.; Sun, J.; and Gao, A. (1993). "The population status of the baiji in the lower reaches of the Yangtze." Working paper presented to Baiji Population and Habitat Viability Workshop, Nanjing, China, June 1–4 1993.

# Sources

AFP (2007)."White dolphin appears from the brink." Discovery Channel, August 29. http://dsc.discovery.com/news/2007/08/29/whitedolphin_ani.html?category=animals&guid=20070824140030.

Animalinfo.org (2006). "Animal info—baiji." http://www.animalinfo.org/species/cetacean/lipovexi.htm.

Anonymous (2007). "Millions forced out by China dam." BBC News, October 13. http://news.bbc.co.uk/2/hi/asia-pacific/7042660.stm.

Anonymous (2002). "Rescue plan prepared for Yangtze River dolphins." *China Daily*, July 11. http://www.china.org.cn/english/environment/36657.htm.

Anonymous (2007). "China dam to displace millions more." Mwcnews.net, October 13. http://mwcnews.net/content/view/17341&Itemid=1.

Black, Richard (2006). "Last chance for China's dolphin." BBC News, June 27. http://news.bbc.co.uk/2/hi/science/nature/5122074.stm.

Blanchard, Ben (2006). "Interview: Chinese river dolphin almost certainly extinct." Reuters, December 13. http://www.alertnet.org/thenews/newsdesk/PEK307754.htm.

Brahic, Catherine (2007). "Yangtze river dolphin is almost certainly extinct." *New Scientist*, August 8. http://www.newscientist.com/article/dn12434-yangtze-river-dolphin-is-almost-certainly-extinct.html.

EDGE of Existence, http://www.edgeofexistence.org.

International Union for the Conservation of Nature, 2008 IUCN Red List of Threatened Species, www.iucnredlist.org.

Lin, Yang (2007). "China's Three Gorges Dam under fire." *Time*, October 12. http://www.time.com/time/world/article/0,8599,1671000,00.html.

Reuters (2007). "Rare dolphin seen in China, experts say." *New York Times*, August 30. http://www.nytimes.com/2007/08/30/world/asia/30china.html.

Rogan, C., et al., eds. (2000). "Report of the Standing Sub-Committee on Small Cetaceans." Cambridgeshire, UK: International Whaling Commission Scientific Committee. IWC/52/4. *52nd Meeting of the International Whaling Commission*, Adelaide, Australia.

The Alaska Sea Otter and Steller Sea Lion Commission (n.d.). "Sea otters." http://www.seaotter-sealion.org/seaotter/index.html.

US Fish and Wildlife Service, Marine Mammals Management (2008). "Sea otter: Southwest Alaska Sea Otter Recovery Team (SWAKSORT)." September 10. http://alaska.fws.gov/fisheries/mmm/seaotters/recovery.htm.

World Wildlife Fund (2006). "Chinese river dolphin (baiji) feared extinct, hope remains for finless porpoise." December 15. http://www.worldwildlife.org/who/media/press/2006/WWFPresitem898.html.

Xinhua (2007). "'Extinct' dolphin spotted in Yangtze River." *China Daily*, August 29. http://www.chinadaily.com.cn/china/2007-08/29/content_6066263.htm.

Yangtze Freshwater Dolphin Exhibition 2006 (2006). "The Chinese river dolphin is functionally extinct." December 13. www.baiji.org/fileadmin/pdf/131206_YFDE_Nrelease.pdf.

## Marsupials

Bostanci, A. (2005). "A devil of a disease." *Science* 307 (5712): 1035. PMID: 15718445.

Cronin, L. (1991). *Key Guide to Australian Mammals*. Balgowlah, Australia: Reed Books.

Dasey, Daniel (2005). "Researchers revive plan to clone the Tassie tiger." *Sydney Morning Herald*, May 15. http://www.smh.com.au/news/Science/Clone-again/200 5/05/14/1116024405941.html.

Fisher, D. O., et al. (2001). "The ecological basis of life history variation in marsupials: Appendix A." *Ecology* 82: 3531–3540.

Guiler, E. R. (1970). "Observations on the Tasmanian devil, *Sarcophilus harrisii II*. Reproduction, breeding and growth of pouch young." *Australian Journal of Zoology* 18: 63–70.

Hawkins, C. E.; McCallum, H.; Mooney, N.; Jones, M.; Holdsworth, M. (2008). "*Sarcophilus harrisii*." 2008 IUCN Red List of Threatened Species.

Heberle, Greg (2004). "Reports of alleged thylacine sightings in Western Australia." *Conservation Science Western Australia* 5 (1): 1–5. http://www.dec.wa.gov.au/images/stories/nature/science/cswa/v5n1/1-5.pdf.

Johnson, C. N., and Wroe, S. (2003). "Causes of extinction of vertebrates during the Holocene of mainland Australia: Arrival of the dingo, or human impact?" *Holocene* 13: 941–948.

Leigh, Julia (2002). "Back from the dead." *The Guardian*, May 30. http://www. guardian.co.uk/Archive/Article/0,4273,4424142,00.html.

Owen, David (2004). *Tasmanian Tiger: The Tragic Tale of How the World Lost Its Most Mysterious Predator*. Baltimore: Johns Hopkins University Press.

Pask, A. J.; Behringer, R. R.; Renfree, M. B. (2008). "Resurrection of DNA Function *In Vivo* from an Extinct Genome." *PLoS ONE* 3 (5): e2240. doi:10.1371/journal. pone.0002240.

Pemberton, D., and Renouf, D. (1993). "A field-study of communication and social behaviour of Tasmanian devils at feeding sites." *Australian Journal of Zoology* 41: 507–526.

Quammen, David (2008). "Contagious cancer: The evolution of a killer." *Harper's Magazine*, April. http://www.harpers.org/archive/2008/04/0081988.

Smith, Deborah (2005). "Tassie tiger cloning 'pie-in-the-sky science.'" *Sydney Morning Herald*, April 17. http://www.smh.com.au/news/science/tassie-tiger-cloning-pieinthesky-science/2005/02/16/1108500157295.html.

Strahan, R. (ed.) (1998). *The Mammals of Australia* (2nd ed., rev.). Sydney, Australia: Australian Museum, Reed New Holland.

Williams, Louise (1997). "Tassie tiger sighting claim in Irian Jaya." *Sydney Morning Herald*, April 15. http://www.smh.com.au/news/tassie-tiger/tassie-tiger-sighting-claim-in-irian-jaya/2002/09/25/1032734218360.html.

Woodford, James (1995). "New bush sighting puts tiger hunter back in business." *Sydney Morning Herald*, January 30. http://www.smh.com.au/ articles/2002/09/25/1032734216943.html.

# Sources

Animal Diversity Web, http://animaldiversity.ummz.umich.edu.

Australian Mammal Society, Australian Museum (n.d.). "Dickson's thylacine (*Nimbacinus dicksoni*)." http://www.lostkingdoms.com/facts/factsheet22.htm.

Australian Museum (n.d.). "Powerful thylacine (*Thylacinus potens*)." http://www. lostkingdoms.com/facts/factsheet38.htm.

Bryant, Sally, and Jackson, Jean (1999). *Tasmania's Threatened Fauna Handbook.* Tasmanian Government, Department of Primary Industries, Water, and Environment. pp. 190–193.

Currumbin Wildlife Sanctuary, http://www.cws.org.au.

Currumbin Wildlife Sanctuary (2008). "Little devils on Little Devils Day." May 30. http://www.cws.org.au/getcloser/images/pdf/little_devil_day_release.pdf.

Mercer, Phil (2008). "Hope over Tasmanian devil cancer." BBC News, April 1. http:// news.bbc.co.uk/go/pr/fr/-/2/hi/asia-pacific/7323794.stm.

Salleh, Anna (2004). "Rock art shows attempts to save thylacine." ABC Science Online, December 15. http://www.abc.net.au/science/news/stories/s1265476.htm.

Sanderson, Katharine (2008). "Tasmanian tiger gene lives again." *Nature,* May 20.

Skatssoon, Judy (2005). "Museum ditches thylacine cloning project." ABC Science Online, February 15. http://www.abc.net.au/science/news/stories/s1302459.htm.

Smithsonian National Museum of Natural History (n.d.). "*Ursus arctos:* Brown bear, grizzly bear." North American Mammals. http://www.mnh.si.edu/mna/image_ info.cfm?species_id=416.

Tasmania, Department of Primary Industries and Water (n.d.). "Tasmanian devil— frequently asked questions." http://www.dpiw.tas.gov.au/inter.nsf/WebPages/ BHAN-5372WP.

Tasmania, Department of Primary Industries and Water (2009). "Devil facial tumour disease." May 7. http://www.dpiw.tas.gov.au/inter.nsf/WebPages/LBUN-5QF86G.

Tasmania, Department of Primary Industries, Water, and Environment (2005). "Devil facial tumour disease update." August. www.dpiw.tas.gov.au/inter.nsf/ attachments/lbun-6fc79n/$file/dftdupdate.aug05.pdf.

Tasmania, Department of Primary Industries, Water, and Environment (2005). "Tasmanian devil facial tumor disease (DFTD): Disease management strategy." February. http://www.dpiw.tas.gov.au/inter.nsf/Attachments/LBUN- 6996MH/$FILE/DFTD_DMS_Feb05a.pdf.

Tasmania, Department of Primary Industries, Water, and Environment (2006). *Devil Facial Tumor Disease Newsletter,* March. http://www.dpiw.tas.gov.au/inter.nsf/ Attachments/LBUN-6MW7Y8/$FILE/devilNews_March2006.pdf.

Tasmania, Parks and Wildlife Service (n.d.). "Thylacine." http://www.parks.tas.gov.au/ index.aspx?base=971.

Tasmanian-Tiger.com, http://www.tasmanian-tiger.com.

Tassie Devil Cancer Awareness, www.tassiedevilcancer.com.

Young, Emma (2008). "Tasmanian tiger DNA 'lives' again." *New Scientist,* May 20. http://www.newscientist.com/article/dn13928-tasmanian-tiger-dna-lives-again. html.

## Pachyderms

Dinerstein, Eric (2003). *Return of the Unicorns: The Natural History and Conservation of the Greater One-Horned Rhinoceros*. West Sussex, NY: Columbia University Press.


# Sources

Anonymous (2008). "Chester zoo names its baby eastern black rhino." *Chester Chronicle*, December 16. http://www.chesterchronicle.co.uk/chester-news/chester-breaking-news/2008/12/16/chester-zoo-names-its-baby-eastern-black-rhino-59067-22485773.

Anonymous (2008). "Borneo rhino sanctuary for Tabin." *Daily Express*, December 12. http://www.dailyexpress.com.my/news.cfm?NewsID=61614.

Anonymous (2008). "Hope for rhinos." *Daily Record*, November 14. p. 7.

Anonymous (2008). "Zoo protects rhinos with native giant reed." *Horticulture Week*, December 12. p. 5.

Anonymous (2008). "Displaced by floods, rhinos released back into wild." *India Post*, December 12. http://www.rhinos-irf.org/en/art/352.

Anonymous (2008). "Rhino shot dead at top East Cape reserve." Legalbrief Today, December 16. http://www.legalbrief.co.za/article.php?story=20081216072642481.

Fletcher, Martin (2008). "Zimbabwe: Extinction looms in a paradise lost to guns, greed and hunger." Times Online, December 18. http://www.timesonline.co.uk/tol/news/environment/article5361568.ece.

International Rhino Foundation (n.d.). "Sumatran rhino (*Dicerorhinos sumatrensis*)." http://www.rhinos-irf.org/rhinos/sumatran.

International Rhino Foundation (n.d.) "IRF programs in Asia." http://www.rhinos-irf.org/asia.

International Union for the Conservation of Nature, http://www.iucn.org.

Jumbe, Mwanamkasi (2008). "Tanzania to import black rhinos from South Africa." *Citizen*, December 16. http://thecitizen.co.tz/newe.php?id=9292.

Lewa Wildlife Conservancy, http://www.lewa.org.

Radcliffe, Robin W. (2008). "Rhino conservation medicine program—Namibia update." April 7. http://intlrhinofoundation.wordpress.com/2008/04/07/preparing-to-crate-a-rhino-3.

Saving Rhinos.org (n.d.). "Javan rhino." http://www.savingrhinos.org/Javan-Rhino.html.

Ultimate Ungulate.com (2007). "*Dicerorhinus sumatrensis*: Sumatran rhinoceros." June 28. http://www.ultimateungulate.com/rhinosum.html.

Williams, Matt (2008). "Cheating lover sends rhino on rampage." *Courier Mail* (Australia), December 9. p. 13.


# Mustelidae

Belant, J.; Gober, P.; Biggins, D. (2008). "*Mustela nigripes*." 2008 IUCN Red List of Threatened Species.

Biggens, Dean E., and Kosoy, Michael Y. (2001). "Influences of introduced plague on North American mammals: Implications from ecology of plague in Asia." *Journal of Mammalogy* 82 (4): 906–916.

Lockhart, Michael J.; Thorne, E. Tom; Gober, Donald R. (2005). "A historical perspective on recovery of the black-footed ferret and the biological and political challenges affecting its future." In J. E. Roelle, B. J. Miller, J. L. Godbey, D. E. Biggins (eds.), *Recovery of the Black-Footed Ferret: Progress and Continuing Challenges*. US Geological Survey Scientific Investigations Report #2005-5293.

## Primates

Beck, B. B. (2001). "A vision for reintroduction." *AZA Communique*, September. pp. 20–21.

Castro, M. I.; Beck, B. B.; Kleiman, D. G.; Ruiz-Miranda, C. R.; Rosenberger, A. L. (1998). "Environmental enrichment in a reintroduction program for golden lion tamarins (*Leontopithecus rosalia*)." In D. J. Sheperdson, J. D. Mellen, M. Hutchins (eds.), *Second Nature: Environmental Enrichment for Captive Animals*. Washington, DC: Smithsonian Institution Press. pp 97–128.

Curtis, D. J.; Zaramody, A.; Rabetsimialona, O. D. (1995). "Sighting of the western gentle lemur *Hapalemur griseus occidentalis* in north-west Madagascar." *Oryx* 29: 215–217.

Glander, K. E., et al. (1989). "Consumption of cyanogenic bamboo by a newly discovered species of bamboo lemur." *American Journal of Primatology* 19: 119–124.

Goodman, S. M.; O'Conner, S.; Langrand, O. (1993). "A review of predation on lemurs: Implications for the evolution of social behavior in small, nocturnal primates." In Peter M. Kappeler and Jörg U. Ganzhorn (eds.), *Lemur Social Systems and their Ecological Basis*. New York: Plenum Press. pp. 51–66.

Grassi, C (2000). "Variability in habitat, diet, and social structure of *Hapalemur griseus griseus*." *American Journal of Physical Anthropology* Suppl. 30: 164.

Hawkins, A. F. A.; Chapman, P.; Ganzhorn, J. U.; Bloxam, Q. M. C.; Barlow, S. C.; Tonge, S. J. (1990). "Vertebrate conservation in Ankarana Special Reserve, northern Madagascar." *Biological Conservation* 54: 83–110.

Hawkins, A. F. A.; Durbin, J. C.; Reid, D. B. (1998). "The primates of the Baly Bay area, north-western Madagascar." *Folia Primatologica* 69: 337–345.

Jolly, A., et al. (2000). "Infant killing, wounding and predation in Eulemur and Lemur." *International Journal of Primatology* 21: (1) 20–40.

Kierulff, M. C. M.; Rylands, A. B.; de Oliveira, M. M. (2008). "*Leontopithecus rosalia*." 2008 IUCN Red List of Threatened Species.

Locantore, Jill, and Horton, Brendan (2002). "What primates think." *Zoogoer* 31 (4). http://nationalzoo.si.edu/Publications/ZooGoer/2002/4/primatethink.cfm.

Mahr, Krista (2008). "Do monkeys pay for sex?" *Time*, January 7.

McKee, Linda (2008). "Half world's primates are facing extinction." *Belfast Telegraph*, August 7.

Menzel, C. R., and Beck, B. B. (2000). "Homing and detour behavior in golden lion tamarin social groups." In S. Boinski and P. Garber (eds.), *On the Move: How and Why Animals Travel in Groups*. Chicago: University of Chicago Press. pp. 299–326.

Mittermeier, Russell A.; Konstant, William R.; Hawkins, Frank. (2005). *The Lemurs of Madagascar* (2nd ed.). Washington, DC: Conservation International. pp. 104-107

Petter, J. J., and Andriatsarafara, S. (1987). "Conservation status and distribution of lemurs in west and north-west Madagascar." *Primate Conservation* 8: 169–171.

Rakotondravony, D., and Goodman, S. M. (1998). "Predation on *Hapalemur griseus griseus* by *Boa manditra* (Boidae) in the littoral forest of eastern Madagascar." *Folia Primatologica* 69 (6) 405–408.

Rowe, Noel (1996). *The Pictorial Guide to the Living Primates.* East Hampton, NY: Pogonias Press.

Ruiz-Miranda, C. R.; Kleiman, D. G.; Dietz, J. M.; Moraes, E.; Grativol, A. D.; Baker, A. J.; Beck, B. B. (1999). "Food transfers in wild and reintroduced golden lion tamarins, *Leontopithecus rosalia*." *American Journal of Primatology* 48: 305–320.

Rylands, A. B.; Mittermeier, R. A.; Coimbra-Filho, A. F.; Heymann, E. W.; de la Torre, S.; Silva Jr., J. de S.; Kierulff, M. C. M.; Noronha, M. de A.; Röhe, F. (2008). *Marmosets and Tamarins Pocket Identification Guide.* Conservation International Tropical Pocket Guide Series #5. Arlington, VA: Conservation International.

Stoinski, T. S., and Beck, B. B. (2001). "Spontaneous tool use in captive, free-ranging golden lion tamarins." *Primates* 42 (4): 319–326.

Stoinski, T. S., and Beck, B. B. (2001). "Behavioral differences between captive-born golden lion tamarins and their wild-born offspring." *Annual Meeting of the International Society of Primatologists*, Adelaide, Australia, 7–12 January.

Tan, Chia L. (2000). "Patterns of resource use in three sympatric *Hapalemur* species in Ranomafana National Park, Madagascar." *American Journal of Physical Anthropology* Suppl. 30: 299.

Tan, Chia L. (1999). "Life history and infant rearing strategies of three *Hapalemur* species." *Primate Report* 54-1.

Tattersall, I. (1982). *The Primates of Madagascar.* New York: Columbia University Press.

Thalmann, U., and Rakotoarison, N. (1994). "Distribution of lemurs in central western Madagascar, with a regional distribution hypothesis." *Folia Primatologica* 64: 156–161.

Wright, P. C. (1999). "Lemur traits and Madagascar ecology: Coping with an island environment." *Yearbook of Physical Anthropology* 42: 31–72.

Wright, P. C. (1990). "Patterns of parental care in primates." *International Journal of Primatology* 11: (2) 89–102.

Wright, P. C., and Randriamanantena, M. (1989). "Behavioral ecology of three sympatric bamboo lemurs in Madagascar." *American Journal of Physical Anthropology* 78: 327.

# Sources

Andrainarivo, C., et al. (2009). "*Hapalemur griseus*." 2009 IUCN Red List of Threatened Species. http://www.iucnredlist.org/details/9673/0.

Andrainarivo, C., et al. (2009). "*Hapalemur alaotrensis*." 2009 IUCN Red List of Threatened Species. http://www.iucnredlist.org/details/9676/0.

Andrainarivo, C., et al. (2009). "*Hapalemur occidentalis*." 2009 IUCN Red List of Threatened Species. http://www.iucnredlist.org/details/9678/0.

Andrainarivo, C., et al. (2009). "*Hapalemur meridionalis*." 2009 IUCN Red List of Threatened Species. http://www.iucnredlist.org/details/136384/0.

Anonymous (2008). "Africa: Continent-wide UN action plan seeks to save the gorilla." AllAfrica.com, December 1. http://allafrica.com/stories/200812011245.html.

Anonymous (n.d.). "Lesser bamboo lemur, grey gentle lemur." BBC Science and Nature. http://www.bbc.co.uk/nature/wildfacts/factfiles/337.shtml.

Association of Zoos and Aquariums, Species Survival Plan Program, http://www.aza.org/ConScience/ConScienceSSPFact.
Gallay E. (1999). "*Hapalemur aureus*." Animal Diversity Web. http://animaldiversity.ummz.umich.edu/site/accounts/information/Hapalemur_aureus.html.

International Union for the Conservation of Nature, 2008 Red List of Threatened Species, http://www.iucnredlist.org

Jane Goodall Institute, http://www.janegoodall.org.

Smithsonian National Zoological Park (n.d.). "Golden lion tamarin conservation program." http://nationalzoo.si.edu/ConservationAndScience/EndangeredSpecies/GLTProgram/Learn/BasicFacts.cfm.
Smithsonian National Zoological Park (n.d.). "Small mammals." http://nationalzoo.si.edu/Animals/SmallMammals/default.cfm.

World Association of Zoos and Aquariums (n.d.). "2009—Year of the Gorilla." http://www.waza.org/conservation/campaigns21.php?view=campaigns&id=9.

## Reptiles

Behler, J. (1993). "Species survival plan for the Chinese alligator." *Crocodile Specialist Group Newsletter* 12 (4): 18.

Chen, B. (1990). "Preliminary studies of the home range of the Chinese alligator." In *Crocodiles: Proceedings of the 10th Working Meeting of the Crocodile Specialist Group*. Gland, Switzerland: International Union for the Conservation of Nature. pp. 43–46.

Fenwick, Treeva (2008). "Joy at giant tortoise eggs." BBC News, July 23. http://news.bbc.co.uk/1/hi/sci/tech/7522573.stm.

Gardner, Simon (2001). "Lonesome George faces own Galapagos tortoise curse." Planet Ark, February 6. http://www.planetark.com/dailynewsstory.cfm/newsid/9708/newsDate/06-Feb-2001/story.htm.

Jinzhong, F. (1994). "Conservation, management and farming of crocodiles in China." In *Crocodiles: Proceedings of the 2nd Regional Meeting of the Crocodile Specialist Group*. Gland, Switzerland: International Union for the Conservation of Nature and Conservation Commission of the Northern Territory, Australia.

Levy, Charles K. (1991). *Crocodiles and Alligators*. London: Apple Press.

Nicholls, Henry (2006). *Lonesome George: The Life and Loves of a Conservation Icon*. London: Macmillan Science.

Ross, C. (1989). *Crocodiles and Alligators*. New York: Facts on File.

Russello, Michael A.; Beheregaray, Luciano B.; Gibbs, James P.; Fritts, Thomas; Havill, Nathan; Powell, Jeffrey R.; Caccone, Adalgisa (2007). "Lonesome George is not alone among Galápagos tortoises." *Current Biology* 17 (9): R317–R318.

Soto, Alonso (2008). "Lonesome George may end bachelor days on Galapagos." Reuters, July 22. http://www.reuters.com/article/environmentNews/idUSN2247458920080722.

Townsend, Charles Haskins (1925). *1859–1944, The Galapagos Tortoises in Their Relation to the Whaling Industry*. New York: New York Zoological Society. pp. 55–135.

# Sources

Florida Museum of National History (n.d.). "Crocodilians: Natural history and conservation." http://flmnh.ufl.edu/cnhc.

National Audubon Society (1994). *Field Guide to North American Reptiles and Amphibians*. New York: Alfred A. Knopf.

Tortoise and Freshwater Specialist Group (2009). "*Geochelone nigra*." 2009 IUCN Red List of Threatened Species. http://www.iucnredlist.org/search/details.php/9011/summ.

University of Florida, Gainesville (n.d.). "The American alligator." http://agrigator.ifas.ufl.edu/gators.

# RESOURCES

## General Wildlife Conservation

**African Wildlife Foundation (AWF)**

www.awf.org

*The African Wildlife Foundation is dedicated to protecting the wildlife and wildlands of Africa. Find out more about its conservation programs, news and education, donation options, and how to get involved with your local chapter.*

**ARKive**

www.arkive.org

*Learn more about your favorite animals on this multimedia site featuring a wealth of animal information, including an extensive list of threatened species, as well as images and videos.*

**Association of Zoos and Aquariums (AZA)**

www.aza.org
8403 Colesville Road
Suite 710
Silver Spring, MD 20910-3314
Phone: 301-562-0777

*Discover how the AZA's animal management and conservation programs help animals around the world and find out how to get involved by becoming a member.*

**Audubon**

www.audubon.org
National Audubon Society
225 Varick Street
7th Floor
New York, NY 10014
Phone: 212-979-3000

*Find a wealth of information, including news and education, issues and action, donation and membership, and a listing of local chapters of this acclaimed, historic organization dedicated to the restoration of vital ecosystems.*

**Bushmeat-free Eastern Africa Network**

www.bushmeatnetwork.org

*Find out how you can help to create a bushmeat-free eastern Africa. Learn how this organization is increasing protection, seeking alternatives, and raising awareness to conserve the region's rich biodiversity.*

## Born Free Foundation

www.bornfree.org.uk
3 Grove House
Foundry Lane
Horsham
West Sussex
RH13 5PL
United Kingdom
E-mail: info@bornfree.org.uk

*Learn how this international wildlife charity is working throughout the world to stop the suffering of wild animals and protect threatened species in the wild.*

## Bushmeat Crisis Task Force

www.bushmeat.org

*Find out how you can assist this task force in building a public, professional, and government constituency to identify and support solutions that effectively respond to the bushmeat crisis in Africa and around the world.*

## Convention on International Trade in Endangered Species of Wild Fauna and Flora (CITES)

www.cites.org
CITES Secretariat
International Environment House
11 Chemin des Anémones
CH-1219 Châtelaine, Geneva
Switzerland
Phone: +41-(0)-22-917-81-39
E-mail: info@cites.org

*Access a broad array of information and resources related to CITES's aim to ensure that international trade in specimens of wild animals and plants does not threaten their survival.*

## Critical Ecosystem Partnership Fund (CEPF)

www.cepf.net
Conservation International
2011 Crystal Drive
Suite 500
Arlington, VA 22202
Phone: 703-341-2400

*Find out how you can apply for a grant to protect a vital ecosystem, access the CEPF project database, and visit the online resource center.*

## Defenders of Wildlife

www.defenders.org
1130 17th Street, NW
Washington, DC 20036
Phone: 800-385-9712

*Learn about this organization's programs and policies to conserve wildlife and habitats, discover how you can support the wildlife adoption center, and check out links to additional resources.*

## Endangered Wildlife Trust

www.ewt.org.za

*Participate in upcoming conservation events for threatened species and ecosystems and get information on working groups and partnerships, membership, and donation.*

## Field Trip Earth

www.fieldtripearth.org

*Access this global resource to read field researcher interviews and field reports, participate in discussion groups, and take multimedia "field trips" describing several different animals and conservation projects throughout the world.*

## The International Union for the Conservation of Nature Red List of Threatened Species (IUCN)

www.iucnredlist.org

*Get taxonomic and conservation status information on plants and animals facing a high risk of global extinction, as well as species that are categorized as extinct or extinct in the wild.*

## International Council for Game and Wildlife Conservation

www.cic-wildlife.org
PO Box 82
H-2092 Budakeszi
Hungary
Phone: +36-23-453-830

*Find news and information supporting the conservation and sustainable use of wildlife.*

## International Wildlife Conservation Society

www.internationalwildlife.org
PO Box 34
Pacific Palisades, CA 90272
Phone: 310-476-9305

*Virtually visit the 200,000-acre Sukila Phanta, or White Grass Plains, Wildlife Reserve in Pacific Palisades, California.*

## National Wildlife Federation (NWF)

www.nwf.org
11100 Wildlife Center Drive
Reston, VA 20190
Phone: 800-822-9919

*Discover a wealth of educational information, learn about the wildlife adoption program, visit the online store, and check out the link to regional NWF field offices.*

## The Nature Conservancy

www.nature.org
Worldwide Office
4245 North Fairfax Drive, Suite 100
Arlington, VA 22203-1606
Phone: 703-841-5300

*Participate in online conservation activities; get volunteer information; and find out where and how the Nature Conservancy works to preserve the plants, animals, and natural communities.*

## Smithsonian's National Zoological Park

www.nationalzoo.si.edu
National Zoo
3001 Connecticut Avenue NW
Washington, DC 20008
Phone: 202-633-3038

*Virtually visit our nation's zoo, learn about endangered species and amphibian conservation efforts, read about conservation research, and find out about internships and volunteer opportunities.*

## United Nations Environment Programme World Conservation Monitoring Centre

www.unep-wcmc.org
UNEP World Conservation Monitoring Centre
219 Huntingdon Road
Cambridge CB3 0DL
United Kingdom
Phone: +44 (0) 1223 277314

*Learn about threatened species, biodiversity and climate change, conservation programs, international policy and trade agreements, and news and events.*

## US Fish and Wildlife Service (USFWS)

www.fws.gov
Phone: 800-344-WILD

*Find detailed information on US conservation issues, including US conservation history, endangered species information, and links to state and local USFWS offices.*

## US Geological Survey

www.usgs.gov
USGS National Center
12201 Sunrise Valley Drive
Reston, VA 20192
Phone: 703-648-4000

*Access reliable scientific information on earth sciences; learn about water management and biological, energy, and mineral resources; and discover how this organization works to minimize loss of life and property from natural disasters.*

## Ventana Wildlife Society (VWS)

www.ventanaws.org
VWS Administrative Office
19045 Portola Drive, Suite F1
Salinas, CA 93908
Phone: 831-455-9514
E-mail: info@ventanaws.org

*Discover how this California-based conservation group is succeeding with species recovery projects, including one for the California condor.*

## Wildlife Conservation Society

www.wcs.org
2300 Southern Boulevard
Bronx, NY 10460
Phone: 718-220-5100

*Learn about local and global conservation efforts and get news, educational resources, and tips for getting involved in wildlife conservation.*

## World Association of Zoos and Aquariums (WAZA)

www.waza.org
WAZA Executive Office
Lindenrain 3
3012 Bern
Switzerland
E-mail: secretariat@waza.org

*Tour a virtual zoo and access a comprehensive listing of zoos and aquariums worldwide.*

## World Wildlife Fund (WWF)

www.wwf.org

*Find out how WWF is building a future where people live in harmony with nature and how you can get involved.*

# Amphibians

### Association of Zoos and Aquariums (AZA)
www.aza.org/ConScience/Amphibians_Intro

*Get information on the AZA's Amphibian Conservation Program.*

### Panama Golden Frog and Harlequin Frog
### Atelopus
### Encyclopedia of Life
www.eol.org/taxa/17194849

*Find general species information.*

### Project Golden Frog/*Atelopus* Conservation Trust
www.ranadorada.org/goldenfrog.html

*Learn about grants for research for and conservation of Panamanian golden frogs and other harlequin frogs.*

### Smithsonian National Zoological Park
www.nationalzoo.si.edu/Animals/ReptilesAmphibians/NewsEvents/golden_frog.cfm

*Learn about the zoo's captive-breeding program.*

### Golden Toad
### Animal Diversity Web (University of Michigan Museum of Zoology)
http://animaldiversity.ummz.umich.edu/site/accounts/information/Bufo_periglenes.html

*Get general species information.*

### WWF International
www.panda.org/about_our_earth/best_place_species/too_late/golden_toad.cfm

*Get a golden toad fact sheet.*

### Puerto Rican Crested Toad
### Puerto Rican Crested Toad Species Survival Plan

www.crestedtoadssp.org
1989 Colonial Parkway
Fort Worth, TX 76110
Phone: 817-759-7180

*Find species and conservation information.*

# Bears

**International Association for Bear Research and Management**

www.bearbiology.com

*Find news and information on conservation of all bear species.*

## Giant Panda
### Defenders of Wildlife

www.defenders.org/wildlife_and_habitat/wildlife/panda.php

*Learn about giant pandas, listen to a panda sound clip, investigate the adoption program, and find out about international and habitat conservation efforts.*

**Giant Panda Species Survival Plan**

www.giantpandaonline.org

*Get news, results of research studies, and information about the history of the giant panda and learn about captive management, giant panda conservation, and the management plan working in conjunction with the American Zoo and Aquarium Association.*

**Pandas International**

www.pandasinternational.org
PO Box 620335
Littleton, CO 80162
Phone: 303-933-2365
E-mail: info@pandasinternational.org

*Find educational information, FAQs, news, and research, much of which is geared toward children.*

**Smithsonian National Zoological Park**

http://nationalzoo.si.edu/Animals/GiantPandas

*Watch pandas on the panda cams, visit the photo gallery, get detailed species information, check out the online journal of the Fujifilm Giant Panda Habitat, and learn about the adopt a panda program.*

**Wolong Panda Club**

www.pandaclub.net

*Get general species and club information, news, pictures, research and conservation information and activities, and photos, and watch pandas at the Wolong Nature Reserve on a webcam.*

## WWF International

www.panda.org/about_wwf/what_we_do/species/about_species/species_factsheets/
giant_panda/index.cfm

*Get a giant panda fact sheet.*

# Birds

## BirdLife International

www.birdlife.org
Wellbrook Court
Girton Road
Cambridge CB3 0NA
United Kingdom
Phone: +44-(0)-1223-277-318
E-mail: birdlife@birdlife.org

*Learn about a wide variety of bird species and conservation efforts, get the latest news, and find out how to get involved with programs like the BirdLife Preventing Extinctions Programme and how to become a BirdLife Species Champion.*

## Peregrine Fund Global Raptor Information Network

www.globalraptors.org

*Access the raptor information database maintained by the Peregrine Fund.*

## The Peregrine Fund, World Center for Birds of Prey

www.peregrinefund.org
5668 West Flying Hawk Lane
Boise, ID 83709
Phone: 208-362-3716.
E-mail: tpf@peregrinefund.org

*Find a wealth of information on birds of prey; learn about conservation projects, avian biology, and conservation research; access the research library; check out the visitor center; and visit the online store.*

## California Condor
### BirdLife International

www.birdlife.org/datazone/species/index.html?action=SpcHTMDetails.
asp&sid=3821&m=0

*Get a California condor species fact sheet.*

## California Condor Conservation

www.cacondorconservation.org

*Find general species information, learn about the California Condor Recovery Program, get news, sign up for the newsletter, and get donation information.*

## The Peregrine Fund

www.peregrinefund.org/Explore_Raptors/vultures/cacondor.html

*Get general species information on the California condor.*

## Ventana Wildlife Society

www.ventanaws.org

*Learn about the organization's condor recovery projects.*

## Hawaiian Crow
### ARKive

www.arkive.org/hawaiian-crow/corvus-hawaiiensis/info.html

*Find detailed species information, including facts and status, range and habitat, threats and conservation, and videos and images.*

### Audubon

www.audubon2.org/watchlist/viewSpecies.jsp?id=98

*Get general species information on the Hawaiian crow.*

### BirdLife International

www.birdlife.org/datazone/species/index.html?action=SpcHTMDetails.
   asp&sid=5793&m=0

*Read a Hawaiian crow species fact sheet.*

## American Bald Eagle
### American Bald Eagle Foundation

www.baldeagles.org
PO Box 49
113 Haines Highway
Haines, AK 99827
Phone: 907-766-3094
E-mail: info@baldeagles.org

*Check out the American bald eagle nest cam; learn about bald eagles and this foundation; and get information on membership, the bald eagle preserve, and the Alaska Bald Eagle Festival.*

RESOURCES

## Cascades Raptor Center

www.eraptors.org
32275 Fox Hollow Road
PO Box 5386
Eugene, OR 97405
Phone: 541-485-1320

*Learn how this nonprofit nature center and wildlife hospital is helping to preserve raptors; view photos; find descriptions, history, and news articles; and learn about the resident raptor program and support and volunteer opportunities.*

## National Eagle Center

www.nationaleaglecenter.org
50 Pembroke Avenue/Box 242
Wabasha, MN 55981-0242
Phone: 877-332-4537

*Get general news and information on bald eagles, plus information on visiting the National Eagle Center in Wabasha, Minnesota.*

## Ventana Wildlife Society

www.ventanaws.org

*Find information about the organization's bald eagle recovery projects.*

## Harpy Eagle
### The Peregrine Fund

www.peregrinefund.org/explore_raptors/eagles/harpyeag.html

*Get general harpy eagle information*

### Smithsonian National Zoological Park, Migratory Bird Center

http://nationalzoo.si.edu/ConservationAndScience/MigratoryBirds/Science_Article/default.cfm?id=32

*Find general species information on the harpy eagle.*

## Mauritius Kestrel
### ARKive

www.arkive.org/mauritius-kestrel/falco-punctatus/info.html

*Find detailed species information, including facts and status, range and habitat, threats and conservation, and videos and images.*

**The Peregrine Fund**

www.peregrinefund.org/Explore_Raptors/falcons/mauritus.html

*Learn general species information about the Mauritius kestrel.*

**BirdLife International**

www.birdlife.org/datazone/species/index.html?action=SpcHTMDetails.
    asp&sid=3592&m=0

*Get a Mauritius kestrel fact sheet.*

**Maui Forest Bird Recovery Project**

www.mauiforestbird.org
2465 Olinda Road
Makawao, HI 96768
Phone: 808-573-0280
E-mail: poouli@hawaiiantel.net

*Learn about Maui forest birds, including conservation efforts, research, and habitat; get donation information; and access links to associated organizations and other conservation organizations on Maui.*

# Canines

**California Wolf Center**

www.californiawolfcenter.org
PO Box 1389
Julian, CA 92036
Phone: 619-234-WOLF
E-mail: info@californiawolfcenter.org

*Watch wolves on the wolf cam, find general information on wolves and wolf recovery projects, and learn about the conservation center in San Diego County, including visitor information, tours, and events.*

**International Wolf Center**

www.wolf.org

*Find news and educational and conservation program information, and learn about upcoming events and how you can get involved.*

# RESOURCES

## The Red Wolf Sanctuary

www.redwolf.org
PO Box 202
Rising Sun, IN 47040
Phone: 812-438-2306
E-mail: info@redwolf.org

*Learn about the Red Wolf Sanctuary; get progress and development updates; and find out about adoption programs, membership, and how to make donations.*

## Mexican Gray Wolf
### Cheyenne Mountain Zoo

www.cmzoo.org/conservation/programs/mexicanGrayWolves.asp

*Get general species information on the Mexican gray wolf.*

### Field Trip Earth

www.fieldtripearth.org/div_index.xml?id=11

*Visit Field Trip Earth's Mexican wolf information page, where you'll find species, project, and regional information; research information; and a media gallery.*

### US Fish and Wildlife Service

www.fws.gov/southwest/es/mexicanwolf

*Learn about the US Fish and Wildlife Service's Mexican Gray Wolf Recovery Program and find out how to get involved.*

## Red Wolf
### Defenders of Wildlife

www.defenders.org/wildlife_and_habitat/wildlife/red_wolf.php

*Get general species information, find out about the adoption program, and watch the video clip.*

### Field Trip Earth

www.fieldtripearth.org/div_index.xml?id=2

*Find information about the red wolf species and conservation projects, and visit the media gallery.*

RESOURCES

### The Red Wolf Coalition (RWC)

www.redwolves.com
PO Box 96
Columbia, NC 27925
Phone: 252-796-5600
E-mail: redwolf@redwolves.com

*Learn about the red wolf and the RWC's work to save this species, including its campaigns and projects, and get information on "Red Wolf Howling Safaris."*

### US Fish and Wildlife Service

www.fws.gov/redwolf

*Find information about the US Fish and Wildlife Service's Red Wolf Recovery Project, including news and reports, publications, resources, and ways to get involved.*

### Timber Wolf
### Conservation Science Institute

www.conservationinstitute.org/pcn/pcn_gray_wolf.htm

*Find general species information about the timber wolf.*

### Timber Wolf Information Network (TWIN)

www.timberwolfinformation.org
E110 Emmons Creek Road
Waupaca, WI 54981

*Find detailed wolf information, news, information on TWIN programs and its organizational background, and links to other sites.*

## Felines

### Big Cat Rescue

www.bigcatrescue.org
12802 Easy Street
Tampa, FL 33625
Phone: 813-920-4130
E-mail: info@bigcatrescue.org

*Learn about big cats; see images and videos; check out the kids' page; find out how this organization rescues and provides permanent homes for exotic cats that have been abused and abandoned; and find out how you can help.*

RESOURCES

**Lion Conservation Fund**

www.lionconservationfund.org
PO Box 380170
Cambridge, MA 02138

*Find out about the holistic approach being used to conserve and restore lion species, learn about projects, and get lion news and membership information.*

**Lion Research Center**

www.lionresearch.org

*Access a broad range of news and information focusing on research projects related to lions.*

**Save the Tiger Fund**

www.savethetigerfund.org
National Fish and Wildlife Foundation
1133 15th Street, NW, Suite 1100
Washington, DC 20005
Phone: 202-857-0166

*Get news and information on tigers and the conservation of various species and their habitats, and learn about research and initiatives to save the tiger.*

**The Tiger Foundation**

www.tigers.ca

*Hear tigers roar, tour the photo gallery, get detailed information on tiger species and conservation, and learn about the adopt-a-wild-tiger program.*

**Tigers in Crisis**

www.tigersincrisis.com

*Learn about the eight tiger subspecies; get news, status reports, and conservation information; and check out the online tiger journal and recommended books.*

**Asiatic Cheetah**
**Cheetah Conservation Fund**

www.cheetah.org
PO Box 2496
Alexandria, VA 22301-0496
Phone: 866-909-3399
E-mail: info@cheetah.org

*Access research and educational materials on cheetahs and their ecosystems, view cheetah videos, visit the online library, check out the Kids4Cheetahs page, and learn about sponsorship opportunities.*

**De Wildt Cheetah and Wildlife Trust**

www.dewildt.org.za

*Find information on the trust, its Wild Cheetah Project, and its research and education programs; news; an adoption program; a photo gallery; and tour information.*

**African Lion**

**Defenders of Wildlife**

www.defenders.org/wildlife_and_habitat/wildlife/lion.php

*Learn about African lions and find out about the adoption program.*

**Asiatic Lion**

**ARKive**

www.arkive.org/lion/panthera-leo/info.html

*Get detailed species information on the Asiatic lion, including facts and status, range and habitat, and threats and conservation efforts.*

**Asiatic Lion**

www.asiaticlion.org
Wildlife Conservation Trust of India
128, Star Plaza
Phulchhab Chowk
Rajkot—360 001
(Gujarat) India
Phone: +91-281-2444074
E-mail: info@asiaticlion.org

*Learn about the Asiatic lions, their habitats, the Gir Forest, and other endangered animals residing in Gir.*

**The Asiatic Lion Information Centre**

www.asiatic-lion.org

*Virtually visit the home of the European Asiatic Lion Breeding Programme, learn more about this species and conservation efforts, get the latest news, and check out the photo gallery.*

**Iberian Lynx**

**ARKive**

www.arkive.org/iberian-lynx/lynx-pardinus

*Get detailed species information on the Iberian lynx; view videos and images; and find facts and status, range and habitat, and threats and conservation efforts.*

**International Union for the Conservation of Nature, Species Survival Commission, Cat Specialist Group: Iberian Lynx Compendium**

www.catsg.org/iberianlynx/20_il-compendium/home/index_en.htm

*Access the latest news, status reports, and information from conferences and research studies.*

**SOS Lynx**

www.soslynx.org
SOS Lynx ADFF
Apartado 182
8550-909 Monchique
Portugal
E-mail: enquiries@soslynx.org

*Access the Iberian lynx video database, view photos, stay apprised of conservation news, and find out how to get involved.*

**Florida Panther**
**Defenders of Wildlife**

www.defenders.org/wildlife_and_habitat/wildlife/ panther.php

*Check out the Florida panther video and sound clips, learn more about the species, and find out about the adoption program.*

**Florida Panther National Wildlife Refuge**

www.fws.gov/floridapanther

**Florida Panther Net**

www.floridaconservation.org/panther

*Find detailed information on Florida panthers and their habitats, threats, and conservation efforts.*

**The Florida Panther Society**

www.panthersociety.org
PO Box 358683
Gainesville, FL 32635-8683
Phone: 386-397-2945

*Read recovery news about the Florida panther, learn more about the species, check out the Just for Kids page, and view photos.*

# RESOURCES

## Bengal Tiger
### Save the Tiger Fund

www.savethetigerfund.org/Content/NavigationMenu2/Community/TigerSubspecies/
BengalTigers/default.htm

*Learn more about the Bengal tiger species.*

### The Tiger Foundation

www.tigers.ca/home/world.html

*Find out about the plight of tigers worldwide and learn more about the Bengal tiger.*

## Siberian Tiger
### AMUR

www.amur.org.uk
Heathfield House
Ross Road
LEDBURY
Herefordshire HR8 2LE
United Kingdom
Phone: 0044-(0)-1225-851251

*Read about the conservation efforts for the Amur (Siberian) tiger and leopard, learn
more about the species, visit the online store, and find out about upcoming events.*

### The Tiger Foundation

www.tigers.ca/home/world.html

*Get general species information on the Siberian tiger.*

### Wildlife Conservation Society (WCS)

www.wcs.org/globalconservation/Asia/russia/siberiantigerproject

*Find out about the WCS's Siberian Tiger Project and how you can help.*

## South China Tiger
### Save China's Tigers

www.english.savechinastigers.org

*Learn about this conservation group's program to breed and rewild the remaining tiger
subspecies, get news and information, see images and videos, and learn about the adopt-
a-tiger program.*

RESOURCES

### Save the Tiger Fund

www.savethetigerfund.org/Content/NavigationMenu2/Community/TigerSubspecies/
SouthChinaTigers/default.htm

*Get general species information on the South China tiger.*

### The South China Tiger Project

www.tigers.ca/Foundation overview/TSCTP1.htm

*Learn about the Chinese State Forest Industry's South China Tiger Project, including a project overview, notes from the field, a travelogue, and news.*

### The Tiger Foundation

www.tigers.ca/Tigerworld/southchina.html

*Find general species information on the South China tiger.*

## Sumatran Tiger

### The Sumatran Tiger Trust

www.tigertrust.info
South Lakes Wild Animal Park
Broughton Road,
Dalton-in-Furness
Cumbria
LA15 8JR
United Kingdom
Phone: 01229-466086
E-mail: enquiries@tigertrust.info

*Discover how this organization is conserving the Sumatran and other tiger subspecies and learn about how you can help through their adoption program.*

### The Tiger Foundation

www.tigers.ca/Tigerworld/W3A1.html

*Get general species information on the Sumatran tiger.*

### WWF International

www.panda.org/about_wwf/what_we_do/species/about_species/species_factsheets/
tigers/sumatran_tiger/index.cfm

*Get a Sumatran tiger fact sheet.*

# Marine Mammals

## Polar Bear

International Association for Bear Research and Management, International Union for the Conservation of Nature, Species Survival Commission, Bear Specialist Group

www.bearbiology.com

*Read news and information about the conservation of all bear species.*

### National Snow and Ice Data Center, Arctic Sea Ice News and Analysis

http://nsidc.org/arcticseaicenews/index.html

*Find detailed information on the conditions of the Arctic climate and sea ice, which have a direct impact on polar bears.*

### National Wildlife Federation Adoption Center

https://online.nwf.org/site/Ecommerce/?VIEW_PRODUCT=true&product_
    id=3381&store_id=1681

*Get general polar bear species information and read about the adopt-a-polar-bear program.*

### Polar Bears International

www.polarbearsalive.org
105 Morris Street, Suite 188
Sebastopol, CA 95472

*Watch the polar bear webcam, get news and announcements, find out about the latest research, pick up teaching tools, and visit the gift shop.*

### International Union for the Conservation of Nature, Species Survival Commission, Polar Bear Specialist Group

http://pbsg.npolar.no

*Learn about the efforts of the Norwegian polar bear conservation group.*

### US Fish and Wildlife Service Alaska Regional Office

http://alaska.fws.gov/fisheries/mmm/polarbear/issues.htm
1011 East Tudor Road
Anchorage, AK 99503
Phone: 907-786-3309

*Get general species information about polar bears and conservation issues affecting them.*

## Yangtze River Dolphin

### The Nature Conservancy

www.nature.org/animals/mammals/animals/yangtzedolphin.html

*Find general species information on the Yangtze River dolphin.*

### WWF International

www.panda.org/what_we_do/endangered_species/endangered_species_list/cetaceans/about/river_dolphins/

*Get a fact sheet on river dolphins.*

## Sea Otter

### Defenders of Wildlife

www.defenders.org/wildlife_and_habitat/wildlife/sea_otter.php

*Find general species information about sea otters and learn about the adoption program.*

### Monterey Bay Aquarium

www.montereybayaquarium.org/efc/otter.asp

*Watch sea otters on the aquarium's webcam and get information on sea otters and conservation plans.*

### US Geological Survey, Western Ecological Research Center (WERC)

www.werc.usgs.gov/otters
M. Tim Tinker, PhD, Research Biologist
USGS WERC Santa Cruz Field Station
Long Marine Laboratory, UCSC
100 Shaffer Road
Santa Cruz, CA 95060
Phone: 831-459-2357
E-mail: ttinker@usgs.gov

*Get detailed information on the WERC sea otter research study.*

### Vancouver Aquarium

www.vanaqua.org

*Check out the "real-time" sea otter webcam.*

## Mediterranean Monk Seal

### The Monachus Guardian

www.monachus-guardian.org
M. Schnellmann
Wernerstrasse 26
CH-3006 Bern
Switzerland
E-mail: editor@monachus-guardian.org

*Discover more about the Mediterranean monk seal and its threatened habitats, learn what this organization is doing to save it, and see the international list of monk seal conservation organizations.*

### WWF International

www.panda.org/what_we_do/where_we_work/mediterranean/about/marine/monk_
seal_project/monk_seals

*Get a Mediterranean monk seal fact sheet.*

## Marsupials

### Department of Sustainability and Environment, Victoria, Australia

www.dpi.vic.gov.au
Phone: 61-3-5332-5000

*Get general species and conservation information on marsupials.*

### Tasmania Parks and Wildlife Service

www.parks.tas.gov.au
GPO Box 1751
Hobart, Tasmania 7001
Australia

*Learn about parks and reserves, recreation, nature and conservation, education, and how to get involved to preserve Tasmania's wildlife.*

## Tasmanian Devil

### Tasmanian Devil Appeal

www.utas.edu.au/foundation/devil.htm
University of Tasmania Foundation
Private Bag 40
Hobart, Tasmania 7001
Australia
Phone: +61-3-6226 7521
university.foundation@utas.edu.au

*Learn more about Tasmanian devils and the disease threatening their existence, plus find out where to see a Tasmanian devil and how you can help save them from extinction.*

**Tasmania Parks and Wildlife Service**

www.parks.tas.gov.au/index.aspx?base=387

*Get general species information about the Tasmanian devil.*

## Tasmanian Tiger
**American Museum of Natural History**

www.amnh.org/exhibitions/expeditions/treasure_fossil/Treasures/Tasmanian_Wolf/tasmania.html?50

*Learn more about the Tasmanian tiger species.*

**ARKive**

www.arkive.org/thylacine/thylacinus-cynocephalus/ /

*Get detailed species information, watch videos, and view images of this now-extinct species*

# Mustelidae

## Black-Footed Ferret
**Black-Footed Ferret Recovery Program**

www.blackfootedferret.org

*Watch black-footed ferret videos and learn more about this species and the conservation efforts to save it.*

**Prairie Wildlife Research**

www.prairiewildlife.org

*Get news and information on conserving the black-footed ferret, including links to news, research articles, and other sites, and learn how you can get involved.*

# Pachyderms

## Elephants
**Elephant Information Repository**

http://elephant.elehost.com

*Find resources and in-depth information related to elephants and the conservation of their species.*

### Elephant Care International

www.elephantcare.org
166 Limo View Lane
Hohenwald, TN 38462
931-796-7102

*Access and share information and data with other professionals in conservation.*

### Rhinos

### The Rhino Resource Center

www.rhinoresourcecenter.com

*Learn more about rhinos, view images, find out about the discussion forums, and access additional resource links.*

### International Rhino Foundation (IRF)

www.rhinos-irf.org

*Find detailed information on different rhino species, conservation and research, and ways to support the IRF's conservation programs.*

### SOS Rhino

www.sosrhino.org
SOS Rhino Borneo Bhd
Lot 15, Block B, 2nd Floor
Visa Light Industrial Center
Mile 5-1/2 Tuaran Road
88856 Inanam
Sabah, Malaysia
Phone: 60-88-388-405

*Get information on the foundation, the five different rhino species, and the Tabin Wildlife Resort; read news from the field; and learn about donation and volunteer opportunities.*

### WWF International

www.panda.org/what_we_do/endangered_species/endangered_species_list/rhinoceros/
african_rhinos/the_african_rhino_programme

*Get a rhino fact sheet.*

### Black Rhino
**ARKive**

www.arkive.org/black-rhinoceros/diceros-bicornis

*View videos and images and find detailed black rhino species information, including facts and status, range and habitat, and threats and conservation.*

### International Rhino Foundation

www.rhinos-irf.org/black

*Get general black rhino species information.*

### Javan Rhino
**ARKive**

www.arkive.org/javan-rhinoceros/rhinoceros-sondaicus

*Learn more about the Javan rhino, including range and habitat, facts and status, primary threats, and conservation plans.*

### International Rhino Foundation

www.rhinos-irf.org/javan

*Get general species information on the Javan rhino.*

### Sumatran Rhino
**ARKive**

www.arkive.org/sumatran-rhinoceros/dicerorhinus-sumatrensis

*Access facts on and the status of the Sumatran rhino, learn about its range and habitat, check out images and watch videos, and find out about current threats and conservation work.*

### International Rhino Foundation

www.rhinos-irf.org/sumatran

*Find general species information on the Sumatran rhino.*

### White Rhino
**ARKive**

www.arkive.org/white-rhinoceros/ceratotherium-simum

*Learn more about the white rhino including the most pressing threats to its survival, and get currents facts and status and information on range and habitat.*

**International Rhino Foundation**

www.rhinos-irf.org/white

*Find general species information on the white rhino.*

## Primates

**GRASP**

**Great Apes Survival Partnership (GRASP)**

http://whrc.org/africa/grasp/index.htm

*Learn how GRASP is using innovative measures and the combined efforts of the United Nations Environment Programme and the United Nations Educational, Scientific, and Cultural Organization to lift the threat of imminent extinction faced by gorillas, chimpanzees, bonobos, and orangutans.*

### Chimpanzees
**The Jane Goodall Institute**

www.janegoodall.org

*Learn more about chimpanzees and learn about the institute's objectives to increase habitat conservation for primates, expand research that is noninvasive to chimpanzees and other primates, and increase awareness of the primate's plight.*

### Gorillas
**American Wildlife Foundation**

www.awf.org/content/wildlife/detail/mountaingorilla

*Listen to a gorilla sound clip and get general species information on gorillas.*

**International Gorilla Conservation Programme**

www.igcp.org
African Wildlife Foundation
1400 Sixteenth Street, NW
Suite 120
Washington, DC 20036
Phone: 202-939 3333
E-mail: africanwildlife@awf.org

*Find species descriptions, learn more about threats to gorilla survival, check out the photo gallery, and get the latest news.*

### Wildlife Conservation Society (WCS)

www.congogorillaforest.com

*Take an online tour of the Congo Gorilla Forest exhibit at the Bronx Zoo, and learn about the WCS Gorilla Conservation program and how you can help.*

### Wildlife Direct, Gorilla Protection

www.gorilla.wildlifedirect.org

*Read a daily news blog covering gorilla conservation in Africa.*

## Orangutans
### Borneo Orangutan Survival International (BOS)

www.savetheorangutan.org
BOS International
Noerre Farimagsgade 37, 1.
1364 Copenhagen K
Denmark

*Find organization and species information, learn about BOS projects and membership, visit the online store, and access links to other BOS branches.*

### The Great Orangutan Project

www.orangutanproject.com
Great Orangutan Project—Way Out Experiences
Studio 6, 8 High Street
Harpenden, Herts, AL5 2TB
United Kingdom
Phone: ++44-(0)-845-371-3070
E-mail: orangutan@w-o-x.com

*Learn more about orangutans, find project information, check out the photo and video galleries, take a virtual tour, get information on resident apes, shop the online store, and learn about volunteer opportunities.*

### Orangutan Appeal UK

www.orangutan-appeal.org.uk

*Get information about the appeal, projects involving orangutans in general, and the Sepilok Rehabilitation Centre, plus news, an online store, and donation information.*

## Orangutan Foundation International (OFI)

www.orangutan.org
824 S Wellesley Avenue
Los Angeles, CA 90049
Phone: 310-820-4906
E-mail: ofi@orangutan.org

*Find detailed information on orangutans, review facts and figures, read the latest news, learn about upcoming events, learn about OFI Borneo rainforest tours, and find out how you can get involved personally and financially.*

## Orangutan Outreach

www.redapes.org
419 Lafayette Street, 2nd Floor
New York, NY 10003
Phone: 646-723-1450

*Access an extensive menu of orangutan-related information, including species and conservation information, video clips and slide shows, and details of the adoption program.*

# Golden-Headed Lion Tamarin
## ARKive

www.arkive.org/golden-headed-lion-tamarin/leontopithecus-chrysomelas/info.html

*Find detailed species information, including facts and status, range and habitat, threats and conservation, and visit the photo gallery.*

## Bristol Zoo Gardens

www.bristolzoo.org.uk/learning/animals/mammals/gold head-tamarin

*Get general species information about the golden-headed lion tamarin.*

## International Union for the Conservation of Nature Red List of Threatened Species

www.iucnredlist.org/details/40643

*Learn more about the golden-headed lion tamarin and threats facing it, get information on its geographic range and habitats, and find out about conservation actions.*

# Reptiles

International Union for the Conservation of Nature, Species Survival Commission, Crocodile Specialist Group

www.iucncsg.org/ph1/modules/Home

*Learn how a worldwide network of biologists, government officials, independent researchers, farmers, traders, fashion leaders, and more are actively involved in the conservation of the world's 23 living species of alligators, crocodiles, caimans, and gharials.*

## American Alligator
### Florida Museum of Natural History

www.flmnh.ufl.edu/natsci/herpetology/brittoncrocs/csp_amis.htm

*Learn more about the American alligator and current conservation efforts.*

### US Fish and Wildlife Service

www.fws.gov/southwest/es/oklahoma/gator.htm

*Get general species information about the American alligator and listen to a sound clip of alligator hissing and bellowing at www.fws.gov/video/sound.htm.*

## Chinese Alligator
### The Crocodile Specialist Group's Chinese Alligator Fund

www.flmnh.ufl.edu/alligatorfund

*Find information on how to help save the Chinese alligator, including species information, donation information, and progress reports.*

### Wildlife Conservation Society

www.savingwildplaces.com/swp-home/swp-crocodile/3631558

*Learn more about the Chinese alligator, including the captive-breeding program run in conjunction with the American Zoo and Aquarium Association.*

## Gharial
### Gharial Conservation Alliance

www.gharialconservation.org

*Learn more about the gharial and conservation efforts, read notes from the field, access resources, visit the kids' gharial gallery, and find tips on getting involved.*

## Abbington Island Tortoise

**Galapagos Conservation Trust**

www.gct.org
5 Derby Street
London
W1J 7AB
United Kingdom
Phone: +44-(0)-20-7629-5049
E-mail: gct@gct.org

*Find general organizational information, plus detailed information about the Galápogos Islands, conservation efforts, news and events, and visiting, and find a Junior Zone learning center geared toward children and young adults.*

## Galapagos Conservancy

www.galapagos.org
Galapagos Conservancy
11150 Fairfax Boulevard, Suite 408
Fairfax, VA 22030
Phone: 703-383-0077

*Get information on conservation efforts, read the latest news, find travel information, and learn about supporting the conservancy.*

# INDEX